The Careers Leader Handbook

Second edition

How to create an outstanding careers programme for your school or college

David Andrews and Tristram Hooley

trotman | **t**

The Careers Leader Handbook: How to create an outstanding careers programme for your school or college

This second edition published in 2022 by Trotman Indigo Publishing, 21d Charles Street, Bath BA1 1HX

© Trotman Indigo Publishing 2022

© Crimson Publishing Ltd 2018, 2019

Authors: David Andrews and Tristram Hooley

British Library Cataloguing in Publication Data
A catalogue record for this book is available from the British Library

ISBN: 978 1 91294 374 6

Please note that all websites given in this book are subject to change so you may find that some of these sites in time may be renamed, merge with other sites or disappear.

Designed by Marc Burville-Riley
Printed and bound in Malta by Gutenberg Press Ltd

Contents

Figures and tables

Figures

Tables

Introducing the authors

Both authors are very excited that '*careers leadership*' is an idea whose time has come in schools and colleges across England and beyond. When they published the first edition of this book, the number of careers leaders was growing across England. With the publication of the second edition, we are now in the position where almost every school has a careers leader. In the intervening years, there has been a transformation in the quality and quantity of careers provision in schools and colleges. But, there is still much to do; as we come out of the pandemic into an increasingly turbulent labour market, career education has never been more important, and there is a greater need than ever for high-quality professional careers leaders.

David and Tristram have continued to be active in pointing out the importance of careers leadership to politicians and civil servants and are heartened to see increasing amounts of support for the idea of careers leadership from above. But policy alone can't transform the education system. At the end of the day the real battle takes place in the school or college. That is where careers leaders are figuring out how to make a difference, arguing for resources, designing programmes and engaging their colleagues.

This is why they have written this book and revised it for a new second edition. They hope that it can be a key resource for a new generation of careers leaders as well as offering existing careers leaders some food for thought.

David Andrews is a consultant, trainer and writer specialising in careers education and guidance. He started his 'career in careers' as head of careers at St Ivo School in Cambridgeshire and then went on to work as an advisory teacher in Cambridgeshire Careers Service and a school adviser/inspector in Hertfordshire. He has spent the past 36 years supporting careers leaders in schools and colleges through leading CPD and offering advice and consultancy. Throughout his professional life he has campaigned for a nationally funded training programme for careers leaders, and at last it is happening!

Tristram Hooley is a researcher and writer specialising in career and career guidance. He is Professor of Career Education and divides his time between the University of Derby in the UK and the Inland Norway University of Applied Science. He writes the Adventures in Careers Development blog at **https:// adventuresincareerdevelopment.wordpress.com**. He believes that everyone has a career and that a key purpose of the education system is to help people make the most of their career.

Acknowledgements

We'd like to thank the hundreds of careers leaders that we've spoken with over the course of our careers. You will find your ideas, struggles, challenges and brilliant solutions showcased in this book. We'd also like to thank the new generation of careers leaders who are coming through. You have inspired us to write and revise this book – we hope that it is useful to you.

We would like to thank colleagues in the CDI's community of interest for careers education and at The Careers & Enterprise Company for their helpful suggestions as we updated and revised the content for the second edition.

We'd also like to thank our families for giving us the time to write and revise this book.

Finally, we'd like to thank Trotman for believing in this project and encouraging us to write a second edition.

A note on resources, endnotes, tools and URLs

In this book we have referred to a wide range of resources. We believe that these resources will be helpful to you in your new role as a careers leader. We want to give you access to the collective wisdom of the careers world and to allow you to stand on the shoulders of those who have gone before you. However, with a few exceptions none of this material is essential. This book alone should give you everything that you need to become an excellent careers leader. Anything that we refer to is just designed to give you the opportunity to extend your knowledge.

We don't 'endorse' all of the resources that we include. In some cases, we have provided you with a range of links to offer different perspectives. You will have to decide which ones you agree with. In other cases, we offer examples of products that are currently available. These are designed to give you a starting point, but you would be advised to do your own research before you buy!

In most cases where we highlight a resource we include it in a box. If it is a book we include the author, full title and publisher. This should make it easy for you to find on Amazon or any other book retailer. If it is a website or online resource we provide a URL. We have checked and updated all of the resources while preparing the second edition, but websites are changing all the time and so URLs will sometimes change. If this happens, we are sure that you can find the resource (or something very like it) with a bit of careful Googling.

This is not designed to be an academic book and so we won't be providing evidence for every point that we make. However, we have tried to provide references to all the important material that we have used in putting the book together. If you are interested in finding out more you can follow the references to the endnotes that are located at the back of the book. Again, most of the time it isn't important that you do this, but further information is available if you are interested.

Finally, we have provided several tools for you. These are generally things like forms or checklists that we think that you'll find useful as you undertake the role of a careers leader. We have gathered all of these tools together at https://indigo.careers/clh/.

Foreword to the second edition by Oli de Botton

When I was a headteacher, I believed the purpose of school was to connect the past, present and future for young people. The 'past' was shorthand for the important knowledge children needed, the 'present' stood for supporting social and emotional wellbeing and 'the future' involved getting young people ready for what comes next.

As Chief Executive of The Careers & Enterprise Company, it's clear to me that, at its best, careers education takes care of the 'future' part – helping young people find their best next step through experiences, learning and guidance.

From margins to mainstream

Thanks to the hard work of schools, colleges and employers, there's been real progress in the development of careers education in recent years. Careers leaders across the country have been tirelessly driving this – innovating, orchestrating, inspiring.

The next challenge is to make sure careers is embedded in the mainstream of every school and college – front and centre in the minds of headteachers, governors, teachers and, most importantly, young people.

The blueprint already exists. Important cross-cutting areas like safeguarding and literacy are now central to everyone's thinking. This is not as a result of one person working by themselves, but because there is a whole-school and -college approach. There's no reason this can't be true of careers education. As this book demonstrates, it's careers leaders who will make this happen.

Careers leaders, leading

As with anything durable in education, leadership matters. Since this book was first published, careers leaders have grown in authority, sophistication and impact. They are the focal point for high-quality, high-impact careers education.

We know the more training, support and time careers leaders have, the better the outcomes they deliver for young people. This is especially true for young people who battle the odds. As careers leaders build deeper connections with employers, they expose young people to inspiring futures. As they support their colleagues to show the real-world applications of their subjects, they open up new possibilities. And when they get a whole school thinking about careers, they make sure no young person misses out.

This book is essential reading for careers leaders who are leading the charge and want to understand more about what excellence looks like. It is full of hard-earned know-how as well as brilliant resources and toolkits. But it's not just that. It's proof of the need to continue to invest in and support the role. As we understand more about what works and the difference careers leaders make, the argument for continued investment in training and support becomes even more compelling.

I'd like to take this opportunity to thank all career leaders for their incredible work and the difference you all make in helping prepare young people for the future so they can find their next best step.

Oli de Botton, CEO, The Careers & Enterprise Company, June 2022

Foreword to the first edition by Sir John Holman

Career guidance is one of the keys to social mobility. The first place that children usually look for advice is in their home. This is natural and right: parents and carers are the people who know their children best. But the guidance they get will of course be partial and often it may be stereotyped. If there is no-one at home with experience of skilled employment, or even of any kind of employment, the horizons for the advice may be limited. In these circumstances, their best, and maybe only chance of good guidance is their school or college.

In 2013, the Gatsby Foundation asked me to seek the answer to the question 'What does career guidance look like when it is good?' An international study and a close look at best practice led to my 2014 report 'Good Career Guidance' which identifies the eight benchmarks that are now the framework behind the English government's Careers Strategy. I'm pleased to see the benchmarks are at the heart of this book.

In 2015–17, Gatsby tested the benchmarks in a pilot study in 16 schools and colleges in the North East of England. The spectacular progress made by those schools and colleges showed the difference that having a clear framework, and a way of measuring progress against it, can make. In particular, it showed schools and employers how to co-ordinate their efforts together. But it also showed that the benchmarks alone are not enough: for a school or college to make such progress needs leadership from what we now call the *careers leader*, backed by the school's senior leaders.

In many ways this is not at all surprising: any business guru will tell you that you can't have success without good leadership. But careers leadership has some important differences. More than any other middle leadership role in a school, it involves a wide range of stakeholders both inside and outside the school, and in some ways it is like conducting an orchestra. It requires skills in co-ordination and networking as well as in management and leadership.

This book by David Andrews and Tristram Hooley is extraordinarily timely, as the government introduces its new Careers Strategy and recognises the importance of careers leaders. For a long time, schools have had people who co-ordinate their careers activities, but until now the importance of active leadership has not been recognised. This clear and accessible book not only explains what a careers leader needs to do: it also describes how you can develop the skills to carry out this multifaceted role. These are skills that will stand you in good stead throughout your own career.

Careers guidance has not always been given the central role in UK schools and colleges that it needs and deserves. This is in contrast to many successful overseas administrations, where roles like the *schooldekaan* (careers leader) in the Netherlands are seen as central to the work of the school. My ambition is that the role of the careers leader will become known, understood and respected, not only in every school and college, but at a national level. I want careers leaders to become a well-defined professional group with the respect and the networks of exchange and support that every strong profession has. This book is an important step towards that goal.

Sir John Holman, The University of York, August 2018

Glossary of key terms and acronyms

A levels. A levels are the traditional (academic) qualifications that are offered by schools and colleges in England for students aged between 16 and 19.

Academy. The term 'academy' has a specific meaning in the English school system. An academy is a state-funded school which receives its funding direct from central government and is independent of local authority control and management.

Benchmarks. Refers to the Gatsby Benchmarks. The key framework for practice in school- or college-based careers education and guidance.

Career. The individual's pathway through life, learning and work.

Career and labour market information. See *labour market information*.

Career Development Institute (CDI). The professional association for everyone working in careers education and guidance in the UK. If you are not based in the UK you will be able to find a similar organisation in your country.

Career guidance. Sometimes used to describe a one-to-one interaction between a careers professional and a young person (see *personal guidance*). Increasingly being used as a generic term to describe all careers interventions that take place in a school or college.

Career management skills. The skills that individuals need to research opportunities, make choices, secure places on courses or jobs and plan and develop their *career* across their life. Sometimes called career development skills or career competencies.

Careers adviser. A careers professional trained to degree level or above. Will typically be focused on delivering *personal guidance* but will also be able to make a range of other contributions to a *careers programme*.

Careers education. The process of teaching others about their *career*. Usually used to describe learning taking place in group settings in the classroom.

Careers education, information, advice and guidance (CEIAG). A catch-all term that is used to describe the full range of careers interventions. Increasingly falling out of favour and being replaced with '*career guidance*' as a generic term.

(The) Careers & Enterprise Company. A government-funded agency responsible for managing programmes to support the implementation and development of careers work in schools and colleges in England, including a centrally funded programme of training for careers leaders. If you are not in England you may still find some of the resources produced by the organisation useful, but most of the funding and programmes will be different. You should become familiar with your country's public careers service.

Careers hub. A careers hub is a local network supported by The Careers & Enterprise Company which brings together schools, colleges, employers and apprenticeship providers to work collaboratively on developing their careers programmes and to share practice.

Careers leader. The individual responsible and accountable for leading a school's or college's *careers programme*.

Careers programme. The collection of careers activities organised by a school or college.

Careers Strategy. A major policy initiative to improve careers support for everyone in England, published by the *Department for Education* in December 2017. The strategy included several developments aimed at young people, not least that every school and college must have a named *careers leader*. Although the period covered by the strategy is now over, it remains an influential document and is the most comprehensive articulation of how the government hopes that career guidance will develop in England.

Continuing professional development (CPD). The process of gaining further knowledge, understanding and skills relevant to your job role. Sometimes referred to as staff development or in-service training.

Curriculum. The way in which formal learning is organised and delivered.

Department for Education (DfE). The government department responsible for careers education and guidance policy in England. In other countries it may be a department of education that leads on careers policy, but it could also be a department of business, labour or some other configuration. As a *careers leader* it is important for you to know where careers policy comes from.

Destinations data. Statistics collected by schools, colleges and local authorities, about where students go after they leave school or college at the age of 16 or 18. This includes information on the progression routes in education, training and employment.

Development plan. A working document, reviewed at least annually, setting out plans and proposals for enhancing and improving the *careers programme*. The Careers & Enterprise Company in England refers to this as a Strategic Careers Plan.

Disclosure and Barring Service (DBS). A government service which runs criminal record checks to prevent unsuitable people from working with vulnerable groups, including children. The service was established in 2012 to undertake functions carried out previously by the Criminal Records Bureau (CRB) and the Independent Safeguarding Authority. It is responsible for processing requests for checks in England, Wales, the Channel Islands and the Isle of Man.

EHC (Education, Health and Care) Plan. An Education, Health and Care (EHC) Plan is for children and young people aged up to 25 with special educational needs and disabilities (*SEND*). EHC plans identify educational, health and social needs, and set out the additional support to be provided to meet those needs.

Employability skills. The generic skills required to succeed in the workplace, in any job.

Employer encounters. Opportunities for young people to meet with employers or working people and discuss the world of work. These usually take place in the context of school or college.

Enterprise Adviser. An employer volunteer who works with a school or college in England to support their *careers programme*. Enterprise Advisers are usually more senior volunteers who focus on strategic issues. They are recruited by *Enterprise Co-ordinators*, who will work with the *careers leader* to match the right Enterprise Adviser to the school.

Enterprise Co-ordinator. A professional who works with schools, colleges, employers and careers organisations to build a local network and ensure that an area has high-quality careers provision. A key responsibility is recruiting *Enterprise Advisers* and connecting them to education.

Enterprise skills. The skills required to develop new initiatives, start businesses and make a success of self-employment and employing others.

Further education (FE). Any education received once someone has left school that leads to qualifications other than degrees. It includes both academic and vocational provision, for young people (16–19) and for adults.

Gatsby. The Gatsby Charitable Foundation is a charity with a particular interest in science and education. It funded the research which defined the eight Gatsby Benchmarks.

GCSE (General Certificate of Secondary Education). The examinations taken by all pupils in England at age 16, the end of compulsory schooling.

Governors. Elected and nominated volunteers who provide strategic direction to the school or college, hold the head teacher or principal to account for its educational performance and oversee its financial management.

Higher education (HE). Education leading to degree-level qualifications. Frequently, but not always, delivered in universities.

Information, advice and guidance (IAG). The term IAG is sometimes used to describe *personal guidance* and sometimes to describe a wider range of interventions. The use of this term has become less frequent over recent years.

Key stage. Term used in the English education system to describe a phase of education, e.g. key stage 3 covers the education of young people from the age of 11 to 14.

Labour Market Information (LMI). Information about the labour market, education system and related issues that can support an individual to make good career decisions. This might include information about salaries, qualifications and future trends. It can include government information and statistics as well as information produced by companies, recruiters and other bodies. Sometimes also called Career and Labour Market Information (CLMI).

Local Enterprise Partnerships (LEPs). Voluntary partnerships between local authorities and local private sector businesses in England, which play a central role in determining local economic priorities and undertaking activities to drive economic growth and job creation, improve infrastructure and raise workforce skills within the local area. There are 38 LEPs covering the country.

MAT (multi-academy trust). A multi-academy trust is a single entity established to improve and maintain high educational standards across several academies. A group of academies form a single MAT which has overarching responsibility for their governance.

Middle leader. The term used to describe members of staff who lead and manage particular aspects of the school's or college's work. Examples include heads of department, heads of year, course leaders and, of course, *careers leaders*.

NEET. An acronym used to describe individuals who are Not in Education, Employment or Training.

Ofsted. The organisation responsible for external inspections of state-funded education in England.

Personal guidance. A structured career conversation between a careers professional and a young person. This usually takes place face-to-face and one-to-one.

Personal, Social, Health and Economic (PSHE) Education. The area of the school *curriculum* in England where pupils learn the knowledge, skills and attributes they need to keep themselves healthy and safe and to prepare for life and work in modern Britain. This is a common location for careers education lessons.

Portfolio. A collection of evidence of tasks completed as part of a *careers programme*, maintained by the student. Kept in electronic (e-portfolio) or paper formats.

Provider access statement. This is a policy in which schools set out how they will ensure that students have access to information on a range of post-16 and post-18 education and training options. This should include giving students opportunities to directly meet with providers of technical education qualifications, apprenticeships and other forms of vocational learning.

Referral. The process by which students are passed from one professional to another. For example, a teacher might send a student to see a *careers adviser* following a conversation with them about their *career*. In other cases, a *careers adviser* might refer to another professional, e.g. the *SENCO* (see below) for more specialist support. Typically, a school or college will have in place systems for students to self-refer as well as referral between different professionals. Referral should be accompanied by good record keeping and information exchange.

SENCO (Special Educational Needs Co-ordinator). The member of school staff who is responsible for ensuring that all pupils with special educational needs or learning difficulties and/or disabilities are supported to access fully the *curriculum* and other provision, including the careers programme. The equivalent role in colleges is the Head of Learner Support.

SEND. An acronym used to describe individuals who have special educational needs and disabilities.

Senior Leadership Team (SLT). The group of senior managers responsible for managing a school or college.

Sixth form. The term given to the final two years of an 11–18 secondary school (or 13–18 upper school) in England. This typically includes young people aged 16–18.

STEM. An acronym used as shorthand for the subjects science, technology, engineering and mathematics.

Studio school. A new type of secondary school in England, for students aged 14 to 19, and designed to focus on practical skills for the workplace as well as teaching the national *curriculum*. Studio schools are sponsored by existing schools, colleges and community groups, and are designed to be small, with a maximum of 300 students.

T levels. T levels are technical qualifications offered in England that are developed in collaboration with employers and businesses. T levels are two-year courses that are typically studied by students aged 16–18.

UCAS (Universities and Colleges Admissions Service). A UK-based organisation whose main role is to operate a central applications process for British universities.

University technical college (UTC). A new type of secondary school in England, for students aged 14 to 19, and designed to focus on practical skills for the workplace as well as teaching the national *curriculum*. UTCs are sponsored by a university and their most distinctive feature is that they offer technically oriented courses of study, combining the national *curriculum* requirements with technical and vocational elements.

Virtual encounter. Any encounter between a young person and an employer or learning provider that takes place online.

Work experience, experience of the workplace. An opportunity for a young person to gain actual experience of workplaces or of undertaking work. This could include visits to workplaces and job shadowing as well as actual work experience.

Year group. In England the years of compulsory schooling are designated Year 1 (when pupils reach the age of 5) to Year 11 (when pupils reach the age of 16).

About the second edition

We published the first edition of *The Careers Leader Handbook* in 2018. At that time, the idea of careers leadership was a new one, albeit one with some long historical roots, as we will describe. But things moved quickly, and over the past four or five years we have seen the role becoming embedded into the English school system. We have also seen a lot of interest in careers leaders from other countries.

While the position of careers leadership has been strengthening, there have also been one or two other things going on in the world. In the UK we've had a new government and five (so far) new ministers of education. This has led to changes in the statutory guidance, in Ofsted inspections and in the services provided by The Careers & Enterprise Company. The evidence base has also continued to develop and evolve. Finally, and probably most importantly, we've also experienced the pandemic, a lot of economic ups and downs and the war in Ukraine.

All of this change in the education system and beyond led us to conclude that it would be useful to refresh *The Careers Leader Handbook*. We wanted to ensure that the book could support careers leaders to be ready for the challenges of the new normal in which we are all living.

As we went through the book we made too many changes to list here. Overall, the book has grown by 16 pages. The main things that we changed involved:

- updating the book to reflect the changes in the policy, educational and economic context in which careers leaders are now working
- describing the new and addition forms of support, resources and other help that are now available to careers leader
- reflecting on new evidence and what we have learnt about careers leadership over the last five years
- adding new material designed to make the book more useful to careers leaders outside of England
- double-checking and updating all of the links, resources and books that we recommend to ensure they are still current and relevant
- responding to feedback and suggestions from readers of the first edition.

Thank you to the thousands of careers leaders who have bought and used the first edition of the book. We hope that the second edition will be even more useful to you, and that it will inspire a whole new generation of careers leaders to transform the lives of the young people that they work with.

Section 1:
Introduction

Introduction

'Career' is our journey through life, learning and work. Paid work is an important part of this journey, but there are so many other elements that make up a career. Careers ensure that we can put food on the table, but they are also where we enact our values (or at least try to), where we participate in our communities, help others, achieve our goals and dream our dreams. Careers are not lived in a simple straight line, but rather built like crazy paving which allows us to move forwards, but also sideways and backwards.

Career is not just important to individuals, it also matters for families, communities and societies. Where people are able to effectively manage their careers it helps governments to ensure that the education system works effectively and that the skills we develop in learning are useful in the workplace. Putting it simply, career matters for everybody's livelihood and wellbeing, and what is more it underpins the effective functioning of education, the labour market and society.

Given the importance of our careers, it is strange that many people spend very little time thinking about them. Although in some ways this is hardly surprising, as we spend so little time devoted to careers education at school and college. The possessive apostrophe, trigonometry, the oxbow lake and the Tudor kings all rightfully have an enduring place in the curriculum. But learning about the different educational routes available, the range of occupations and sectors that make up the labour market and considering how you choose a job, secure it and do well in it are typically pushed to the margins of education.

We believe that it is time for a change and that in fact we are already seeing this change starting to take place. Across the world there are calls to bring the worlds of education and employment into closer dialogue. This is not about turning the education system into a production line for employment. Rather it is about ensuring that young people emerge from the education system with the skills and knowledge that enable them to critically participate in post-compulsory education, in working life, and to become the workers, leaders, entrepreneurs and citizens of the future. This is the careers education that we would like everyone to experience, and this is what we are going to try to help you to deliver as a careers leader in your school or college.

A career is pursued in the context of the world. You can learn more about career, develop your skills and knowledge and build networks to support you – but you can't ever be certain that your career will work out exactly as planned. Career is about managing complexity and learning to do the best with what you've got. As a careers educator, you can't promise all your students that everything will turn out in the way that they plan, but you can ensure that they have the personal resources and critical understanding of the world that will give them the best chance. The evidence is strong that careers education and guidance can make a difference to young people, and as we will see in this book it is also increasingly clear what good careers education and guidance looks like.[1]

So, you're a careers leader now

If you've bought this book, you are probably just about to become a careers leader or you have already begun doing the job. Being a careers leader is about taking responsibility for the careers programme (or programmes) that are run within your school or college. This is a big job and it is often one that people will begin with little training or experience. This is why we decided to write this book. We wanted to draw on everything that we've learned from previous generations of careers leaders and make it available to you.

We understand that for many people becoming a careers leader wasn't a longstanding ambition, or even something that they planned for at all. As careers education is becoming more important in schools and colleges, many senior leaders are looking around for willing people to take on the role of the careers leader. Whether you planned to become a careers leader or fell into it by accident, we are sure that you will find it an interesting and challenging role. Since we wrote the first edition of this book, the position of the careers leader has become even more strongly embedded in the English school system and also begun to pop up in other countries. So, you are now part of a large and growing number of educators across the world doing the job.

The last few years have been extremely challenging for schools, colleges, teachers and young people. The world has been in constant flux with Brexit, elections, Covid-19, economic crashes, environmental catastrophes, and war. In the middle of this, schools and colleges have been trying to keep young people's education progressing while also being on the frontline of dealing with the concerns of young people about the world that they are moving into. Among these concerns about wellbeing, attainment and mental health, it has sometimes been difficult to keep the careers programme on track. But now is no time to retreat from running a high-quality careers programme. In an uncertain world, young people need more help with their career than ever, and this is why it is so important for the careers leader to step up and be assertive about placing careers at the heart of the school's or college's mission.

We'll move on to look at what careers leaders do (in Section 2), at the nature of the careers leader role (in Section 3) and at how you can ensure continuous improvement (in Section 4). Before we get there, it is useful to have a look at some of the key theories and ideas that underpin careers work.

Underpinning thinking

Modern careers work has its origins in the late 19th and early 20th centuries. Social reformers like Frank Parsons in Boston, USA were keen to ensure that society worked harmoniously and that people found their 'vocation' in life.[2] To help ensure this, they set up vocational guidance bureaus or careers centres to help people find their way in life.

In its early days, careers work was often seen as a fairly simple process of matching people's skills and attributes to the opportunities around them. If you could understand what someone was interested in, well suited to and good at you would then be able to match them to appropriate jobs and improve their chance of happiness and success. John Holland was one of the people who developed these kinds of ideas the furthest.[3] He made the argument that individuals' personalities and jobs could both be classified as being made up of the following traits: realistic, investigative, artistic, social, enterprising and conventional. If you could find out which combination of these you favoured it would be a really useful guide to the right job for you.

As the careers field grew, it increasingly became integrated into the education system in the hope that people could find their vocation before they left education. The problem was that young people tended to change and develop and so, just as you thought that you had matched them to the ideal career, they would learn to do something new or develop a new facet to their personality. The psychologist Donald Super was one of the people who thought through this new, developmentalist perspective.[4] Perhaps careers wasn't just about matching people to the ideal job, but rather about helping them to develop throughout life and manage all of the different jobs and roles that they would need to fulfil?

As careers began to develop further as an academic field, people started to disagree with each other and bring in all sorts of new ideas. Careers research and practice drew together psychology, sociology, education and economics and each of these had different perspectives and emphasised different things. Psychologists like Mark Savickas argued that individuals were able to construct their own careers as part of what he called 'life design'.[5] Meanwhile, sociologists argued that opportunities were structured by class and the economic system, which meant that many people have very limited choices in their career.[6]

The debates continue to rage on.[7] What they tell us is that when we are dealing with people's careers we are dealing with something complex that sits in the eye of the hurricane of different social and psychological factors. For educators working with young people these debates present challenges. Careers is not a subject where there is a clear right answer. It has moral dimensions as well as educational ones. For example, do you encourage young people to leave their communities to pursue their careers or to stay with their families? How should we respond to different government initiatives that encourage young people to pursue university education, STEM (science, technology, engineering and mathematics) subjects or apprenticeships and vocational education? What constitutes career success? Is it about high salaries, positive social impact, personal happiness and wellbeing or something else?

The questions go on, and as you work with young people on career issues you will find more and more complexity and shades of grey. We think that this is one of the most interesting things about careers. It allows you to talk about everything, from your dreams of scoring the winning goal for England to the politics of globalisation. And in the middle of all of this complexity you are trying to help people to make intensely practical choices about things like what qualification to study, whether to go to university and how to apply for a job.

This is not a book of theory, it is a book about practice. We'll be aiming to be as practical as we can throughout and to help you to figure out how you and the young people that you work with can manage the complexity of their careers. But, as you'll see, we will periodically be dipping into research and theory where this can help to explain what you need to do as a careers leader.

💡 Resources: Career theory

There are lots of good books and resources that address career theory and some of the research and evidence that sits behind the field. Some good places to start include:

Careers New Zealand (**www.careers.govt.nz/resources/career-practice/career-theory-models**) – excellent resources on career theory and models.

Running in a Forest (**https://runninginaforest.wordpress.com**) – a blog by Tom Staunton (University of Derby) that regularly covers the latest in career theory.

Introduction to career theory: A self study course (**https://adventuresincareer development.wordpress.com/2020/09/17/introduction-to-career-theory-a-self-study-course**) – an online series of video lectures provided by Tristram to introduce people to some of the key career theories.

Oxford Handbook of Career Development by Peter Robertson, Tristram Hooley and Phil McCash (Oxford University Press) – a comprehensive new book covering the latest in theory, research and practice.

Who is this book for?

We have written this book for careers leaders in schools and colleges. We are particularly interested in supporting new careers leaders, but we hope that it will also be of interest to more experienced colleagues. We've covered both schools and colleges equally, and have drawn on examples from both. But, to avoid repetition, we have not provided two separate examples for every point that we make. We realise that leading careers in colleges and schools can be different, and so at times you may need to translate the point that we make to ensure that it works for your context.

Similarly, we have covered both mainstream and SEND schools. We know that there are several different types of special school but supporting young people with SEND to prepare for independent living and to progress to some form of further education, training or work is a priority in all such settings. The purpose of career guidance is fundamentally the same in all schools, and a lot of the points we make apply to both mainstream and SEND schools. We recognise, however, that careers leaders in special schools will need to interpret some of those points for their particular pupils, and on various occasions throughout the book we have added particular notes where there is something distinctive to say about career guidance practice for young people with SEND.

The idea of translating the examples in the book is likely to be true for everyone. All schools and colleges are different, and all careers leaders will bring different experience, skills and knowledge. The examples we give are designed to be illustrative and inspirational, and you should think through how best to apply them in your context.

The book has emerged out of some major shifts in the position of careers leadership in England's schools. We both live in England and we have mainly, but not exclusively, referred to the English policy context and landscape. If you are reading this book in another country you may need to do some further translation to make it relevant for you. However, the basic principles that underpin the book will be relevant across the world and particularly relevant in any system that has a school- or college-based model of careers education and guidance.

We had a great reaction to the first edition, and were contacted by people from all over the world. We noticed that the organisation of career education and guidance in other countries typically falls into one of two categories.

In some countries, schools can call on support from an external careers service. This service works with the school to support them to deliver a careers programme, typically by delivering personal guidance, but often by providing other forms of support such as access to careers and labour market information and training for careers teachers. This is the case in other UK nations (Scotland, Wales and Northern Ireland), where the partnership organisation is a dedicated national careers service. In some other countries, such as Germany and Estonia, schools work closely with the public employment service. In these countries, the role of the careers leader is often quite weak, as careers is typically left to the external partner. We believe that it is great to be able to call on an external careers service, but that schools and colleges are still going to need a careers leader to ensure that the provision of careers information and careers education in the school and that the support from the external service form a coherent and integrated programme for that institution's students.

In other countries, careers is typically the responsibility of a guidance counsellor. Guidance counsellors in these countries have responsibility for delivering careers, but also for things like pastoral support, supporting academic achievement, managing pathway choices, delivering health education and managing crises for individuals and the school. Importantly, the guidance counsellor will also typically be responsible for delivering personal guidance. The guidance counsellor role is very demanding, and it can be difficult to find enough time in it to give careers the focus that it needs. We've seen this sort of system in a wide range of countries, including Australia, Ireland, Norway and the USA. In these countries, schools need to figure out whether they want the guidance counsellor to become a careers leader, or whether careers leadership is a new role. If guidance counsellors are going to take on the role of careers leader, they will need more time and resource (perhaps through the appointment of an assistant); if the careers leader is to be a separate role, then they will need to work with the guidance counsellor very closely.

As we go through the book, we will focus on the experience in England, but also try and provide some thoughts on how other countries might approach the issues we discuss.

How to read this book

We have organised this book into five sections as follows.

You are currently reading **Section 1**. In this section we introduce the book and explain why careers education and guidance is important.

Section 2 is a much longer section consisting of eight chapters. In this section you will be introduced to the Gatsby Benchmarks which, we will argue, offer an evidence-based framework for the careers programme that you need to organise. We devote a chapter to each of these Benchmarks and provide ideas about how you can implement each of them to a high standard.

Section 3 looks at the role of the careers leader in delivering the careers programme. It argues that careers leaders need to be good at leading others, managing teams and projects, co-ordinating staff across the school or college and networking with external contacts. This section contains four chapters, respectively focusing on leadership, management, co-ordination and networking.

Section 4 examines the idea of continuous improvement. It explores how you can evaluate your programme and looks at how you can access continuing professional development (CPD) and make training and other development opportunities available to your colleagues. It finishes by looking at what happens when you start to think about moving on from being a careers leader, both asking how you can make the most of this experience in your own career and thinking about how you can leave the school or college with the best succession plan. This section also has four chapters which focus on evaluation, your CPD, the CPD of others and moving on.

Finally, in **Section 5** we ask you to reflect on what you have learned.

You are free to read this book however you choose. You might want to read it from beginning to end or dip into different sections as suits you. You may be using it as part of a formal course of study, in which case you will probably want to make note of some of the references and sources that we use – or you may be using it as a 'how to' guide, in which case you are free to cherry-pick out anything that is useful. As you read, you will notice the following features.

Each chapter starts with a **summary** of what the chapter is going to cover, usually comprising of one or two paragraphs and some bullet points.

Each chapter concludes with a section called **In a nutshell** which highlights the key learning that we hope that you will take out of the chapter.

Throughout the chapters you will find the following.

Resources. Set out places where you can find out more and extend the learning that you have gained from the book.

Links to Gatsby Benchmarks. Highlight points that link to the framework for practice that is covered in Section 2.

Case studies. Provide worked examples of some of the points that we are making in the chapter. These case studies are fictional, but they draw on our experiences with real schools and colleges.

Tools. Summarise some of the tools that we have made available to you on the website that is linked to the book: **https://indigo. careers/clh**.

International reflections. Explore how some of our key points might be addressed in countries outside England. We don't talk about individual countries, but we often highlight where there are differences between systems that have external careers services and those that have guidance counsellors.

We hope that you find the book useful and that it will enable you to be the best careers leader that you are capable of being. As you will see, there is a lot to learn, but you don't have to learn it all in one go. A good place to start is in thinking about what a good careers programme looks like – so this is what we will now focus on in Section 2.

Section 2:
Delivering an outstanding careers programme

Introduction

This book is designed to support you to become an outstanding careers leader. The most important place for us to start is by thinking about what an outstanding careers programme looks like. The chapters in this section of the book set out what constitutes good practice in such a programme and provide you with all the support that you will need to make it a reality in your school or college.

Over the last few decades, the time that it takes young people to move from education to employment has steadily lengthened while the number of pathways has grown and become more complex.[1] Because of this it is more important than ever to provide young people with education, information and other forms of support to help them to make transitions and manage their careers. However, there are a lot of different ways to do this and as a careers leader it can be difficult to know what is most effective and how to organise this support.

You may have heard that it is important to give young people direct access to employers, that you should take everyone to visit a university campus, teach them about the possibility of self-employment or make sure that every student gets time with a professional careers adviser. But, which of these options is most important and how do you put them all into practice?

The answer is probably that a very wide range of careers activities have a value and that you should try to make sure that your students have the opportunity to experience as many of them as possible. There is also good evidence that the volume of activities makes a big difference, with, broadly speaking, the more career education the better![2]

In a very important piece of research published in 2014 the Gatsby Charitable Foundation argued that *'there is no single "magic bullet" for good career guidance: it is about doing a number of things, identified in our benchmarks, consistently and well'*.[3] So, good careers provision is not just about picking the right activity, rather it is about building a programme of activities. We'll be returning to Gatsby and its benchmarks in a minute, so make a note of these as they are going to be very important!

CASE STUDY

Rita has recently been appointed as the careers leader for Dunchester Progress Academy. She's a maths teacher and has been teaching for about five years. The governors have decided that they want to see big improvements in the school's careers provision, so they created the careers leader role to drive this. Rita teaches maths three days a week, and leads careers for two days a week. However, she doesn't know very much about careers.

She starts by doing some reading about careers and talking to the staff about what is currently going on in the school. Lots of the documents and research that she reads talk about 'careers programmes', but when she looks around the school she doesn't really see anything that you could call a programme. There is a careers adviser, some lessons in PSHE and a few trips and visits and so on, but it is all a bit fragmented. Rita resolves to start by mapping what is there and trying to figure out how she can piece it all together better.

Reflective questions: How did you get the job of careers leader? Where do you think is the best place for a new careers leader to start?

Quantity, diversity, quality and context

We are learning about our careers all the time. The next time you stand up in front of a class, some students will be deciding that they want to be a teacher or a careers professional, while others will be deciding that this is something that they definitely don't want to do. Pretty much everything that happens in our life has the potential to influence our thinking about our career. Young people are soaking up these influences all the time, from the internet, the TV, their parents and their friends. But these kinds of influences tend to be limited by young people's own networks and by the media that they are exposed to. This means that there are whole areas of the labour market that young people never hear about and that lots of what they do learn about how work operates is second hand and filtered through fairly unreliable sources. TV is full of dramas and comedies about hospitals and various kinds of cop shows, but your students would be well advised to view these as, at best, a very partial source of careers information. This is even true of the so-called 'reality' shows which students might be inclined to trust more. Your careers programme should engage with these media representations, but also offer some alternatives.

Resources: Using the media

Although it is a very bad idea to get all of your careers information from the popular media, this doesn't mean that you should ignore it altogether. TV programmes and internet memes have a huge influence on young people and it is worth spending time in your careers programme reflecting on what messages young people are receiving. Sometimes this might be about helping young people to realise the dreams that TV programmes have inspired them to, at other times it might be about correcting misinformation or providing a bit of wider context. Most importantly you should be trying to develop young people's skills to explore, critique, supplement and act on the careers information that they find in the media.

One simple thing that you can be doing as a careers leader is trying to make sure that young people are exposed to opportunities to find out about and experience careers and educational routes that they might not otherwise have experienced. There are real benefits for those young people who experience more, and more diverse, careers support. A lot of learning comes through repetition and through building on previous experiences. So, hearing from one employer might not have an impact, but regular encounters with employers throughout education starts to make a real difference.[4]

However, just increasing the quantity and diversity of careers support is not enough. It is also important to attend to the quality of the support that is offered. We'll be talking a lot more in this section about what good-quality careers support looks like. But there are a few questions that you should be asking about any activity, encounter or experience that you organise so as to ensure that it is good quality.

- What is this activity designed to achieve?
- How will we maximise students' opportunity to learn from this activity?
- How does this activity fit with everything else that students have done in the careers programme and in the wider curriculum?
- Are we doing this often enough and for long enough to make a difference?
- Have we done this before and how well did it work?
- What is the role that we are asking the students to play in this activity?
- Who is going to lead this activity?
- How can we involve employers and/or learning providers in delivering this activity?
- How can we adapt this activity so that it addresses the needs of different students?
- How will we provide participants with feedback on what they have done?

As a careers leader you need to work to ensure that your students get access to a wide range of high-quality career learning activities. However, there is a danger that as the number of careers activities grows they become repetitive and confusing for students. Increasingly frantic activity doesn't necessarily result in more career learning. In fact, sometimes the opposite can be the case as students get lost in a blizzard of information. This highlights your most important role as a careers leader: you are the person who designs the programme of careers education and who provides the glue that sticks all of the different pieces of your programme together.

A good careers programme is progressive. It links together different activities in a logical order, ensuring that each experience builds on previous learning, and creates a pathway for students to learn about their careers. How you design your school or college's careers programme is up to you. You should be influenced by the type of institution, the level of engagement of the staff, the proximity of employers and universities and a host of other factors. This means that every careers programme will be different.

What careers support do students need?

An individual's career is their lifelong journey through learning and work. Our education system requires young people to make choices while they are still in school or college that have implications for their future progression opportunities. Once they leave secondary or further education they will face further decisions, about future study options and jobs. Their career beyond full-time education will consist of a series of moves between different jobs and is likely to include several changes in occupation. Schools and colleges therefore need to help students with the choices and transitions they have within the school or college, but also need to equip them with the knowledge and skills to deal with the career decisions they will face beyond the school or college. Students need information, advice and guidance to help with the immediate choices, plus a set of career management, employability and independent learning skills to progress successfully through their lifelong careers. A careers programme should include: the provision of careers information; access to timely advice and guidance; and careers education within the curriculum.

Although you should make sure that your programme meets your students' needs, you don't need to start from scratch. Try to meet and talk to other careers leaders and learn from their mistakes and successes. This book is built out of the distilled wisdom of generations of careers leaders and so we've tried to pull many of the good ideas together for you. We are also lucky to be able to build on a growing consensus in research and policy about what constitutes good practice in career guidance.

We've already mentioned the Gatsby Charitable Foundation. In 2014 this organisation published *Good Career Guidance*, which drew together existing research, policy and practice to propose a framework of eight benchmarks for careers programmes in schools. In 2018 a version of the benchmarks for further education (FE) colleges was published, and in 2019 the organisation published further guidance for the special education needs and disabilities (SEND) sector. The *Gatsby Benchmarks* have become increasingly influential around the world. In England they form the basis of the government's statutory guidance[5] and they have influenced thinking in several other countries. Most importantly, we think that they are useful for careers leaders, and so we have placed the Gatsby Benchmarks at the heart of this book.

Introducing the Gatsby Benchmarks

The Gatsby Benchmarks were developed out of a research project led by Professor Sir John Holman for the Gatsby Charitable Foundation. In this project, Sir John worked with researchers from the International Centre for Guidance Studies at the University of Derby to explore what 'good career guidance' really looked like. Together they reviewed the existing research, visited the Netherlands, Germany, Hong Kong, Canada, Finland and Ireland, looked at practice in independent schools and surveyed state schools in England.

Out of this mass of evidence, and with advice from key experts and stakeholders, they synthesised this information and came up with eight areas that all schools and colleges should be focusing on (the Gatsby Benchmarks).

The Gatsby Benchmarks

1. A stable careers programme	Every school and college should have an embedded programme of career education and guidance that is known and understood by students, parents, teachers, governors and employers.
2. Learning from career and labour market information	Every student, and their parents, should have access to good quality information about future study options and labour market opportunities. They will need the support of an informed adviser to make best use of available information.
3. Addressing the needs of each student	Students have different career guidance needs at different stages. Opportunities for advice and support need to be tailored to the needs of each student. A careers programme should embed equality and diversity considerations throughout.
4. Linking curriculum learning to careers	All teachers should link curriculum learning with careers. STEM subject teachers should highlight the relevance of STEM subjects for a wide range of future career paths.
5. Encounters with employers and employees	Every student should have multiple opportunities to learn from employers about work, employment and the skills that are valued in the workplace. This can be through a range of enrichment activities including visiting speakers, mentoring and enterprise schemes.
6. Experiences of workplaces	Every student should have first-hand experiences of the workplace through work visits, work shadowing and/or work experience to help their exploration of career opportunities, and expand their networks.
7. Encounters with further and higher education	All students should understand the full range of learning opportunities that are available to them. This includes both academic and vocational routes and learning in schools, colleges, universities and in the workplace.
8. Personal guidance	Every student should have opportunities for guidance interviews with a career adviser, who could be internal (a member of school or college staff) or external, provided they are trained to an appropriate level. These should be available whenever significant study or career choices are being made.

Gatsby then trialled its Benchmarks with 16 schools and colleges in north-east England. A major evaluation conducted by the University of Derby found that the pilot was very successful, with all participating institutions massively improving their careers programme through engaging with the Benchmarks.[6] They also found that the Benchmarks resulted in improved career readiness, more engaged students and better GCSE attainment. Importantly, the study also found that that the identification of a careers leader was a critical condition required to successfully implement the Benchmarks. These Benchmarks provide a useful template for how to organise your school or college's careers provision, and are summarised in the table on pages 16–17.

While it is useful to attend to each of the Gatsby Benchmarks individually, it is also important to recognise that they describe an integrated programme of activity. Each of the Benchmarks is connected to all the others, and throughout the book we emphasise these links to highlight how you can strengthen the coherence of your programme. The table on pages 16–17 illustrates how the Benchmarks interrelate and gives examples of how different activities contribute to more than one Benchmark.

Resources: The Good Career Guidance website

The Gatsby Charitable Foundation has created a website (**www.goodcareerguidance.org.uk**) which provides further details on the Benchmarks and includes lots of ideas and inspirations from schools and colleges that have already implemented them.

Careers leaders working in special schools will find a useful guide to the Benchmarks for the SEND sector on the website (**www.goodcareerguidance.org.uk/assets/file?filePath=send/good-career-guidance-perspectives-from-the-send-sector.pdf**).

The Gatsby Foundation has also published a guide to the Benchmarks for young people in colleges (**www.gatsby.org.uk/uploads/education/final-0099-gcg-college-booklet-a5-4pp-rgb-aw1.pdf**).

The rest of this section will work through these Benchmarks in turn and look at how you can develop your programme in each of these areas and meet the standards set out in the Benchmarks. However, it is important to remember that you are creating a single programme and not a series of eight distinct activities.

Relationships between the Gatsby Benchmarks

	1. A stable careers programme	2. Learning from career and labour market information	3. Addressing the needs of each student	4. Linking curriculum learning to careers
1. A stable careers programme		All students should have access to information on the full range of options and progression routes open to them.	Careers activities should be planned with sufficient differentiation to ensure that all students are able to access the learning.	Careers education is an integral component of an embedded careers programme.
2. Learning from career and labour market information			The information provided to students should cover all the opportunities available and be offered in a variety of formats.	An important element of careers education is teaching students how to access, evaluate and use careers information.
3. Addressing the needs of each student				Careers education programmes should include activities on challenging stereotyping in career choices and overcoming barriers to progression.
4. Linking curriculum learning to careers				
5. Encounters with employers and employees				
6. Experiences of workplaces				
7. Encounters with further and higher education				
8. Personal guidance				

5. Encounters with employers and employees	6. Experiences of workplaces	7. Encounters with further and higher education	8. Personal guidance
Employers can provide careers information and advice on how to get into particular careers and can add real-life context to careers education.	The workplace is a rich resource for learning about careers.	Enabling students to hear from, and have direct experience of, providers of future study options is a key component of a careers programme.	All students should have access to career guidance from a qualified careers adviser at times when they need it.
Employers can provide careers information, through talks and networking events in school or college.	Workplace visits, and work experience and work shadowing placements provide opportunities for student to gain careers information first hand.	Students can gain information on future study options from talks from colleges, universities and apprenticeship providers, and by visits and taster sessions.	Careers advisers can provide careers information specific to a student's individual interests.
Introducing students to employers from sectors they may have dismissed can help to challenge stereotypical career choices.	Different workplace experiences might be arranged for different students, depending on their courses of study and careers aspirations.	Visits to universities in key stage 3 can help to promote higher education to students who may not have considered it as an option.	Effective links with tutorial and pastoral staff can help to identify when students might benefit from access to guidance.
Employers may offer CV writing sessions and employability skills workshops within careers education programmes.	To maximise the learning from work experience, preparation and debriefing activities should be planned in the careers education programme.	Careers education programmes should include taster sessions at colleges and universities.	Within careers education students should learn how to access and make good use of career guidance services.
	Some of the encounters with employers may take place in the workplace.	Visits to colleges and universities could be enhanced with brief talks from employers who recruit from their courses.	Careers advisers may suggest that students contact particular employers to research opportunities.
		Students could learn about apprenticeships by shadowing an apprentice in the workplace.	Careers advisers may suggest students arrange a placement to find out more about the nature of the work.
			Careers advisers will draw on students' knowledge of future study options during guidance interviews.

International reflections: The Gatsby Benchmarks

A number of countries across the world are looking at the Gatsby Benchmarks and thinking about whether they could provide a framework for their provision of career guidance for young people. The eight Benchmarks are sufficiently generic to be applicable in different national contexts: the differences are likely to be in who delivers which element. However, as the Benchmarks have travelled to different countries, there have also been some attempts to embed them in the local culture and add new elements. This process of embedding and adaptation is a good one, which we would encourage any countries interested in the Benchmarks to do. But, in this book we will continue to use the original eight Benchmarks, so it is worth exploring how these might work in different contexts.

In countries with an external careers service, that service will lead on Benchmark 8, and may have a big impact into Benchmark 1 as they negotiate a partnership agreement with the school. This will usually leave the school to lead on the other six Benchmarks, although in some countries the partnership organisation may also have a strong involvement in other Benchmarks as well, e.g. in the production of labour market information.

In countries where schools employ guidance counsellors, the school will lead on all eight benchmarks. In this case, the big question is what Benchmarks are the sole responsibility of the guidance counsellor and where should responsibilities be shared across the whole school staff?

In both cases, the Benchmarks can provide a framework for planning the whole careers programme and thinking about how the elements fit together.

The role of the careers leader

We will finish our discussion of each of the Benchmarks by looking at the role that careers leaders should play in implementing each of them. However, your most important role as a careers leader is at the top level, looking at how your whole programme works, at how the different Benchmarks and activities work together, and ensuring that all of the stakeholders (SLT, teachers, students, parents, employers and learning providers) are on board and playing their role.

To ensure that all of this happens Benchmark 1, which looks at how you build a 'stable careers programme', is critical. So it is now time to dive into the Benchmarks and start building your programme.

2.1 A stable careers programme

Every school and college should have a careers programme that is coherent, which supports young people to move through their education and on to the next stage of their life and equips them to manage their future progression through learning and work. This programme is not just a collection of activities but a progressive pathway through a range of different career learning opportunities. It should be possible to describe what your school or college's programme looks like and publish it in a way that makes it transparent for young people, their parents, employers and other key stakeholders.

Building a careers programme doesn't happen overnight. In many ways this is the most difficult of the Gatsby Benchmarks, as it is the one that ties everything together. In this chapter, we are going to tell you how to get started on building your programme and also how to create the processes that you need to ensure that your programme is well regarded, sustainable and effective.

This chapter will cover:

- assessing your current programme
- increasing your understanding about what is expected and required for a good careers programme
- engaging the key stakeholders in supporting and delivering your programme
- deciding whether the programme is effective and how it can be improved
- reflecting on your role as the careers leader.

Introduction

We've already talked about how your most important role as a careers leader is to oversee the whole careers programme and help to organise everyone involved in it. The first of the Gatsby Benchmarks is focused on this and provides some useful guidance which will help you to ensure the coherence and effectiveness of your programme.

In this chapter we are going to take you through a process of programme development which will help you to build an outstanding programme. The Careers & Enterprise Company in England refers to this process as preparing a Strategic Careers Plan. Such a plan will typically span two or three years and set out both a vision for career guidance in the school or college and plans for implementing the proposed programme. It is equivalent to a departmental or faculty development plan, and should feed into the whole school or college improvement plan.

Where are you already?

The first task in building your careers programme is deciding where you and the school or college are already. Key to this is taking a hard look at yourself and considering whether you have the skills and knowledge that you need to drive the programme forwards. We'll be looking at your continuing professional development further in Chapter 4.2, but for now start by asking yourself the following questions.

- What is your experience of careers education and guidance?
- What do you feel your strengths and weaknesses are as you assume the role of careers leader?
- Who do you have that you can ask for help and advice?
- Do you feel that you know what careers activities are taking place in the school or college already? If not, how can you find this out?
- What do you think that the school or college does well or badly with respect to careers?
- What policies, programmes and documents are written down already about careers in your school or college?
- What kind of profile does your careers programme have within the school/college and with external stakeholders?

💡 Resources: Compass

Compass is a voluntary self-review tool for assessing your careers programme. It is hosted by The Careers & Enterprise Company and designed to provide you with a quick assessment of how you are doing against the Gatsby Benchmarks.

You can use Compass for free at **www.careersandenterprise.co.uk/careers-leaders/tools-resources/**.

Ideally, you will complete Compass at least once a year and use the feedback that it gives you to drive your development plan. As you start to get more confident, you will also want to move on to use Compass+, which allows you to manage and track student progress; but, for now, just get started with Compass.

CASE STUDY

Once she starts getting into the role of careers leader, Rita starts to look around for sources of help. One of the first things that she finds is the Compass tool, which allows her to benchmark the school against Gatsby. She is fairly horrified by the result that she gets – the school isn't meeting any of the Benchmarks. So she looks down the feedback in the report and identifies a few tasks that look easy to fix.

Within Benchmark 1, the school needs to have a careers programme that is written down, on its website and communicated to key stakeholders. 'This should be easy', thinks Rita and she starts typing up what the school does for each year group. However, there are some areas where she isn't sure, so she has to speak to her colleagues. As she works her way through the draft document she is amazed to realise the number of people that she has had to talk to in the school. But, gradually it takes shape, and as she talks to people she starts to get ideas and offers of help. She starts to see that she is not just going to be managing a programme, but actually leading a dispersed careers team drawn from all parts of the school and beyond.

Reflective questions: How many of the Gatsby Benchmarks does your school meet? What is it most urgent to fix quickly? Where are your quick wins? What are some of your longer-term goals?

Where do you need to be? Examining the key drivers

We hope that the moral arguments that we've made for the importance of careers work have convinced you that you should put this at the centre of your school or college. However, you'll also need to convince everyone else that careers is important, and so it can be useful to have a few carrots and sticks up your sleeve. In this section we're going to talk about some of the key policies and drivers that influence the provision of careers in England. If you are not based in England, then it is important that you do the research for yourself to see what government policies and other key drivers exist that you should take into account when you are developing your careers programme.

We've already talked about the importance of the Gatsby Benchmarks as a framework for activities. When the Department for Education (DfE) in England launched its Careers Strategy in December 2017, it placed the Benchmarks at its heart, setting an expectation that all schools and colleges should use the framework to guide the development of their careers programmes. We've organised this book around the Benchmarks, so you should be able to work through the book and be confident that you've covered everything that you need to. The Benchmarks are an influential framework that describes good practice; although they aren't a legal requirement, they do underpin what Ofsted, the Quality in Careers Standard and others who might review your careers programme look for.

Ofsted

In England, all educators have to pay attention to Ofsted. In recent years, Ofsted has become increasingly interested in careers provision in schools and colleges, and the Education Inspection Framework contains four key judgement areas that need to be considered from the perspective of a careers programme. In some areas, Ofsted specifically highlights successful careers programmes as a feature that will typify Good or Outstanding provision:

- **Quality of education.** Is your careers programme coherently planned and able to provide learners with the knowledge and skills that they need to progress to the next stage of their lives? What is your intent for the programme and how are you measuring its impact?
- **Behaviour and attitudes.** Are you developing learners with a positive attitude to learning and work and who are resilient and able to manage challenges and setbacks?
- **Personal development.** Are students receiving a rounded career education (based on the Gatsby Benchmarks) that supports them to progress to a positive destination after school? Do curricular, extra-curricular and enrichment activities develop a wide range of capabilities in students? Does the school use destinations data to inform its provision and check on its students' progression?
- **Leadership and management.** Does the school comply with appropriate guidance and regulation? Is there evidence of clear leadership for the careers programme based around a strong vision?

Taken together, these areas mean that there are a lot of aspects of your careers programme that you might get asked about when your school or college is inspected. They focus you to think about how the programme is embedded into the curriculum, how you support students' educational decision making and transitions beyond school or college and also how you connect careers provision to wider citizenship learning and personal development. The idea of thinking about what 'contribution' young people want to make to society is a very helpful one when we are talking about their careers. For more information on Ofsted's inspections see **www.gov.uk/topic/ schools-colleges-childrens-services/inspections**.

💡 Resources: Ofsted

The Careers & Enterprise Company has published a useful guide to help you to prepare for Ofsted inspection. It is called 'The education inspection framework guide for careers leaders, school leaders and the enterprise adviser network'. It can be found at https://resources.careersandenterprise.co.uk/sites/default/ files/2020-09/1276_ofsted_guidance-digital.pdf.

For more information on Ofsted's Education Inspection Framework, see www. gov.uk/government/publications/education-inspection-framework.

Destinations data

A good careers programme should influence what students do after they leave school. Tracking former students and talking to them after they leave can provide a very useful critical perspective on your school and the curriculum that you teach. This is important information for the careers programme, but should also encourage your school or college to think more broadly about whether students are getting the skills, experiences and knowledge that they need for their lives after they leave school.

The government records and publishes information about your students' destinations after they leave school or college. Data are published on the number of NEETs (Not in Employment, Education or Training) and the number of students who progress to apprenticeships and universities. This allows comparisons to be made between your school/college and others.

As well as focusing you on your students' careers this driver also means that you need to share data with the local authority and the Department for Education to make sure that the information that they have on your school or college is accurate. For more information see **www.gov.uk/government/collections/statistics-destinations**.

Education Act 2011

The Education Act 2011[7] provides the legal basis for any demands that are made on your school or college with respect to careers. It says that your school or college 'must secure that all registered pupils [students] at the school [college], from Year 8 to age 18, are provided with independent career guidance during the relevant phase of their education'. Government legislation of this kind is notoriously difficult to understand, which is why governments then issue statutory guidance to help to explain what it means. We'll come to that in a minute, but for now, it is just important to recognise that you have a legal requirement to provide your students with some careers support. For more information see **www.legislation.gov.uk/ukpga/2011/21/part/4/crossheading/careers-education-and-guidance**.

Technical and Further Education Act 2017

The Technical and Further Education Act 2017[8] requires all schools and academies to ensure that there is an opportunity for a range of education and training providers to access all pupils in year 8 to year 13. This is designed to ensure that all pupils are given information about technical education and apprenticeships. Again, this is a formal legal requirement for schools, and in addition to ensuring that providers have access to your school you also have to publish a provider access statement on your website saying how you are doing this. The duty has been further strengthened through the Skills and Post-16 Education Act 2022,[9] which specifies the number of such sessions with providers that schools must arrange, and which pupils must attend, in different year groups.

Education (Careers Guidance in Schools) Act 2022

This piece of legislation[10] extends the scope of the statutory requirement of schools to secure access to independent careers guidance to cover all pupils in secondary education – bringing in pupils in Year 7 for the first time and all academies – with effect from September 2022.

Statutory guidance

Statutory guidance is designed to help schools and colleges to interpret what their legal obligations really mean in practice. In effect it gives government a second chance to tell you what you need to do and to try to do it more clearly. Government changes the statutory guidance most years, but normally it evolves fairly slowly with minor changes. Of course, once in a while, like in 2017–18, it makes some major changes.

The current version of the statutory guidance strongly endorses the Gatsby Benchmarks and requires all schools and colleges to appoint a careers leader (hence the creation of this book!). It also requires schools and colleges to publish information about their careers provision on their website. At a minimum, this should include the name and contact details of the careers leader, a summary of the careers programme and information about how the school or college measures the impact of the programme on students. So, if you follow the advice that we give you in the book you should be meeting the statutory guidance. For more information, see **www.gov.uk/ government/publications/careers-guidance-provision-for-young-people-in-schools**.

Quality in Careers Standard

The Quality in Careers Standard is a voluntary external assessment of your school or college's provision. Although it is voluntary it is 'strongly recommended' in the statutory guidance, and your school will probably get a lot out of engaging with the Standard. There is a cost to accreditation through the Standard, so you will need to decide whether it is worth the investment. The Quality in Careers Standard focuses on ensuring that your school or college has a good careers programme, is meeting the Gatsby Benchmarks and is committed to continuous improvement. It can provide public, externally assessed evidence that your school's programme is of high quality. Further information about Quality in Careers Standard is available at **www. qualityincareers.org.uk**.

International reflections: Key drivers

The drivers described above are specific to England; if you are working in a school or college in another country, it will be important to find out what the policy and accountability measures are for career guidance for young people.

Start by looking at national government policies in the area, but also think about local government and what they are looking for. It is also important to remember that drivers do not just come from government; they also emerge from business, the community and from parents and students.

Spending time thinking about what the world outside your school is looking for from your careers programme will help you to develop your strategy.

Building your programme

Once you've figured out where you are already and have reviewed the various drivers that exist, you are ready to start putting together your programme. Schools and colleges often construct a detailed document which sets out what careers activity they are going to do with each year group, when it will take place, who is involved and how they will monitor or evaluate it.

There are a few key principles that you will want to keep in mind when you are designing your programme. Your programme should be …

Universal. Every student should get access to all aspects of your careers programme. So, all students should meet employers, visit a university, do work experience, have a careers interview and so on. You need to build this universal coverage into the way that you design the programme.

Progressive. The programme should cover every year of secondary education (year 7 to year 13). Careers is not something that can be left until key decision points (like choosing GCSEs) or until the end of school or college. It should happen throughout education and care should be taken to ensure that the activities that take place in each year build on those in the previous year.

Student centred. Students are at the heart of your careers programme and all activities should be organised to maximise students' career learning.

Outcome focused. It is important for you to think about what kinds of outcomes your programme is really trying to achieve and then to monitor how far you are successful in meeting these outcomes. We will be looking at setting learning outcomes in Chapter 2.4, using the Career Development Framework and other relevant learning frameworks. We will also be looking at identifying the outcomes of your programme more widely and considering how you can monitor against these outcomes in Chapter 4.1.

Link to Gatsby Benchmarks 1–8
Your careers programme should link to ALL of the other Gatsby Benchmarks. It should explain how the whole thing fits together, but also provide evidence that you are addressing each of the Benchmarks.

The most important thing when you are building a careers programme is to think about what young people need to be successful in their careers. The Gatsby Benchmarks provide a useful summary of this, but you will need to go deeper and provide more detail as you build your programme. The Benchmarks give a broad indication of what activities to provide in a careers programme, but they need to be aligned to a set of learning outcomes for the students. So, the Gatsby Benchmarks set out the aspiration that every young person should have an encounter with an employer every year. Your careers programme will look at what this means in detail, answering the question of what kind of encounter Year 8 will get, when it will happen and how it fits into your wider programme. Most importantly, you will need to think about what educational purpose this encounter serves and how it might be useful to the young person.

Resources: Tracker

The Careers & Enterprise Company provides a free online tool called Tracker. Tracker helps you to build and manage your careers programme and keep track of it all in one place. It also produces downloads which are designed to help you to share your plan with colleagues and other stakeholders. You can access Tracker at https://tracker.careersandenterprise.co.uk/info.

If you are not going to use Tracker you can create a spreadsheet to achieve a similar outcome. At its most basic this might just look like this …

Summarising your careers programme

Gatsby Benchmarks								
	1	2	3	4	5	6	7	8
Year 7	School careers prog-ramme	Using labour market data in maths	Discussion of stereotyping and gender roles – PSHE	Use of heritage industry materials in history	Employer assembly talks	Visit to the box factory	Assembly talks from current students and apprentices	Intro-ductory group session from careers adviser
Year 8	...							

Showing your programme to the world

Planning your programme and writing it down is only the start of the process. It is really useful to use Tracker or a detailed spreadsheet to keep track of what you do internally, but you should also produce an external version of your plan. If you are doing all of these fantastic things, you want to make sure that you can show them to the world!

Schools in England are required to present their careers programme as a section of their website. This summary can then link to a more detailed document that sets out what happens in each year. Some of the best schools also present detailed pages divided by the audience group that they are aimed at: pupils, parents, employers and so on. The important thing is to make sure that you are clearly communicating what your school does in a way that is meaningful to the relevant audience.

As you start to develop your programme you will probably want to include more details, such as your contact information for employers and other stakeholders. It is best to communicate your programme to others concisely on one or two pages.

Resources: Examples of careers programmes from real schools

Bedford Academy **www.bedfordacademy.co.uk/careers/24.html**.

Biddenham **www.biddenham.beds.sch.uk/careers-education/**.

Beaumont Leys School **www.beaumontleys.leicester.sch.uk/Our-School/Careers-at-BLS/**.

The Misbourne **www.themisbourne.co.uk/1238/careers-education-2**.

John Hampden Grammar School **www.jhgs.bucks.sch.uk/44/careers-resources**.

You are also required to publish a *provider access statement* as part of your careers programme. This should set out how you will ensure that *all* students will be able to learn about *all* educational routes including further education, higher education, apprenticeships and other forms of work-based learning. Typically, this should happen through students having direct access to a range of different providers. The provider access statement was introduced because the government was worried that schools were overly focused on sixth form and university routes and often ignored technical alternatives.

Link to Gatsby Benchmark 7

Publishing a provider access statement is closely linked to Benchmark 7, which asks you to ensure that students have encounters with further and higher education. As you plan the activities that relate to Benchmark 7 you will in effect be putting together your provider access statement.

Get your colleagues involved

Writing a careers programme is not something that you should just beaver away at on your own. The creation of your programme offers you an opportunity to get key people involved in your school or college. A careers programme needs to be a whole school/college endeavour, it can't be your private project. So when you are creating the programme you should meet with the following people, get their input and sign them up to support the programme that you are creating.

Head teacher/college principal. It is really important that the top person sees the importance of careers and has the opportunity to provide some input. In most cases you wouldn't expect a head teacher or college principal to be involved in the day-to-day running of the careers programme, but it is important that they understand the rationale for the programme, what the Gatsby Benchmarks are and what they mean for careers provision in your school/college.

Senior leadership team (SLT). As with the head/principal, it is important the SLT understands the rationale for the careers programme and the broad approach to delivery that you have taken. In addition to the specific purposes of preparing young people for future study and work and helping them to decide on the next best steps, a good careers programme can also contribute to the wider aims of the school or college. Interest in the ways in which careers education and guidance can support school and college improvement goals has been recognised in recent years. For example, students who have a clear idea of their next steps are better motivated to study and are likely to achieve higher grades.[11] It is important that the careers leader explores these links with the SLT. It is also critical that you identify one person on the SLT (unless you are on the SLT yourself) who has accountability for careers at the top level; this person is your senior champion and should work closely with you on the strategy for the careers programme.

Governors. Many of the responsibilities that schools and colleges have with respect to careers are actually the responsibilities of the governing body. The governing body has the duty to make sure that the school or college delivers excellent career guidance. This should mean that you send your careers programme to the board of governors for scrutiny, that you present it and receive feedback and that the governors hold the school or college accountable for delivery. To make this work effectively it is very helpful if a *link governor* is appointed whom you can connect with more regularly and who has an interest in the careers programme.

Teaching/lecturing staff. Careers needs to become the responsibility of the whole school/college. This means that you need to engage as many teachers/lecturers as possible. Every teacher/lecturer should understand that they should be making links within their subject, supporting young people through the tutorial system and making a contribution to the wider careers programme.

Careers advisers. Careers advisers are one of the most important partners in the delivery of your careers programme. As well as leading on Benchmark 8, they will also have knowledge and expertise to put into all the other Benchmarks. Getting their input to your programme should be invaluable.

SENCO or SEND lead. You need to make sure that your careers programme works for all students. To ensure that you are not missing anyone out, it can be useful to seek input from the school's SENCO or whoever is responsible for leading on special educational needs and disabilities in your school.

Other school/college staff. Depending on how your school or college is organised you might have a wide range of other staff. Some of these, such as the librarian, will have key roles to play in operationalising your careers programme. But it is important that all staff in the school/college are aware of the programme and that you encourage them to support it by talking to students about careers and getting involved in the activities that you are organising.

Students. Ultimately the programme that you are running is designed to meet student need. It can be really valuable to talk to students in advance, to hear their experiences of careers so far and see what ideas they have about what would be useful.

Parents. Parents and carers are intensely interested in their children's future and are a major influence on their plans. It is good practice to engage parents in your careers programme, so it is useful also to collect their views about the programme and what they see as important. Parents of young people with SEND often feel particularly anxious about their child moving on from school, and careers leaders in special schools find it helpful to engage parents in the programme from an early stage.

All of these different stakeholders have a role to play in shaping your careers programme. As well as talking to them when you are putting the programme together, it is also important to have a process for gathering systematic feedback from them over the course of the year. This feedback and evaluation is discussed further in Chapter 4.1.

International reflections: Colleagues

Depending on the country that you are in, the key professional roles in your school may be configured differently. The key point is that this is not a lone activity, and it is important to involve your colleagues. If you are in a system based on a guidance counsellor model you can probably draw on the relationships that the guidance counsellor has built around other issues. If you are in a system that relies on an external careers organisation to deliver some of the elements of the programme, it is important to involve that organisation at the planning stage.

Get people involved beyond your school

By its nature, careers work is about learning about and moving into new opportunities beyond the school/college. This requires you to involve other individuals and organisations and to give students the opportunity to meet employers, employees, students and learning providers. We discuss this further in Chapters 2.5, 2.6 and 2.7 (involving employers and education and training providers), and in Chapter 3.4 (the role of the careers leader as a networker).

Benchmark 1 asks a lot less of your networking skills. All it requires you to do is to make sure that all of the key stakeholders in your programme (students, parents, teachers, employers and learning providers) are aware that your school/college runs a careers programme and that they are clear about what is in it. They should also be able to find a point of contact (i.e. you!) and have an opportunity to give you feedback on how the programme is working. This is one of the reasons why it is so important for you to publish your careers programme on your website. By doing this, you are telling the world that your school or college cares about careers and that you want people to come and work with you to support young people.

Every area has an Enterprise Co-ordinator whose job it is to work with the local schools and colleges to improve their careers programme and make a meaningful link to business. If you don't know your local contact, you can get involved by signing up on The Careers & Enterprise website: **www.careersandenterprise.co.uk/careers-hub/join-the-network**.

Once you connect to the Enterprise Co-ordinator, they will help you to find an Enterprise Adviser to work closely with your school or college to develop your careers programme. An Enterprise Adviser is a volunteer from the business community whose role is to support your school or college to increase its connection to local employers and to make a strong connection to the world of work and to improve your careers programme.

Developing your programme

The final stage in building your careers programme is to think about how you are going to be sure that what you are doing is working. We'll be covering this in more detail in Chapter 4.1, but for now the key thing is to make sure that you have written a commitment into the document that you produce to seek feedback and evaluation of your programme. This should include a list of key evaluation activities that you are going to undertake and also state when you intend to update your careers programme and produce a new version of it (usually annually). Of course, you will always be shaping, improving and tweaking your programme as you go along. If you find something that doesn't work, then change it as you go along. But it is also useful to have a moment when you stand back and think about it more strategically.

The role of the careers leader

Benchmark 1 is the most important area for the careers leader to focus on. It is here that you create both the vision of what your school or college wants to achieve and the plan for operationalising this vision. It can be tempting to approach this as a solitary process where you list everything that you are planning to do, but when you are putting together your programme is the ideal time to engage everyone in the school/college and beyond and get them to commit to the ways that they are going to support you.

Because of this, you will need to recognise that creating your careers programme is going to take time and that achieving your full vision will probably take you a few years.

The key jobs for careers leaders in relation to Benchmark 1 include:

- leading the team of teachers, administrators, external partners and others who deliver career guidance
- advising the SLT team on policy, strategy and resources for career guidance and showing how these meet the Gatsby Benchmarks
- formulating a vision for career guidance in the school/college and getting it endorsed by the SLT and governors
- preparing and implementing a career guidance development plan and ensuring that details of the careers programme are published on the school's or college's website
- understanding the implications of a changing education landscape and labour market for career guidance, e.g. technical education reform, employment trends
- monitoring delivery of career guidance across the eight Gatsby Benchmarks, using the Compass evaluation tool.

In a nutshell

You need to develop a careers programme for your school or college and communicate it to the world. To do this you will need to:

- reflect on the existing provision and on whether you have the skills and knowledge to drive change
- find out about what is expected of the school or college by examining all of the drivers, regulations and requirements that exist
- create a plan that builds on the Gatsby Benchmarks and describes what you are going to do for every year group
- think about how you will communicate your programme to the key stakeholders
- use the development of the plan as an opportunity to engage both internal and external stakeholders in what you are trying to do
- plan to gather feedback and to evaluate your programme to help you to continue to develop it.

2.2 Career and labour market information

The foundation of all careers support is access to good-quality information about the opportunities available and the progression options that follow from them. Without such information young people cannot make informed choices about their future pathways.

Career and labour market information includes information on future study options, such as GCSE and A level examination courses, vocational programmes and technical education qualifications, such as T levels, in schools and FE colleges, apprenticeships and higher education, as well as information on jobs and the labour market. It also encompasses information on related matters such as student finance and sources of advice and guidance.

This chapter will cover:

- sources of careers information
- the principles of providing good-quality careers information
- teaching young people career research skills.

Introduction

Career and labour market information sits at the heart of careers programmes in schools and colleges. It describes the world within which young people are going to pursue their careers. Careers programmes should help young people to gain a broad overview of the education system and of how the world of work is organised.

Careers advisers providing personal guidance, and tutors and mentors offering initial information and advice, need access to career and labour market information to enable them to support young people and ensure that the guidance they offer is informed by the realities of the opportunities available. Information on study options and jobs should also be provided to parents, so that informal discussions with their sons and daughters are informed by accurate knowledge and understanding of the options and pathways available.

You cannot possibly give information on each and every opportunity to all students and their parents. Nor can you expect that every staff member in your school or college will have an encyclopaedic knowledge of the education and employment system. Your responsibilities are to make career and labour market information available and to help students to develop the skills to access the information and to use it effectively.

Key decision points

Students will need access to information on future study options and opportunities in the world of work. There are some key decision points when career and labour market information is particularly critical.

> **Years 8 or 9.** Students in schools make choices about GCSE and other options in Year 9, or in some schools in Year 8. They will need information on the courses available in their own school and any opportunities available at age 14 in local colleges, university technical colleges (UTCs) or studio schools. They will also need to start thinking about what the careers and educational implications are of choosing particular combinations of GCSEs. This means that it is important to provide information on the qualification requirements of different occupations and courses.

> **Year 11.** A further, significant decision point comes in Year 11, when students make choices about continuing study post-16. At this stage they will need information on courses available in their own school, if it has a sixth form, and any other local schools with which their current school may be working in a collaborative arrangement, on courses at local further education colleges and sixth form colleges and on apprenticeships and other forms of work-based training. Again, this kind of immediate information also needs to be supplemented with career and labour market information that provides a longer view on what qualifications can be used for.

> **Year 13.** All students are required to continue in education or training up to age 18. Post-18 study options include both higher education and further education courses, and apprenticeships. Schools and colleges should make information available on all these options. After 18 some young people will make the move into employment and so they will need career and labour market information that supports the transition directly into work.

There are, therefore, three key transition points during 11–18 education and at each stage students, and their parents, should be given information on not only the courses and qualifications open to them, and the progression routes that follow, but also the institutions where they might be studying.

International reflections

The key decision and transition points for young people will be different in each country. It is important for you to consider when they are in your context and also to think about when it is important to start preparing young people for these key choices (usually it is long before they actually have to make any decisions). Young people should know when they are required to make a decision, what they are deciding between and how the processes of decision making and transition work.

Link to Gatsby Benchmark 7

Providing information on future study options links with Benchmark 7, which addresses information and experiences of further study (see Chapter 2.7).

Defining career and labour market information

Throughout their time at school and college students should have access to information on different jobs and occupations, and on the labour market at local, regional, national and international levels.

Career and labour market information (CLMI, or sometimes just LMI) is what distinguishes career guidance from other, more generic forms of information, advice and guidance. It refers to data available from surveys and reported in tables and charts, as well as more qualitative information, such as narratives from employees. Sometimes people use the term 'labour market intelligence': this relates to the interpretation of CLMI and the consideration of what it means for individuals' careers.

Careers and labour market information (CLMI) describes a broader range of information, encompassing not only economic factors and jobs but also opportunities and progression routes in education and training, and other careers-related matters such as financial support and sources of information, advice and guidance.

CLMI and school or college careers programmes

There are three broad considerations with regard to using career and labour market information in designing and delivering your careers programme. Firstly, you should use CLMI to inform your strategic careers plan, to ensure that your programme reflects the range of progression opportunities open to your pupils and students. Secondly, young people should learn about the world of work and opportunities available in education, training and employment. Thirdly, young people need to know where to find career and labour market information, how to access relevant sources and how to use LMI effectively in their career planning.

Providing career and labour market information can often be about providing students with basic definitions and terms that will allow them to understand what people are talking about when they are discussing the world of work. It can be a useful exercise to get students to brainstorm a list of terms that they have heard used, and to work through these to discuss what they really mean.

There are lots of terms that it is helpful for young people to understand. Below, we suggest 10 key terms that we think it is particularly essential that you talk through with your students.

1. **CV or curriculum vitae.** A CV is a document that you use to communicate your skills, qualifications and experiences to potential employers. The term comes from curriculum vitae which is Latin for 'the course of my life'. It is also known as a resumé.

2. **Employment.** A relationship between two parties (an employer and an employee). In it the employee agrees to give up their time to do something that the employer wants done, in exchange for money. Where someone wants to work but cannot find an employer they become **unemployed**. However, if you are able to earn money without an employer, for example by selling services direct to customers, then you are **self-employed**.

3. **Labour market.** The world of work can be thought of as a marketplace in which some people (employers) are buying and others (employees) are selling their time and effort (labour).

4. **Occupation.** An occupation describes a type of job or a series of closely related jobs. It describes what someone does but doesn't describe where someone works (see *sector* below). So computer programmer is an occupation but the information technology (IT) industry is a sector.

5. **Recruitment.** The process of finding employees to fill vacant job opportunities.

6. **Salary.** A regular payment made to someone for the work that they do. It is usually described in job adverts as an annual figure. However, this annual figure will normally be described as a **gross** figure (the whole amount paid by the employer) rather than as a **net figure** (the amount that the employee actually takes home after they have paid taxes, pensions and other deductions).

7. **Sector.** The type of organisation that you work for. It doesn't describe the jobs that individual workers do. So, a university is in the education sector, but it will employ accountants, cleaners, managers and security guards as well as educators.

8. **STEM.** The term STEM describes qualifications and jobs that relate to science, technology, engineering and mathematics. This is a very broad category, but it is important because lots of commentators argue that we don't have enough workers with STEM qualifications.

9. **Trends.** Economists look at what has happened in the past to make a guess about what might happen in the future. For example, they might look at how many agricultural workers are about to retire and how many are being trained to suggest whether there is going to be a need for more agricultural workers in

the future. Such information is based on careful analysis, but is best seen as an informed guess rather than a fact.

10. **Work.** This term describes anything that an individual does which takes their time and energy. It is different from *employment*, as we are not always paid for work. So work can include volunteer work and work that people might do towards a future career, e.g. an aspiring artist who paints a picture.

So, career and labour market information covers not only the nature of jobs, qualifications and training, pay levels and so on but also details about the employers and organisations providing the jobs and information about the wider economy. Such information should cover all forms of work, including paid employment (full-time and part-time), self-employment and voluntary work.

Link to Gatsby Benchmark 4

Examining career and labour market information offers all sorts of opportunities for careers education and making links to the curriculum (Benchmark 4 – see Chapter 2.4).

It is important not just to view career and labour market information as a series of straightforward answers to questions. If we make critical use of it, and encourage our students to think critically about what it says, it can open up some big questions about how the world of work operates and how we know what we know.

Sources of career and labour market information

Careers information exists in a variety of different forms. Schools and colleges should provide the information in different formats to allow for students' preferences in how to access it. The list of possible sources of careers information includes:

- booklets, produced by the school or college
- books and directories, produced by careers publishers
- careers fairs
- careers talks
- college and university open days
- networking events
- newspapers and magazines
- occupational leaflets, produced by careers publishers, professional and trades associations, employers, sector bodies etc.
- online services, including the National Careers Service website and helpline, commercial subscription packages, Local Enterprise Partnership websites, school and college and university websites
- option information evenings for students and parents

- taster courses at colleges, apprenticeship providers and universities
- vacancy information on job boards
- workplace visits.

💡 Resources: Career and labour market information

There is a wide range of sources of career and labour market information available online. Some of the most commonly used include:

- iCould **https://icould.com**
- National Careers Service **http://nationalcareers.service.gov.uk**
- Nomis **www.nomisweb.co.uk**
- Office for National Statistics **www.ons.gov.uk/employmentandlabourmarket**
- Prospects **www.prospects.ac.uk**
- Salary Stats **www.adunza.co.uk./jobs/salaries**
- Where the Work Is **wheretheworkis.org**.

However, it can also be useful to branch out a bit and look at some other sources of information. The following sources of information can be used to get students to think critically about what is going on in the labour market.

- Corporate Watch **https://corporatewatch.org**.
- Guardian Careers **www.theguardian.com/careers**.
- Living wage employers **www.livingwage.org.uk/accredited-living-wage-employers**.
- Resolution Foundation **www.resolutionfoundation.org**.
- TUC blogs **www.tuc.org.uk/blogs**.

Many of the best careers websites make use of the government's LMI for All resource (**www.lmiforall.org.uk**). LMI for All is an online data portal which draws together existing sources of high quality, reliable labour market information and makes them available in a way that can be easily embedded into other careers websites and apps. You are probably not likely to use the LMI for All website directly, but you should look for it on other sites as a guarantee that the site is reliable and up to date.

Careers resource centres

Each school and college needs to have a physical area where students can access careers information. When you took on the job of careers leader you may have inherited a careers library with piles of old books and leaflets. These should probably be rationalised, with what you do retain organised carefully to make it easily accessible.

Increasingly, careers information is online and so it is important that you think about how students can best find and access this material. For example, a contemporary careers resource centre should probably provide several work stations to enable students to access information online, as well as guidance on how to start their investigation.

> ### 💡 Resources: Trotman Indigo books, websites and resources
>
> Trotman produces a lot of really useful resources for schools and colleges.
>
> You can download a whole host of free resources from **https://indigo.careers/ free-resources**.
>
> If you have a budget to buy some books, Trotman produces a huge range of subject- and sector-specific titles in print and online, as well as general books on applying to university and the annual *Careers* directory. See **https://trotman. co.uk** for further information. For a yearly subscription, Trotman's digital platform for schools and colleges is loaded with key information for students at each major transition point: **https://indigo.careers**.

A careers resources centre provides a brilliant venue for student self-study and research into careers. It is also somewhere that students can reach out for informal help and advice on their career and where they can have career conversations. Ideally you will have trained the member of staff who supervises the careers resource centre to make sure that they are confident to have career conversations with students.

The three key features of a good-quality careers resource centre are that it should be:
- accessible
- comprehensive
- up to date.

Accessible

Access for students is crucial. While a school or college careers centre is an important source of reference for careers advisers, teachers and tutors, its primary purpose is to provide information for students to use. The first issue to consider is where to locate the centre. Some schools and colleges favour having a separate centre, perhaps close to the rooms used for career guidance interviews. There are, however, strong arguments for creating a space within the main learning resource centre or library. This is likely to increase usage as it will attract not only students who are specifically seeking careers information but also students who chance across the centre when they are in the library for other purposes. It also means that the careers information will be in a space that is large enough to accommodate a class for a lesson on research skills. A further reason for integrating the careers library in the main library is that it makes supervision easier. This also means that it can be open for more hours.

The next issue to consider is how best to promote the resource centre. Of course it will be mentioned in careers lessons and guidance interviews, but use will increase if it is also advertised in subject departments and faculties. As a careers leader you will receive a lot of information, some of which is linked to particular subject areas. It is a good idea to pass this on to subject leaders to display in their areas of the school or college, and it would be simple to add a note advertising the careers resource centre.

Thought needs to be given also to the size and layout of the physical space. Will it be large enough to accommodate a group to teach career research skills? How will the paper-based materials be categorised and displayed? Well-presented signage and labelling will help students to orientate themselves towards the relevant sections.

Comprehensive

The second principle is that the provision of careers information should be comprehensive, i.e. cover the full range of opportunities available to students. This will include general careers reference materials; occupational information including labour market information (LMI); information on further education, higher education and apprenticeships; and information on colleges, apprenticeship providers, universities and employers. Some careers centres also display local vacancies. The centre should also provide information on student finance and how to access careers advice and guidance.

Up to date

The third principle is that the information in the centre should be up to date. Careers information dates very quickly and it is better to have a smaller collection of up-to-date materials than a larger quantity that give inaccurate information. All printed materials need to be date-stamped and part of the ongoing maintenance of the library should involve removing out-of-date literature. It is also important to check that any online material is still active and current. Some schools and colleges make use of student helpers to assist with these tasks.

Creating and linking to online sources

As schools and colleges move on from careers libraries of printed materials to developing resource centres to provide access to online resources, careers leaders are working with website managers to create careers sections on their schools' or colleges' websites.

We discussed the importance of creating a careers section on your website in Chapter 2.1 to communicate information about your careers programme to all of your stakeholders. This provides a brilliant starting point for you to provide careers and labour market information and other resources. This may include information generated within the school or college, particularly about courses and qualifications provided within the school or college or through local partnerships, but should also provide links to several different online sources.

There are a few commercial products that provide portals for organising careers information weblinks in a way that is bespoke to the school or college.

💡 Resources: Bookmarking useful information

It can be useful to get students to establish a system for bookmarking interesting career and labour market information that they want to go back to later. There is a range of online bookmarking tools that you can use for this purpose. Lifewire reviewed a series of the leading bookmarking tools in May 2018 (**www.lifewire.com/best-bookmarking-tools-for-the-web-3486309**).

It can be good to introduce students to a tool like this in a lesson on research skills and then to make sure that they use it whenever they are doing any research.

International reflections: Sources of careers and labour market information

If you work in a school of college in a country other than England it is important that you find out what the reliable sources of local, regional and national careers and labour market information are. In countries that have an external careers service, that service will probably be the most accessible source. Some of the countries in which schools employ guidance counsellors have set up national organisations with a specific remit to provide careers and labour market information to help guidance counsellors keep up to date.

If in doubt, a good starting point is always your country's national statistics service. They will typically publish freely available government data online. Alongside this, you should become familiar with online job sites and vacancy boards that allow you to see the various positions that are currently on offer.

Finally, remember that CLMI is not just about the labour market and should also include information about the education system. So look for sources of information in your country on universities, vocational education and other learning pathways.

Teaching career research skills

There is a wealth of careers information available, but young people need to be helped to access and use it effectively. When The Careers & Enterprise Company commissioned some research about how young people go about making careers choices it found that lack of information is not generally the main problem.[12] The problem is making use of the range and diversity of the information available to them. It concluded that students needed education to build their confidence and capability to make sense of the information. Careers research, or career exploration, skills should be an integral part of a school's or college's programme of careers education.

Link to Gatsby Benchmark 4

Teaching students the skills to access and use careers information links with Benchmark 4, which is covered in Chapter 2.4.

Students are taught research skills in several different parts of the curriculum but they are not always good at transferring the learning from one subject to another. It is important, therefore, to organise activities that teach information research skills in the context of career choices or to help students to transfer their wider research skills to the context of career.

Researching career, like researching any subject, essentially boils down to asking some good questions. The following questions should provide a helpful starting point to your students' research process.

Career research questions

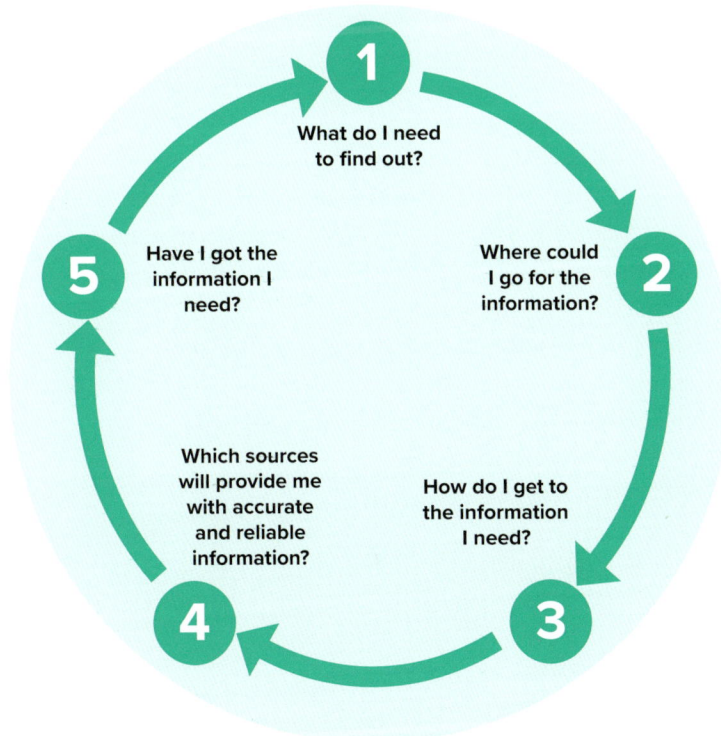

1. **What do I need to find out?** Framing and clarifying the questions you need answers to.

2. **Where could I go for the information?** Considering where you might go and whom you might go to, to find the answers to your questions.

3. **How do I get to the information I need?** Considering how you can get access to the information that you need in an efficient and timely manner.

4. **Which sources will provide me with accurate and reliable information?** Asking critical questions about what the information tells you and what it doesn't. This step is crucial: it involves looking at the date of the information, but also distinguishing between objective information and subjective material that aims to recruit or influence young people. It is important that they learn to distinguish between the two and become alert to potential bias. Students should also have access to subjective views on different options, for example from students currently studying the courses they are considering or from employees working in particular jobs they are investigating. But they need to be taught how to evaluate all sources in order to then make up their own minds about what they want to do.

5. **Have I got the information I need?** The final, review stage includes going back over the information they set out to find and identifying any gaps. Students may well then need to repeat the cycle and look at new sources of information.

Increasingly, a lot of careers research skills are bound up with students' digital literacy. It is important to encourage students to use online sources of careers information, but also to make sure that they have the skills they need to find and retrieve careers information online and evaluate the provenance of such sources. You shouldn't make an assumption that all young people have good digital skills. While most will be active users of IT, very few will ever have made use of these skills in the context of their career. It is also useful to remember that the digital environment is not just about information, it is also a place where it is possible to establish contacts and make applications and these activities also need to be covered in your careers programme.

Activities to teach career research skills should cover the kinds of career and labour market information that are available online and the skills that are needed to make the most of this information.

CASE STUDY

At Dunchester Progress Academy, career exploration skills are taught in all three key stages.

In Year 8, as part of a curriculum day on the world of work, pupils are given a quiz of 20 careers questions that they have to complete by using the careers information centre and talking to the employers leading the other activities. Within the Year 9 PSHE course, pupils work in pairs to draw up a list of things they would want to know about a job. They then have to think of a job that their partner could do and use a variety of sources to find the answers to their questions about that job. The pairs then present the information first to their partner and then to the class. A plenary review discussion focuses on what sources of information they found useful and what information they were unable to find.

At the beginning of Year 11, again as part of the PSHE course, students are asked to research particular post-16 options that they are considering, using a variety of sources of information. After a plenary review of what they have found out, they are then asked to research one example of a job that could follow from one of the study options they looked at.

In the sixth form, all students complete an online guidance tool that explores the higher education options that match their preferences. The results encourage students to undertake further research on the options that the tool suggests. Students complete this research in their own time and then discuss their findings in one of their regular individual reviews with their tutor.

All students also undertake a three-day work shadowing placement as part of their study programme. One of the things they are asked to do is to interview one employee about their job, how they got into it, what they think about it and where they might be moving on to.

Reflective questions: Where in your school or college curriculum are students taught to find CLMI and how to use it to research their own careers? Which subject and course areas could you work with on this?

Working with parents

Throughout this chapter we've referred to the importance of providing information for parents. This is important as young people turn to their parents for careers advice long before they seek the opinion of a teacher or careers adviser. If we can engage parents in the career learning of their children and ensure that they are well informed there are huge benefits. However, it is often easier said than done. It is very easy for resources sent home to parents to languish in the bottom of school bags and never to see the light of day. So it is important that you think creatively about involving parents.

We have seen the following approaches used effectively to ensure that parents have access to careers and labour market information.
- Producing options packs or booklets which provide basic careers and labour market information around option choices.
- Emailing parents with a list of key websites to look at with their children.
- Getting students to interview or involve their parents in career conversations as part of PSHE homework.
- Including a session on careers as part of a parents' evening.
- Running an information session or even a short careers course for parents in the evening.

> ## 💡 Resources: Engaging parents
>
> The Gatsby Foundation has created a toolkit for parents to help them have informed conversations with their children about the different training and education pathways available to them: www.talkingfutures.org.uk.

The role of the careers leader

Part of the role of careers leader is to take responsibility for ensuring that students and parents have access to good-quality information on future study options and career opportunities. You may take on some of the tasks of establishing, maintaining and developing the careers information yourself, but you may also work in partnership with the learning resources manager, or librarian, to manage the provision of careers information. You also need to work with the middle leaders and senior leaders who produce options booklets and organise information evenings on choices at 14, 16 and 18, and form a close relationship with the website manager to help to build, or at least link to, a suite of online resources.

But your role extends beyond making careers information available and accessible: it also involves planning activities to help students develop the important career management skills of using the careers information effectively.

Key tasks for the careers leader relating to careers information include:
- managing the provision of careers information
- planning activities to teach careers information skills.

In a nutshell

As the careers leader you are responsible for ensuring that students, and their parents, are provided with good-quality careers information. You will need to:

- establish and maintain a careers resource centre
- work with middle and senior leaders to ensure that students and their parents are provided with information on all future study options at key points of transition
- work with the PSHE leader and other curriculum leaders, where appropriate, to design activities to teach students career research skills
- keep up to date with reforms in education and training, with changes in the labour market, and with sources of careers information and LMI.

2.3 Addressing the needs of all students

The principles of differentiation are widely applied to curriculum planning and delivery in all subjects, and should be used when planning careers programmes. A career is a highly individual thing so career learning needs to be differentiated. Everyone has different capabilities, career aspirations and motivations, and everyone will pursue a unique path through their life and career.

This means that it is important to expose all students to all opportunities and to make sure that you are clear as to what they have been exposed to by keeping good records on each student.

This chapter will cover:

- thinking about whether your provision is independent and impartial
- avoiding stereotyping and bias in the way that you deliver your programme
- exploring the nature of 'aspirations' and thinking about how you can best support them
- identifying what kind of support students need and making sure it is made available
- keeping good records on the provision that you are offering (at an individual student level)
- tracking your students over the long term
- meeting the needs of young people with special educational needs and disabilities (SEND).

Introduction

One of the key principles that should underpin a good careers programme is the idea that students' career learning should be driven by the needs of the young person rather than those of the school or college. Another is that your careers programme should recognise the differences between students while seeking to support all their aspirations, even where these might be difficult within an unequal society. A third principle is that you should know where the young person is in terms of their career learning and plan your activities to move them forward from that point.

In this chapter we are going to take you through how best to address the needs of all students. In some ways, this Benchmark is one of the more complex and abstract ones. It asks you to think about impartiality, stereotyping, differentiation and tracking the impact of your careers programme. However, it is possible to bring all of these different issues together by focusing on the needs of the student and thinking about practical ways to ensure that these are met.

Independence and impartiality

Once you spend some time in the careers world you will often hear the terms 'independence' and 'impartiality'. These are key terms which are used to encapsulate an important idea that should underpin your careers programme. We can summarise this idea as follows.

Students should be supported to pursue their career aspirations. The school or college should not seek to shape these aspirations in its own interest or in the interests of a particular government policy.

This seems like it should be pretty uncontentious. But, in practice it is a bit trickier than it looks, as the following case studies show.

CASE STUDY

Raj is a careers adviser who is employed by Dunchester Progress Academy. He is in the process of seeing the year 11s about their post-16 choices. One of the students, Suzie, has been to see him three times now, and has been bouncing between leaving school to go to art college or staying on at school to do A levels (including art). Raj has been getting her to think through the different possibilities, encouraging her to visit the art college and write lists of pros and cons. But Suzie keeps changing her mind.

Meanwhile, Sandra, who is the head of art at the academy, comes to see Raj. She tells him that recruitment for the art A level is really weak this year. If they don't get another student it won't run. She mentions Suzie and asks if he can talk to her.

Reflective questions: If you were the careers leader in this school, what would you say to Raj, and what would you say to Sandra?

CASE STUDY

Another of Raj's regular students, Justin, is also in a dilemma, but this time in year 13. He's a high-achieving student who has good grades and is thinking of going on to do engineering at university. But, Raj has also shown him some of the literature from the government about apprenticeships. There are some good opportunities in engineering that he thinks it would be worth Justin thinking about. Government policy is strongly encouraging apprenticeships and the labour market information shows a clear need for more high-achieving apprentices. But, Justin's family are not sure about apprenticeships and feel that university might be the safer opportunity. The question is whether to give Justin a bit of a push …

Reflective questions: How are apprenticeships viewed in your school? What could you do to better inform your colleagues about what contemporary apprenticeships are like?

As both case studies show, the issues are not always clear cut. What is good for the school or in line with government policy aims may also be good for the student, but the student may not always be aware of this. As a careers leader you have lots of opportunities to put possibilities in front of young people, and how you choose to do this may shape the choices that the young people make. You also might be called on to help mediate between a careers adviser like Raj and an anxious subject head like Sandra who is trying to recruit to her A level course. The trick is to try to present as wide a range of possibilities to young people without completely overwhelming them, and to leave the decision making in their hands as much as possible.

It can be helpful to think through the possible stances that can be taken in relation to recommending a particular career option to a student.

Stances when advising students

Independent	Where personal guidance or career support is being given by someone who has no organisational or financial interest in the outcome. This is very difficult, as someone has to pay the wages of careers advisers and normally that is a school, college, university or other party that has a clear interest in the outcome.
Impartial	Where personal guidance or career support is being given by someone who is committed, usually through some kind of professional ethical framework, to serving the interests of the students above those of the organisation that employs them. As a careers leader you should commit to being impartial and support the careers advisers that you work with when they are delivering services impartially.

Transparently partial	There is nothing wrong with a subject lead, college, university or employer trying to recruit students to their organisation. It is good for students to hear a range of perspectives and it is only reasonable that everyone will want to promote their subject, course or career. The important thing is to clearly signal to students that this is just one perspective and to encourage them to recognise that the person telling them how wonderful their course is has a vested interest in saying this.
Offering multiple perspectives	Students should get to hear from and experience multiple different career possibilities. On its own, each one of these perspectives will be partial, but taken together they present enough options to be able to say that a young person has had an impartial careers education.
Fostering criticality	Perhaps most importantly, we should be encouraging our students to think critically about all of the different people that they are interacting with as they consider their careers. Criticality is not about encouraging cynicism but, rather about trying to put what people say and the advice that they give into context. This is about being positive about what everyone says without believing that any one person – whether it is the careers adviser, an inspirational employer or even the careers leader – has all the answers.

Link to Gatsby Benchmark 8

The issue of independence and impartiality is key to the work of professional careers advisers (Benchmark 8) and forms part of their professional ethics.

Stereotyping, bias and injustice

Following on from thoughts about independence and impartiality it is also important to recognise that students are not all the same and that society doesn't treat everyone equally. Career guidance has a strong commitment to social justice and it is important that the work that we do serves to make the world a bit more equal and a bit fairer rather than exacerbating existing inequalities.[13]

The recognition that there is a range of characteristics that influence young people's career thinking is, therefore, an important part of ensuring that you are addressing the needs of all your students. Students should be able to see that your programme takes account of their experience and provides them with career opportunities that they view as relevant. However, the purpose of addressing issues of stereotyping, bias and injustice in your careers programme goes beyond just engaging your students and allows you to explore wider issues about how the world of work operates and what some of the challenges are with that.

The Equality Act 2010[14] recognises nine protected characteristics. In addition to these protected characteristics we should add 'class' or economic background, as we know that this also makes a big difference to people's careers. The table below lists these characteristics and sets out some key questions to ask of your careers programme.

Equality and diversity in careers programmes

Age	How are younger and older people represented in your programme?
Disability	Does your programme provide examples of a range of disabled people doing different jobs?
Gender identity, transgender and inter-sex	Does your programme provide examples of people with different gender identities successfully pursuing their careers?
Marriage and civil partnership	How does your programme represent marriage, partnerships and family life as part of people's careers? Is a range of partnerships and approaches to work–life balance discussed?
Pregnancy, maternity and paternity	Does you careers programme cover the employment rights that exist around pregnancy, maternity and paternity? Are pregnancy, adoption and childcare presented as a normal part of working life?
Race	Is a range of races and ethnicities represented in your careers programme in a range of jobs and careers?
Religion or belief	Does your programme acknowledge the importance of religion and belief to some people's career aspirations? Does it show those with a range of religions and with none in different roles?
Sex	Does your programme discuss the way in which the labour market is organised by sex and gender? Does it seek to encourage young people to question and challenge this?
Sexual orientation	Does your programme represent people with different sexual orientations?
Class	Does your programme discuss the way in which economic advantage can shape people's access to careers? Does it provide young people with the knowledge and tools to challenge this? Does your programme introduce students to people in work from a range of different social and economic backgrounds beyond the students' immediate community and locality?

In relation to how you organise your careers programme it is important to recognise that each of these characteristics might make a difference to the way in which your students think about their careers. For example, despite years of progress on equal pay between men and women there is still a clear 'gender pay gap' and large areas of the labour market remain segregated into 'men's work' and 'women's work'.[15] Young people inevitably pick up on this and it influences their career thinking. Similarly, too often young people think that certain types of work are not for 'the likes of them': a good careers programme should challenge such thinking.

> **Tools: Item 2.3A. Equality and diversity audit.**
> A template for reviewing your provision from an equality and diversity perspective is provided in the online resources accompanying this book: https://indigo.careers/clh/. This asks you to think about how you address each of these issues in your provision.

Career guidance has a difficult task to help people to make their way through the stereotypes associated with different protected characteristics. On the one hand, we want to challenge stereotypes and argue that every job and career should be available to every person. On the other hand, many young people will want to pursue careers where they will find people like them, and will be understandably anxious about being the first woman, first person from an ethnic minority or first gay person into a workplace. Sadly, workplace discrimination is a real phenomenon and we need to help young people to prepare for this and develop strategies to deal with it.

The challenges that we face in supporting young people to break out of stereotypes gets to the heart of one of the main challenges of career guidance. Career guidance helps us both to think about what we want and to learn about what is possible. Sometimes these are in tension, and then career guidance has to help people to resolve this tension.

Sometimes what is possible is absolute. Not all of us are tall enough or talented enough to be professional basketball players. But, more usually we can expand what is possible by working harder and being more focused. Where the limits are placed on us by others through outright prejudice or unconscious bias, we sometimes have to recognise that we need to challenge others' perspectives in order to achieve what we want to in our careers. Sometimes, these limits are not the result of bad behaviour by an individual, but due to how society is structured. Again, it is important to acknowledge these structural issues and to encourage young people to think about what they can do about them.

As a careers leader, this means that you need to design a programme that encourages your students both to expand their ideas about what is possible and to develop strategies to challenge prejudice and power.

CASE STUDY

Rita's cousin is a successful local electrician who has worked on lots of big construction projects in the area. She invites him in to talk about his work and how he trained to be an electrician. She also asks him if he is okay with telling the class that he is gay and talking about some of his experiences in dealing with homophobia at work. He's comfortable about doing this, so they plan out his talk together. The session goes really well, and prompts a lot of debate about how to deal with prejudiced colleagues in the workplace (and in school).

After the session, Ezra comes up to Rita and comes out as trans. He says that he's worried he will face a lot of prejudice in some of the careers that he is thinking of. Rita listens and says she'll see if she can find someone for him to talk to. She contacts the local LGBTQI+ centre, and they agree to talk to Ezra about some of the support that is available for trans young people in the town.

Reflective questions: How are you addressing issues of prejudice and stereotyping in your programme? Can you bring this to life by connecting students with people with lived experiences of these issues? Do you know where to refer students to if they have issues that are beyond your experience?

The intersection between careers and equality can be a fertile area for cross-curricular links and for discussions about citizenship, democracy and the nature of the society in which we live. If careers is focused on thinking about the kind of future that young people want, then it is very difficult to separate this from a discussion about what kind of society we might live in in the future. In a democratic society, everyone has some responsibility for how society is organised. So it can be useful to encourage young people to think about whether our society provides the best environment for them to develop their career in. If not, then the question is what can they and others do about it?

This kind of discussion can feel quite abstract at times, but it is possible to do a lot of practical things to help address stereotyping and other forms of social injustice. Tristram, one of the authors of this book, working with Rie Thomsen and Ronald Sultana has developed the five signposts to socially just career guidance,[16] and these are laid out in the table on pages 52–3.

Signposts to socially just career guidance

Signpost	What you should do
Build critical consciousness	Encourage students to think about the world they live in and how they can change it.
Name oppression	Help students to recognise inequalities and injustices in their lives and the lives of others.
Question what is 'normal'	Encourage students to question stereotypes and their other assumptions about things, such as what a career or career success look like.
Work together	Support students to see that they are not on their own – that their careers are pursued alongside others with whom they often have shared goals.
Work at a range of levels	Help students to see that career is not just conducted on the level of the individual, but that it also takes place in families, organisations and societies. Encourage them to think about what they can do to develop their career by acting at all of these levels.

These conversations open up some big issues for your careers programme. It is probably not possible to address them all within the time that you have available, which is why it is important to work with other teachers on how these issues can be addressed, and given a careers spin, as a cross-curricular theme. This approach to social justice is also well integrated into the Career Development Framework of learning outcomes that you will be introduced to in chapter 2.4.

Examples	Possible curricular links
Encourage students to reflect upon their own aspirations and assumptions about what they can achieve. Talk about how these aspirations have been influenced by their family and background. Encourage students to investigate inequality and injustice that they see in education and in the labour market. Use this to open discussions about what they can do about this.	Business studies, citizenship, geography, history, philosophy, religion and ethics, politics, PSHE, sociology, economics
Spend time talking openly about the challenges and prejudices that exist for people in their careers. Discussing equality and diversity issues in relation to careers shouldn't be about pretending that 'anyone can do anything' without recognising why it is more difficult for some people than others. Discuss strategies that you can use if you see prejudice, discrimination or harassment.	Citizenship, English literature, history, philosophy, religion and ethics, politics, PSHE, sociology, economics
Make sure you routinely represent different types of people undertaking a wide range of roles. Where possible, try to use examples of people pursuing careers that challenge assumptions and expectations.	Citizenship, English literature, geography, history, philosophy, religion and ethics, politics, PSHE, sociology, economics
Encourage peer support, and encourage young people to draw on the resources in their family and community. Provide examples of where collective careering has made a difference to people's lives, e.g. trade unions improving wages and conditions, or social businesses giving people a way to work together for a common aim.	Business studies, citizenship, history, philosophy, religion and ethics, politics, PSHE, sociology, economics
Map the wide range of different influences that shape people's careers and provide examples of the ways in which people have influenced these through making choices, changing minds, changing the way businesses work and lobbying government.	Business studies, citizenship, geography, history, philosophy, religion and ethics, politics, PSHE, sociology, economics

Link to Gatsby Benchmark 4

The five signposts (see above) to socially just career guidance, as well as other resources on equality, diversity and inclusion, show how you can link some of the issues raised by Benchmark 3 to the wider curriculum (see Benchmark 4).

💡 Resources: Equality and social justice

There are a number of resources that can help you to explore some of these difficult issues of equality and social justice in your careers programme.

Career guidance for social justice **https://careerguidancesocialjustice. wordpress.com**.

Equal Choices, Equal Chances (Key stage 2) **www.equalityhumanrights.com/en/ primary-education-resources**.

STEM learning resources on equality and diversity **www.stem.org.uk/resources/ collection/2930/equality-and-diversity**.

Achieving aspirations

When you are doing careers work with young people, you are always working with their aspirations – what they want to do with their lives. People's aspirations are shaped, to some extent, by their background and life experiences.

It has become fashionable for politicians to complain about 'low aspirations' among young people, particularly those from disadvantaged backgrounds. However, most of the evidence tells us that young people have remarkably high aspirations regardless of their backgrounds, and that aspirations alone don't really explain the differences in career outcome experienced by different groups.[17] One way of thinking about this is to make a distinction between aspirations, expectations, plans and behaviour. We would argue that it is valuable to think about all of these things and to track how they change over time – perhaps by using some kind of student reflective portfolio.

Aspirations describe what someone wants to happen in their career. This might include some longshots, e.g. aspiring to be a professional footballer or pop star. However, most young people can distinguish between these high-risk career aspirations and safer choices that might serve as a plan B. When you are talking to them about their aspirations it is important to push them to talk about a variety of these different ideas about what they want to do.

Expectations describe what someone thinks will happen to them in all likelihood. Expectations describe the path of least resistance, but also reveal a lot about how people are thinking about their careers. Talking about expectations can reveal that despite high aspirations some young people are pessimistic about their future. This can be very important to know, as it helps to reveal the kind of support that might be useful for that student.

Plans describe how people think that they can go about achieving their aspirations. For example, a young person might plan to work hard so that they can get good grades and become a doctor.

Behaviours describe what someone is actually doing to bring about their aspirations. For example, are they steadily implementing their plans or ignoring them altogether?

Providing opportunities for your students to think about their aspirations is at the heart of a good careers programme. But it is also important to pay attention to the differences between what people want to happen and what they expect will happen, and to consider how far they are actually doing something proactive to make their aspirations happen.

Identifying and meeting needs

To be able to address the needs of all of your students, it is important to recognise their diversity and to respond to this. The idea of differentiation is not unique to careers, and there are several well-established strategies that you can use.

Differentiation describes the process of tailoring the speed and approach that you use in teaching to suit individual needs. Differentiation in programmes of careers education and other activities should operate in the same way as it does for other areas of the curriculum. You will have determined the intended learning outcomes for the programme or activity and you will need to have assessed the students' current levels of achievement and progress towards those outcomes. You will then be able to plan the lessons and activities to take account of the students' different starting points and make use of different resources or teaching methods to enable them all to work towards outcomes.

Targeting of additional activities. Some students will benefit from additional help to support them to develop their career. This might be because they have special needs or face some other kind of barrier, or because they have a particular interest in a career path that is not easily addressed with a whole group, or for some other reason. In some cases, you may have funding or other drivers that require you to target support at some students. Targeting can be a mixed blessing. Where it works well you can direct help and support to an individual and really help them thrive. For example, by providing a student with a mentor or an additional visit or placement. But it can also be disruptive to whole class activities and lead some students to resent being singled out while others are envious that they are not getting the same amount of help. In general, targeted activities need to be handled carefully, made available as widely as possible and their rationale clearly explained to those who participate in them (and in some cases to the wider student body).

Making effective use of the careers adviser. While the Gatsby framework says that students should have a minimum of two personal guidance interviews, some students will benefit from more interaction with careers advisers. Careers advisers work with individual young people to help them make progress in their thinking about their career plans. They are able to apply strategies for reviewing students' current plans and moving them forward. This can be invaluable for students who are struggling to find a direction, as well as for those who have a very clear direction but need help keeping on track.

As a careers leader you will want to establish a mechanism for identifying when students should be referred to the careers adviser. The best sources of intelligence on students' current career thinking and guidance needs are the people with whom the students have the most regular and frequent contact, their tutors and mentors. Systems for ensuring that students have access to the personal career guidance they need, at times when they need it, should include clear procedures for tutors and mentors to refer students to careers advisers, and should also enable self-referral. This is another reason for maintaining up-to-date records on students' aspirations and plans, and guidance interviews.

Links to Gatsby Benchmarks 4 and 8
We explore these issues further in Chapter 2.4, which looks at careers education and careers in the curriculum and Chapter 2.8, which looks at personal guidance.

Careers support for young people with SEND

The term 'special educational needs and disabilities' (SEND) covers a wide range of learning difficulties, health conditions and disabilities that can prevent individuals from making good progress through education without appropriate support being put in place. The reason why young people with SEND are identified as such is to make sure that the right level and form of support can be put in place.

Some young people with SEND will be identified as needing an Education, Health and Care (EHC) Plan. This tends to be young people with more severe needs and is unlikely to cover all the young people whom your school might identify as having SEND. For young people with less severe needs the school or college will put in place a package of support, possibly helped by the local authority. It is important for you to talk to the special educational needs co-ordinator (SENCO) to understand more about the support available for different students.

Where a young person does have an EHC Plan, it will document their needs and set out the support that should be put in place to meet those needs. Typically, this is about co-ordinating the work of a wide range of different agencies and support services to ensure that it all works together seamlessly and in the best interest of the child. EHC plans can begin at any age from 0 and can continue up to age 25. They are reviewed at least annually.

It is not possible in this book to discuss every possible type of need that young people with SEND might have but we can make some general points about good practice in relation to providing appropriate careers support.

Some students with SEND are in special schools, while others are in mainstream schools but with support. They all face choices about courses and qualifications while at school, and decisions about what routes to follow on leaving school at 16 or at 19. Many school leavers continue with further study at college, either on specialist programmes or a mainstream course with appropriate support. Others may go into work or on to some form of work-based training. The focus of the curriculum in special schools is to prepare pupils for independent living and the transition into further learning or work. In mainstream schools support for pupils with SEND is co-ordinated by the SENCO, and the careers leader needs to work closely with the SENCO to make sure that pupils with SEND are identified and given the support they need.

Since responsibility for career guidance in England was devolved to individual schools in 2012, local authorities have retained a responsibility for supporting young people deemed to be vulnerable and disadvantaged, including those with SEND. Schools and colleges should negotiate a service level agreement with the local authority for support for such young people. In special schools this is likely to be negotiated by the careers leader, in mainstream schools it could be done by either the SENCO or the careers leader. The important point is that as the careers leader you need to work together with the SENCO to ensure that support is secured and made available to the right young people.

There is one further consideration when planning careers support for young people with SEND, and that relates to working with parents. We know that parents play a significant role in influencing their children's career plans but parents of young people with SEND can be particularly anxious about their son's or daughter's future. It is important therefore to communicate regularly with parents about the support being provided and to involve them in the process from the beginning. Planning for transition at 16 or 19 for young people with EHC plans often begins as young as age 13 or 14.

> ### 🔦 Resources: Careers support for young people with SEND
>
> There are quite a few resources that can help you to build effective programmes for young people with SEND.
>
> SEND resources from The Careers & Enterprise Company (**https://resources.careersandenterprise.co.uk/browse-category/send**).
>
> Talentino (**www.talentinocareers.co.uk**). A specialist careers company working with young people with SEND.
>
> The SEND Gatsby Toolkit (**www.talentinocareers.co.uk/cec-gatsby-toolkit-refresh.pdf**). A practical resource pack produced by Talentino, the Career Development Institute (CDI) and The Careers & Enterprise Company.
>
> Transition programmes for young adults with SEND. What works? (**www.careersandenterprise.co.uk/research/transition-programmes-young-adults-send-what-works**). A paper produced by The Careers & Enterprise Company reviewing the research in this area.

> ### 🌍 International reflections: Young people with special educational needs and disabilities
>
> Different countries will have different policies and practices with regard to the support for young people with special educational needs and disabilities, and their parents and carers. You will need to find out what provision is available and how you can best work with that support to provide the career guidance those young people need. Of critical importance is building an effective working relationship with the person or people within your school who have specific responsibility for special educational needs and disabilities.

Keeping good records

We've already talked about two important types of records that schools and colleges should keep to ensure that the careers programme is addressing the needs of individuals. Firstly, your school or college should have records on the equality and diversity characteristics of young people and make use of these to ensure that the programme meets their needs. Secondly, you should make sure that you keep some records about young people's career aspirations, expectations, plans and behaviours. Being able to track how these shift and change is hugely valuable in understanding what support might be useful to them.

Beyond this, there are several other things that you should be keeping records on. Many of these, such as students' family circumstances, attainment, behaviour and so on, will normally be being recorded as part of wider student record systems. It is important that you recognise that these records provide a resource that can support the careers programme.

What is normally not being recorded on standard record systems is students' participation in career guidance activities. This is important for monitoring your programme, for understanding what different students have accessed, and ultimately for ensuring that you are able to evaluate the impact of your programme (see Chapter 4.1).

You should be recording every young person's participation in the careers programme. This might include things like:

- whether they have met employers, and which employers they have met
- which workplaces or post-secondary learning providers they have visited
- how many careers interviews they have had, and information about what was discussed in these interviews
- their participation in any online career learning
- what experiences of the workplace they have participated in
- whether they have a part-time job
- what extra-curricular activities they are involved in.

Ideally, you would be able to adapt your existing student record system to be able to keep track of all of this information. Alternatively, there are a number of online careers products that allow you to keep track of your students' participation in some or all of the careers activities. A key thing to be aware of is whether it is possible to link the specific records that you keep on students with their main student record. If you are looking at online products this is a key question to ask. If you are creating your own record it is a good idea to use the Unique Pupil Number,[18] as this will enable you to link any careers-specific records to your main student record, and potentially to other Department for Education (DfE) data which is held on your students. Your school or college is likely to have a data protection officer who will be able to advise you on data protection issues that exist around any new data you collect, for example those relating to the General Data Protection Regulations (GDPR). The law on data is complex and evolving regularly, and so you should make sure that you are up to date – but there are a few principles that should underpin all data collection.

- **Permission.** Students should know what information you are keeping on them and they and their parents should have given you permission to hold this information.
- **Accuracy.** Information that you keep on students should be accurate and not misrepresent them.
- **Retrievability.** Students and their parents should be able to gain access to the information held on them to allow them to check its accuracy and see what information is held about them.

> ### 💡 Resources: Student-level records
>
> Compass+ (**https://resources.careersandenterprise.co.uk/resources/compass**) is a free tool from The Careers & Enterprise Company which allows you to benchmark, manage, track and report on your school's careers provision at individual student level. Importantly it links with your school's existing student record system. Compass+ is available to eligible secondary schools, special schools, sixth-forms and PRUs in England.

Recent legal developments increasingly make it clear that we have the right to know what information is held on us and to decide what is done with it. Consequently, this places a responsibility on the school or college to make data as open as possible. One way to achieve this in a way that is useful for career learning is to combine records that are kept about students' participation in careers programmes with their own record keeping and reflection. This kind of approach is usually described as an e-portfolio.

E-portfolios

An e-portfolio is an online tool which allows students to record information about their activities and save evidence of their learning. E-portfolios are designed to help students to recognise and reflect on their achievements (as well as the gaps in their learning) and present them to others. Some e-portfolios support students to gather feedback by asking for input from teachers, careers advisers, employers and parents.

Some e-portfolios are designed to facilitate transitions by allowing students to create online resources which can be shown to employers and post-secondary learning providers as part of applications.

> ### 💡 Resources: E-portfolios
>
> There is a variety of different types of e-portfolio on the market at the moment. They all do slightly different things, so it is worth spending some time looking into them to see if they meet your needs. Some starting places include:
>
> Grofar (student careers passports) **https://grofar.com**
>
> PiXL Edge **www.pixl.org.uk/edge**
>
> Start **www.startprofile.com**
>
> Webanywhere **www.webanywhere.co.uk/education/products/portfolio-app**.

Note: An important consideration with all student records and e-portfolios is how portable they are. If a student moves school or college, will they be able to take it with them? Will they be able to access these records after they have left school? Thinking about these issues of long-term access and portability should be an important consideration when you are putting together your approach to maintaining student records.

Tracking destinations

So far we've talked about the importance of keeping records on students while they are in school or college. But, it is equally important to keep records about what happens to your students after they leave your school, as successful transitions are a key outcome for a good careers programme.

You can think about managing your destinations data in the following five stages.

1. **Intentions.** The first thing to do is to talk to all your students to build up a clear picture of what their plans are after they leave school or college. This information should be clearly recorded and should help you to target support to students while they are at school or college. So, if students have no clear and purposeful plans, you should work closely with them to put some plans in place. This intentions data also provides your first set of insights into your students' destinations.

2. **Data sharing.** Once your students have left, you should make sure that you have the right data-sharing partnerships in place with your local authority and post-secondary institutions. Most students will go on to further study, and you should be able to get information about who has enrolled and where. When you compare this with your intentions data, it should reveal where most of your students have gone.

3. **Follow-up.** Some of your students are likely to be 'missing' following the data-sharing stage. For these students, you will need to actively follow them up. This might include making phone calls or visits to their homes or the destination that they reported in your intentions data. This kind of follow-up is critical to improving the quality of your data. However, it is also an important way to direct additional help and support to those students who have failed to make a transition. Intervening with students at this point may prevent an initial stumble in transitions from turning into a fall into long-term NEET status.

4. **Triangulation.** Stages 1–3 should give you a good insight into the destinations of your students. Throughout this process you will be in dialogue with your local authority and with the DfE. The data that you collect will inform the data presented by the DfE as part of its national destinations information.[19] It is useful for you to triangulate your data with that reported by the DfE and to think about why there are any discrepancies.

5. **Dialogue with alumni.** Stages 1–4 describe how you gather the first destination of your students. This is interesting, but it tells us only a little bit about what happens to your students in their career. There is a clear value in building a long-term dialogue with your alumni and trying to keep as many of them connected to your school as possible. This is useful from the perspective of increasing your understanding of the destinations of your students, but it is also important because an alumni network gives you access to a ready-made network of working people who can return to your school or college to provide employer encounters.

The role of the careers leader

Benchmark 3 is one of the more challenging Benchmarks. It asks you to work on the vision of what your careers programme is trying to achieve and to put in place strong systems to ensure that it is working for all of your students. It is one where the role of leadership is particularly critical and where you are likely to have to spend quite a lot of time earlier on to build the correct foundations.

The key jobs for careers leaders in relation to Benchmark 3 include:

- reviewing and evaluating career guidance and providing information for development planning, Ofsted and other purposes
- planning the programme of activity in career guidance
- managing the work of others, e.g. careers advisers and administrative and other staff involved in the delivery of career guidance
- monitoring access to, and take-up of, personal guidance
- liaising with the PSHE leader and other subject leaders to plan their contribution to career guidance
- liaising with tutors, mentors, SENCO and heads of year to identify pupils needing guidance
- establishing and developing links with FE colleges, apprenticeship providers, UTCs and universities
- negotiating a service level agreement with the local authority for support for young people with SEND/EHC plans
- building a network of alumni who can help with the careers programme.

In a nutshell

The careers leader needs to make sure that the careers programme is working for everyone. To do this you will need to do the following.

- Think about who your students are and make sure that your programme serves their diverse needs.
- Consider how your programme challenges stereotypes and injustice.
- Keep track of your students' aspirations, expectations, plans and behaviours.
- Keep track of what careers activities your students have participated in.
- Track and react to the destinations that your students proceed to.

2.4 Careers in the curriculum

Every young person will benefit from thinking about their career while they are at school. One way to ensure that no one gets missed out is to make sure that careers provision is well embedded into the school curriculum, both by organising specific careers lessons and by including careers content in other subjects. This is why the Gatsby Benchmarks recommend that 'all teachers should link curriculum learning with careers'.

Careers can be studied as a subject, as it requires students to develop unique knowledge and skills and to learn how to put them into practice. This subject is sometimes called 'careers education' and there is a lot of benefit in carving out some space for it in the timetable. However, young people are also developing their careers when they are studying all subjects, and so it is also important that you find ways to make these cross-curricular links. In this chapter we will show you how to embed careers education into the curriculum.

This chapter will cover:

- defining careers education and the outcomes that you want to achieve from it
- designing schemes of work and careers education programmes
- different approaches to delivering your programme.

Introduction

There are several different components of a careers programme in a school or college. Young people need access to information, advice and guidance on the opportunities available to them, and they also need to be provided with activities that help them to gain the knowledge, understanding and skills to research and evaluate careers information and make use of it as they transition to further learning and work.

Students build up their knowledge of careers and skills in a similar way to any other subject. They need to acquire factual knowledge, learn from experts, try things out and receive feedback when they get it wrong. But careers is also a uniquely personal subject that students need to be encouraged to explore through the careers curriculum, other subjects and their wider experiences what it all means for them.

> ## ⚲ Resources: Evidence on careers education
>
> There is evidence, from UK and international research, that careers education in the curriculum impacts positively on young people, in three ways in particular: personal effectiveness; career readiness; and educational outcomes.
>
> If you are interested in finding out more about the evidence that supports careers education then you may be interested in viewing a literature review published by The Careers & Enterprise Company which draws together the findings of over 100 published research papers.[20] This paper can be downloaded from **https://resources.careersandenterprise.co.uk/resources/careers-curriculum-what-works**.

What is careers education?

Careers education prepares students for adult and working life. Specifically, it aims to equip young people to play an active part in determining their future roles as learners and workers, helping them to make realistic and informed choices about their careers, to manage the transition to the next phase of education, training or employment and to succeed in further and higher education training and work.

This definition has its origins in what has become known as the 'DOTS framework' for careers education, developed by Bill Law and Tony Watts[21] around the time when careers education first appeared on school timetables. The framework has been refined over the years but the basic principles remain as a sound basis for careers education.

The DOTS framework

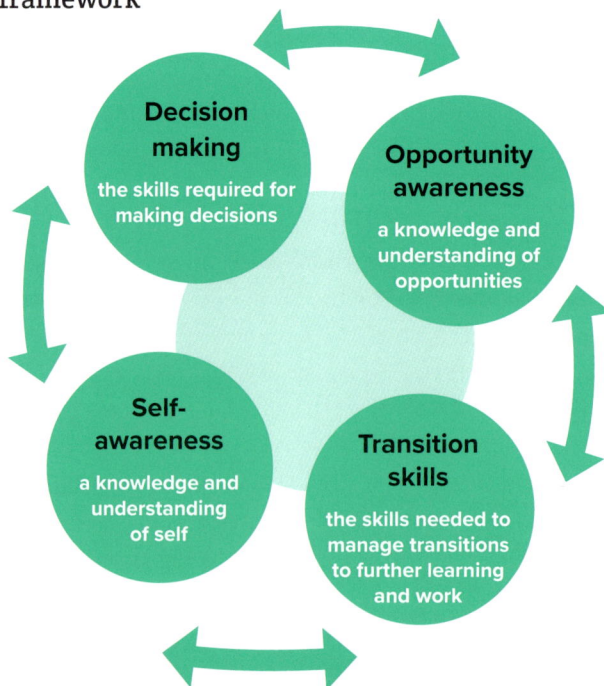

Decision making — the skills required for making decisions

Opportunity awareness — a knowledge and understanding of opportunities

Self-awareness — a knowledge and understanding of self

Transition skills — the skills needed to manage transitions to further learning and work

The DOTS framework offers a basic summary of what are often called *career management skills* (the skills to research opportunities, make choices and secure places on courses or jobs) and *employability skills* (the generic skills required to succeed in the workplace, in any job). More recently there has been an emphasis on the importance of *enterprise skills* (the skills required to develop new initiatives, start businesses and make a success of self-employment and employing others). Collectively, these skills are now referred to as career development skills.

Over the years, many organisations and researchers, both in the UK and across the globe, have sought to bring together lists of career development skills. Almost without exception, they have their origins in the DOTS analysis; but they have also evolved as career patterns have changed and as our understanding of what help individuals need has developed.

The main framework of career development skills in England is the Career Development Framework, produced by the Career Development Institute (CDI), the single professional body for all careers professionals in the UK. The framework can be downloaded from **www.thecdi.net/New-Career-Development-Framework**, and we will be discussing it in more detail later in this chapter. There are various local and national frameworks, as well as frameworks produced by sectoral and employer bodies. So check whether there are other lists you should take account of.

It is important to understand the difference between these frameworks of learning outcomes and the Gatsby Benchmarks. The Benchmarks explain what a careers programme should look like, while the skills frameworks set out what individuals should get out of participating in such a programme.

While a lot of attention is paid to developing these important skills for life, careers education extends beyond the *skills* needed **for** careers. It should also encompass *knowledge and understanding* **about** careers. This is not just information about opportunities in learning and work but also an appreciation of the changing nature of careers themselves and the role that individuals' decisions about learning and work play in shaping society. Careers education should empower young people to understand the world of work and to take control over their future pathways.

CASE STUDY

Dunchester Progress Academy has developed a careers education programme which is delivered in key stage 3 and key stage 4 mainly through a timetabled PSHE course. When she took over running the course, Rita, the school's careers leader, mapped what the PSHE lessons were covering and compared them with the Career Development Framework.

Rita felt that while the PSHE lessons were working well there were some important areas of career learning that weren't being covered. She talked to teachers in other departments and found some additional places where teachers were covering careers content. The humanities department includes several lessons on the local labour market, and how it has changed over time, within its scheme of work in Year 8 and the IT department includes a module on digital career management skills in Year 9. In key stage 4 the English department covers letters of application and targeted CVs as part of its scheme of work focusing on developing the skills of writing for different audiences.

Rita then worked with the leaders and teachers of the other subjects to help them to identify the career learning in the curricula that they were teaching and to encourage them to make these career links explicit for students.

Reflective questions: What elements of the CDI's Career Development Framework are covered in discrete careers or PSHE curriculum time in your school? Which subjects are the most fertile for developing links with careers?

Designing a careers education scheme of work

Teachers will be familiar with the process for curriculum planning and development, and careers advisers will recognise a similar process for planning groupwork sessions. We view this process as a cyclical one. Thinking about the cycle of curriculum development is important if you are going to run careers education as a subject in its own right. It is also critical if you are going to work with subject teachers and heads of department to insert career content into subject schemes of work and course programmes. The curriculum planning and development cycle (see diagram opposite) provides opportunities for you to think about when you can intervene and how you can support subject teachers and course leaders to embed careers content into their teaching.

1. Outline the starting point

Before starting to plan a scheme of work or programme of lessons, it is important to take stock of what students know, understand and can do already. The concept of progression in learning applies just as much in careers education as in any other area of the curriculum.

Understanding what students know already involves more than simply examining the scheme of work for the preceding year. It is important to understand what students have learnt, which is why assessment, monitoring and review (stages 5 and 6 below) are important. The information you need will come from records kept by teachers of careers education, examination of pupils' and students' work, review discussions with teachers, feedback from careers advisers and school or college staff providing advice and guidance to students, and discussions with students themselves.

The curriculum planning and development cycle

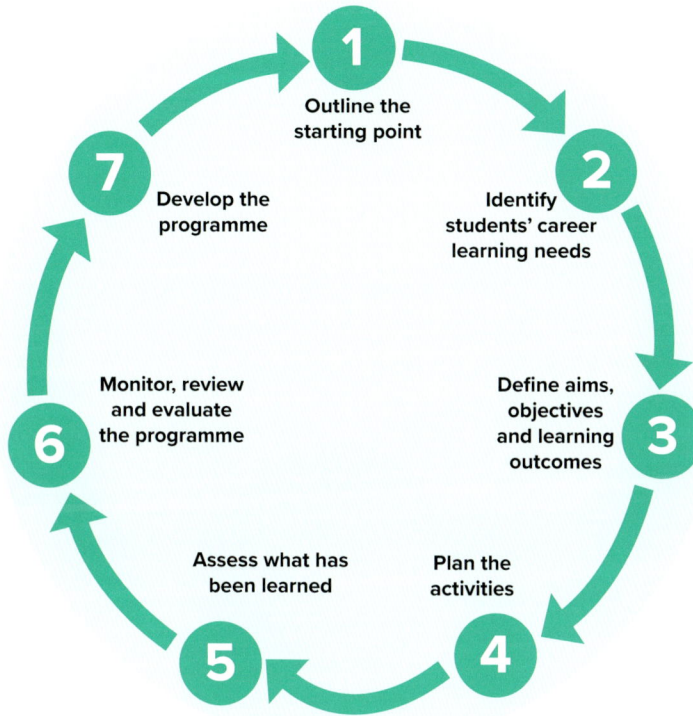

2. Identify students' career learning needs

Once you have gained an overview of what the students have learned thus far (and, perhaps equally importantly, what they don't currently know, don't understand or can't do), you can begin to identify what they need to learn next. This stage of the process will also be informed by where the students are in relation to their progress through school or college and what choices they are approaching.

You need to understand the opportunities available to your students, and gather up-to-date intelligence from employers, training providers, colleges and universities. You may also want to talk to former students and explore the issues that they encountered.

3. Define aims, objectives and learning outcomes

An earlier section of this chapter introduced the overall aims of careers education. We would expand on that by saying that careers education in schools and colleges should help young people to:

- review their personal strengths, interests and aspirations
- understand the influences on their career plans
- gain knowledge of the world of work
- research opportunities in learning and work
- create opportunities by being proactive
- make decisions and plans for their future in learning and work
- know how to find and use sources of advice, guidance and support
- present themselves well in writing, online and in person
- prepare for the next phase of their education, training and work
- balance their life as a worker with other interests and commitments
- become aware of how the economy, politics and society impact on their career.

These are the career development skills that we talked about earlier. In curriculum documents in England[22] these aims are often summarised under six headings as follows.

Learning outcomes for careers education

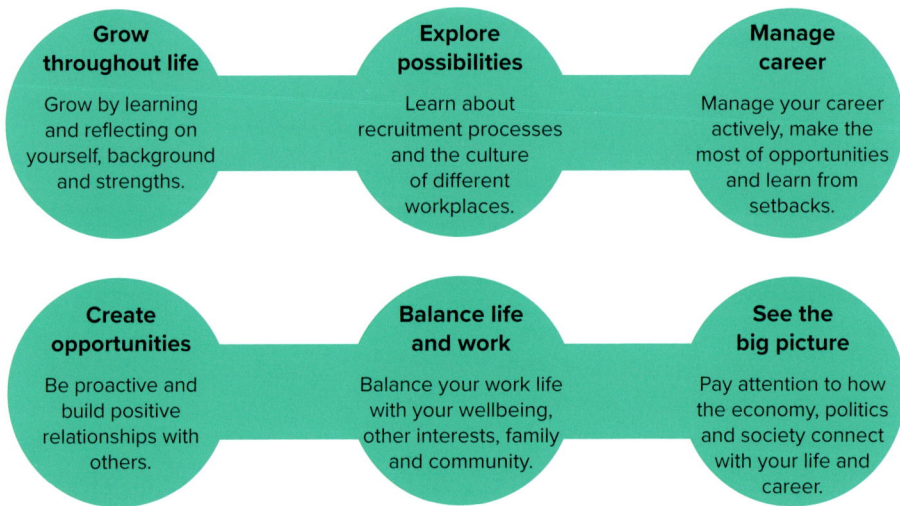

Grow throughout life
Grow by learning and reflecting on yourself, background and strengths.

Explore possibilities
Learn about recruitment processes and the culture of different workplaces.

Manage career
Manage your career actively, make the most of opportunities and learn from setbacks.

Create opportunities
Be proactive and build positive relationships with others.

Balance life and work
Balance your work life with your wellbeing, other interests, family and community.

See the big picture
Pay attention to how the economy, politics and society connect with your life and career.

This stage of the curriculum planning process involves converting the broad career learning needs of your students into a set of specific objectives. It is often the hardest part of the process, but without clear objectives, you cannot be confident that the activities you plan are the right ones for your students, nor assess what they have learned or evaluate its impact.

Fortunately, there are published frameworks of learning objectives that can help you when you are planning the delivery of careers education. None of these is prescriptive: they simply present recommendations and suggestions which you can use when designing your own list, taking into account the prior learning and needs of your pupils and students.

Resources: Framework for careers, employability and enterprise education 7–19

In England the most widely used framework is the CDI's Career Development Framework, mentioned earlier, which can be downloaded from: **www.thecdi.net/ New-Career-Development-Framework**.

From the same link, it is possible to gain access to several different supporting resources, including a handbook for secondary schools and colleges and another for primary schools, plus MS Word documents that can be used for auditing and planning programmes of careers education.

The materials offer comprehensive lists of learning objectives for each of five phases of education: key stages 1 to 4 and post-16. You can take the relevant lists and then tailor and adjust the objectives to produce a bespoke set of objectives for your scheme of work, taking into account the context for the group of students you are working with. Your final list will also be determined by how much curriculum time you have available.

Because discrete careers education sessions are often delivered through PSHE programmes, you should also look at the PSHE programmes of study for further ideas. These can be downloaded from **https://pshe-association.org.uk/ guidance/ks1-5/planning/long-term-planning**.

Skill Builder's universal framework of essential skills offers further suggestions: **www.skillsbuilder.org**.

The final step in this stage is to define learning outcomes for each of the objectives. The objectives are statements of what you intend each student to learn; the outcomes are descriptions of what they could do to demonstrate that the learning has been achieved. Again, the Career Development Framework helps by providing examples of 'I can ...' statements.

International reflections: curriculum frameworks

The status of careers education in the school curriculum varies across different countries. In some, it is part of the statutory curriculum (at least for students of a particular age range) with a prescribed specification; in others it is voluntary, but possibly supported by a recommended framework, such as the Australian Blueprint for Career Development[23] or the Norwegian career competences.[24]

This is another area where you will need to find out what the policy is in your country.

4. Plan the activities

This stage of the process involves taking each of the objectives in turn, and designing lessons or activities to enable students to gain the knowledge, understanding and skills intended. It means paying attention to both content and method.

> **Tools: Item 2.4A. Lesson plan template.**
> A template for planning a careers education lesson, and a completed example, are provided in the online resources accompanying this book: https://indigo.careers/clh.

You may choose to design your own activities. Designing careers education activities is creative and fun and it also helps to engage your students as you know what they are interested in.

> ## Resources: Careers education materials
>
> There is a wide range of published resources available to support careers education.
>
> The Careers & Enterprise Company have produced extensive resources to support careers leaders: https://resources.careersandenterprise.co.uk/all-resources-all-one-place. This includes a range of curriculum resources, lesson plans and other useful stuff.
>
> Some resources are available free of charge, for example the Lifeskills programme produced by Barclays https://barclayslifeskills.com and the Step into the NHS resources www.stepintothenhs.nhs.uk.
>
> Other resources are priced publications: Optimus Education offers an online catalogue covering all the main publishers of careers materials https://optimus-education.com/services/education-resources.

As with any other area of teaching, you will find it useful to share ideas and practice with other careers leaders.

> **Link to Gatsby Benchmark 2**
> One important topic within careers education is helping students to develop the skills to research careers information. This links directly to Benchmark 2, which is covered in Chapter 2.2.

5. Assess what has been learned

Careers education is rarely assessed through formal tests and qualifications, although such forms of external accreditation of students' learning are available.

Nevertheless, as the person responsible for planning the scheme of work, you will want to know what has been learned, to inform both the next stage for this group and the review of the programme for the next group of students.

> ### 💡 Resources: Accrediting careers education
>
> An example of accredited careers education is the ASDAN Certificate of Personal Effectiveness (CoPE) (**www.asdan.org.uk/personal-and-social-effectiveness-level-1-and-2**) used by many SEND schools.

There is a range of ways in which you can assess careers education. These can include discussions with students, observations, tests, written work and oral presentations. We think that one of the most effective is to get students to keep a portfolio of their work in careers education. This may be a simple folder of work completed in careers education lessons or might make use of an e-portfolio (as discussed in Chapter 2.3). These portfolios, perhaps completed with a piece of written reflection, can then be assessed either formally or informally and used to provide feedback.

In most schools and colleges it is common for several members of staff to be teaching the programme of careers education. As careers leader you will need to meet with your colleagues to collect and record their feedback on the progress made by students.

6. Monitor, review and evaluate the programme

This curriculum planning process is a cycle. You will want to take stock of the programme before planning for the next stage and the next group. This will involve monitoring what was delivered, reviewing with your colleagues how the activities worked in practice and evaluating what impact the programme had on the students.

Subject leaders are responsible not only for planning and developing schemes of work, and briefing and supporting teachers delivering the lessons, but also for monitoring what happens in those lessons. In this respect the careers leader is no different from any other subject leader: you have a responsibility to monitor teaching and learning in careers education. The process should be fully consistent with the school's or college's overall policy and approach to monitoring lessons.

Tools: Item 2.4B. Monitoring careers education lessons.
A checklist for monitoring careers education lessons, which is based on Ofsted's criteria for outstanding lessons, is provided in the online resources accompanying this book: **https://indigo.careers/clh**.

Practical approaches to monitoring, review and evaluation are considered in greater depth in Chapter 4.1.

7. Develop the programme

Data collected from assessment, monitoring, review and evaluation will be used to inform the future development of the programme. This may lead to changes to the scheme of work itself, but it may also suggest areas for staff development or changes in the way the careers education programme is organised.

Delivering your careers education programme (pre-16)

A key determinant of the effectiveness of your careers education programme is where in the curriculum it is taught, and by whom. As the careers leader you will be responsible for planning the schemes of work and lessons for careers education, but it is highly likely that you will be teaching only a proportion of the lessons. What your pupils and students experience and learn will be determined by who teaches the lessons and this, in turn, will depend on where in the curriculum the careers education lessons are located. Such decisions are usually made by the senior leaders with overall responsibility for the curriculum and for the timetable, but as the leader for careers you have a role in presenting to these senior leaders proposals for what you consider would be the most effective approach.

In key stages 3 and 4 it is possible to identify six different models adopted by schools. Often a school will employ a combination of more than one approach and it may have different models in key stage 3 and key stage 4. What follows is a brief discussion of the pros and cons of each of the six possibilities.

Discrete careers lessons

Some secondary schools timetable weekly careers lessons, taught by careers teachers, particularly in Years 9, 10 and 11. This approach is fairly rare in England, with the exception of some special schools, but is much more common in other countries.

Modules of careers education within a PSHE carousel

In curriculum terms, careers education can be viewed as part of PSHE, which is concerned with developing young people's knowledge, understanding and skills for the full range of roles they have in life. Many secondary schools, therefore, timetable their careers education as part of the PSHE programme and one approach is to divide the programme into short modules on different aspects of PSHE. The students then move from one module to another, often every half term or term. The advantage of this approach is that the careers education module can be taught by the careers specialist, but the downside is that some pupils will experience the module too early in the year and others too late.

Part of an integrated PSHE course

Research commissioned and published by the DfE shows that PSHE teaching is most effective when organised as an integrated programme, with discrete time on the timetable and taught by teachers who are confident with the subject content.[25] In this approach careers education is organised as an integral part of a PSHE course in the core curriculum taught by a small team of dedicated PSHE teachers, including ideally the careers leader. The teachers deliver the whole course and the careers education elements are covered at the most appropriate times in the school year.

Part of a tutorial programme

Other schools organise their PSHE programme in tutorial time, with the form tutors teaching the whole programme to their group. This allows careers education to be delivered whenever it is appropriate, but relies on each and every tutor being confident in delivering the lessons to the required standard. Further challenges are presented if the tutorial timetable slots are too short or if they get cancelled for administrative and other matters.

Curriculum days

Some schools organise their careers education, and often other elements of PSHE too, as whole days or half days when the normal timetable is suspended. It is certainly the case that you can organise some valuable activities in a session that lasts for two or more hours that would not be possible in a 50–60-minute lesson, but experience suggests that these days should be used as an addition to a more regular series of careers education activities rather than as the sole means of delivery.

Cross-curricular approach

Careers education can be delivered through other subjects but this can be difficult to achieve in practice if it is to be the sole approach. Not every element of careers education fits easily with a particular subject. Experience indicates that a school really needs to have both a discrete element of careers education, often organised as part of PSHE, plus elements integrated into other subjects. Linking subject teaching to careers is a key element of Gatsby Benchmark 4 and is the focus of the last section of this chapter.

> **Tools: Item 2.4C. Curriculum model review.**
> A proforma for reviewing your current curriculum model for careers education is provided in the online resources accompanying this book: https://indigo.careers/clh.

Delivering your careers education programme (post-16)

In post-16 education the overall curriculum structures are different and so, therefore, are the models for delivering careers education. Schools and colleges use one or more of five different models for organising careers education in the curriculum for post-16 students.

Part of a tutorial programme

This approach is very common in the college sector and is also employed by many school sixth forms. Schools and colleges report that delivering careers education within taught tutorial programmes is more effective in post-16 education than it is in the 11–16 sector.

Part of a separately timetabled enrichment programme

This approach is very similar to the tutorial model. The difference is only in where it is located in the timetable and the team of teachers and lecturers who deliver it.

A series of events

Like the curriculum days in key stages 3 and 4, this approach can enhance and complement more regularly timetabled sessions, but a series of talks and one-off activities is insufficient on its own.

Integrated into a main course

Where students are following a particular technical or vocational qualification, or the International Baccalaureate, it is possible to integrate all the elements of the careers education programme into the course and deliver them in context.

Linking subject teaching to careers

Gatsby Benchmark 4 promotes the importance of all teachers linking curriculum learning with careers.

Subject teachers have a significant influence on young people's career plans and there is clearly a role that all teachers can play in helping pupils and students to understand the progression opportunities, in terms both of future study options and of possible careers, that follow from their subject. This important contribution to educating pupils and students about careers can be enhanced further by teachers illustrating how the knowledge, understanding and skills developed through their subjects can be applied in the world of work. This can, in turn, bring relevance to the learning and increase pupils' and students' engagement in the subject lessons.

The careers leader should work with all curriculum areas to help subject leaders to build into their schemes of work activities to enable pupils and students to learn about the career opportunities that can follow from their subjects and about how the learning in their subject can be applied in the world outside the classroom. These elements of careers education within subject teaching can be delivered by teachers themselves but can also be brought to life through working in partnership with employers and employees, both in school and in the workplace, and working with tutors from further education, higher education and apprenticeship providers.

There is a variety of practical approaches to linking subject teaching to careers. Some schools have a designated careers week, when each department is expected to include activities specifically designed to show how their subject links to opportunities in the world of work by inviting in speakers, taking students out on work visits or planning work-related projects jointly with employers. Others expect each curriculum area to organise careers-related activities within their schemes of work for the year, but at times in the school year that are most convenient to them. Practice in relation to linking subject teaching to careers is probably most highly developed in the STEM subjects but it is equally important to show students how their studies in arts and humanities, and in languages, link to the world of work and can open up careers opportunities.

> ### 💡 Resources: Linking curriculum learning to careers
>
> The Careers & Enterprise Company has produced and collected together a suite of materials to support subject areas in embedding careers into their teaching at My Learning, My Future: **https://resources.careersandenterprise.co.uk/my-learning-my-future**.

At the very least, all teachers should be able to answer the following questions and draw on this knowledge while they are teaching their subject.[26]

- **How are the skills and knowledge that you are teaching used outside of school?** Understanding the real-world usefulness of what you are teaching is a powerful way to increase the relevance of your teaching. It also provides resources that you can use to illustrate concepts and encourage further research.
- **What jobs require (or prefer) people to have qualifications in your subject?** It is useful to know the jobs where your subject is central – some of them might surprise students. For example, many trade roles require good

75

mathematics skills. This is an area where you can make use of labour market information and encourage keen students to do some of their own research.

- **What jobs do people who study your subject go on to work in?** Are there obvious, and less obvious, jobs and careers that people who enjoy your subject often move into? Subjects can lead people in surprising directions. It is always worth highlighting examples that show that careers often don't follow a straight line, perhaps by looking at the career stories of celebrities who studied your subject.

Resources: Degree subjects and jobs

The higher education sector body JISC produces an annual summary of what students from different degrees go on to do. It is called *What do graduates do?* and can be downloaded from https://luminate.prospects.ac.uk/what-do-graduates-do.

- **What courses connect to your subject?** The higher education and vocational education and training courses that require or recognise your subject is critical information for you to share with students.
- **Can I involve an employer in my class?** One of the most powerful things that you can do is bring in an employer or working person to your classroom (perhaps a parent or one of your former students). Employers can talk about how they use your subject in their job, and the skills, experience and training they look for in future employees. Making this direct connection will really engage your students.

Helping teachers to understand these questions and develop good answers to them is one of the key roles that you play as a careers leader. We will be discussing how you can support the CPD of others in the school in Chapter 4.3.

Link to Gatsby Benchmarks 5 and 6
Working with employers to enhance careers education within subject lessons links with Benchmarks 5 and 6, which are covered in chapters 2.5 and 2.6.

In addition to these links with all subjects, the careers leader may also work with particular subject areas to deliver some aspects of the scheme of work for careers education in a cross-curricular way. Examples include examining the changing role of women in the workplace in history, researching labour market data in IT lessons and preparing CVs in English.

It is very difficult in practice to deliver an entire careers education programme through other subjects, partly because some elements do not fit easily with any particular subject and are best delivered in a discrete careers education session or as an integral part of a PSHE programme, and also because any cross-curricular element can only be delivered in a subject that all students will take. Delivering some elements of careers education through subjects can bring relevance to subject teaching but needs to be complemented by discrete provision.

In order to establish these various links with the different subject areas, the careers leader will need to be enabled to work with the subject leaders or a nominated link person for careers in each department. For this reason, many schools have identified 'careers champions' in each subject or curriculum area. Such working relationships are made easier if the careers leader is a member of the middle leadership group in the school or college.

The role of the careers leader

The careers leader is the subject leader for careers education. This involves planning a scheme of work for careers education and overseeing its delivery by briefing and supporting teachers, monitoring teaching and learning in careers lessons and keeping the programme under review. The role also includes advising the senior leaders with overall responsibility for the curriculum and for the timetable about the place of careers education in the curriculum and effective models for timetabling the provision.

The careers leader is also trying to extend careers education beyond careers education lessons or curriculum days. Teaching in all subjects should be linked to careers, so the role of careers leader includes working with other subject leaders to embed elements of careers information and careers education within their schemes of work.

Key tasks for the careers leader relating to careers in the curriculum include:
- advising senior leadership on policy, strategy and resources for careers education, including the most appropriate curriculum model and staffing
- reporting to senior leaders and governors on careers education
- reviewing and evaluating the careers education programme
- preparing and implementing a development plan for careers education
- planning a scheme of work for careers education
- briefing and supporting teachers of careers education
- monitoring teaching and learning in careers education
- liaising with the PSHE leader and other subject leaders to plan careers education
- working with subject departments and course programmes to integrate careers learning into curriculum teaching.

In a nutshell

As the careers leader you are the subject leader for careers education in the curriculum. You will need to:

- plan schemes of work for careers education in each year group
- work with the senior leader with overall responsibility for the curriculum and timetable to decide where to deliver the programme in the curriculum and who is best placed to teach it
- work with the PSHE and other subject leaders to support the staff teaching the programme
- monitor the delivery of the programme and keep it under review.

2.5 Encounters with employers and employees

One of the challenges of running a careers programme inside a school is that it can be difficult to really bring the world of work to life. Young people have spent all of their lives in educational institutions and many of their teachers have done the same. To address this it is important to bring in a range of voices and perspectives from outside of the school. The Gatsby Benchmarks suggest that every year, from the age of 11, pupils should participate in at least one meaningful encounter with an employer.

In this chapter we are going to be looking at how you can build employer encounters into your programme. Most of the encounters discussed in this chapter take place within the school or college.

This chapter will cover:

- why employer encounters are important
- what different kinds of activities can constitute an employer encounter
- how you can ensure that you are offering a sufficient quantity of employer encounters
- how you can ensure that the activities that you organise are of sufficient quality.

Introduction

The opportunity to meet with and talk to someone who is working outside of a school or college offers huge value to a young person's career learning. Hearing stories direct from 'the horse's mouth' can engage and inspire your students to consider all sorts of careers that they might not have thought about or heard of before. If you find the right people to talk to your students, their enthusiasm and passion for their jobs will transform the somewhat abstract process of career learning into something real and meaningful.

Employers and employees also have access to unique insights that aren't available in any other way. Do you know the most common reason that the automotive industry rejects applications from apprentices? No? Nor do we! And it is really difficult to find this kind of information through Googling or reading books. But if you get anyone who works in the automotive industry to stand up in front of your class and talk about apprenticeships, they will cover this without even thinking about it. So much information that is relevant for careers is tacit and rarely spoken. By inviting employers in you are giving your students access to this kind of hidden information.

Before we go on, we need to sort out some definitions. People often talk about working with 'employers' or organising 'employer encounters', but it is important to remember that there is a wide range of different types of people from the world of work that you might want to invite to your school or college at some point. People vary by their occupation, by age, seniority and career history as well as by the range of demographic characteristics that everyone varies by (race, gender, sexuality, religion and so on). Ideally you will seek to organise a programme of employer encounters that represents this diversity (see below), but there is another important set of distinctions that you should be mindful of when organising employer encounters.

- Some people are *employers*. Employers actually make decisions about how their organisation works, whom they employ and potentially whom they sack or make redundant. An employer might be the owner of a company or the top boss. You can also see people like human resources directors or recruiters, who come to represent their company rather than themselves and the job that they do, as being employers or employer representatives. It is important for young people to hear directly from employers, as these people set policies and make decisions about employment, promotion and redundancy.

- Some people are *employees* or working people. Many of the people who come to speak at your school or college are not actually employers. Rather, they are working people who are volunteering to tell you about their job and their career. They may be visiting your school on behalf of their employer or they may be doing it in their own time. Employees can provide different kinds of insights from employers. They can tell your students what work is actually like, they can dish the dirt and tell you the tricks of the trade.

- Some people are *self-employed*. Around 15% of the population of the UK are neither employers nor employees.[27] They work for themselves running small businesses, consultancies or services. These people range from people eking out a living through apps like Uber and Deliveroo to wealthy consultants making lots of money from their considerable expertise. Given that this group is such an important part of the labour market it is important that your students encounter them through your careers programme.

We often refer to encounters with all of these different types of people as 'employer encounters'. This is fine as long as we remember that this term masks a myriad of different experiences.

Five surprising 'employer encounters' that you could organise

Employer encounters don't have to just be a string of people standing up and talking about their company or job. There is a lot to learn about the world of work, so be imaginative and include some surprising employer encounters in your programme. The following five ideas are designed to inspire you …

1. Someone who has never worked for anyone else. As we've already seen, self-employment is an important part of the labour market. Most people spend some time working for someone else before they strike out on their own. However, there are a small number of people who set up their first businesses straight from school, college or university. Hearing about this kind of entrepreneurship can be very inspiring for your students.

2. Someone who has set up a business that has failed. There is an old saying that you learn more from failure than from success. If you are able to find someone who will talk to your students about this experience they might be able to avoid making the same mistakes.

3. A trade unionist. Trade unions and workers' rights are an important part of the world of work. If you can bring a trade unionist in to talk about their experiences you will enrich your students' career learning and make links to other curriculum subjects like history, politics and citizenship. Professional associations are also an important part of many people's careers and could also be part of your careers programme.

4. Someone who has experienced discrimination. The world of work isn't always a nice or easy place to be. It is important that young people get a chance to think about what to do when things go wrong. If you can get someone who has experienced discrimination to talk about what it was like and how they dealt with it you will be providing your students with a valuable learning opportunity.

5. A former pupil. There is nothing quite like hearing from someone who sat where you sit now a few years ago. You should make active use of former pupils (both recent and from the distant past) where you can. If your school has an active alumni network, then make use of it for the careers programme. If your school doesn't have a strong alumni network, then you should think about building one – it will pay off in the long run in a host of ways.

Link to Gatsby Benchmark 3
Thinking more broadly about who to include in your programme of employer encounters is part of ensuring that you challenge stereotyping and celebrate diversity (Benchmark 3).

The evidence for employer encounters: a brief detour into social theory

There is a lot of evidence that tells us about the benefits that are attached to employer encounters.[28] It highlights benefits to students' academic performance, to their likelihood of transitioning successfully to work after they finish studying and even suggests that there are some benefits to lifetime salary.

So why is employer engagement so valuable? To answer this we will need to take a brief detour into social theory – so if this isn't your bag you might want to skip to the next section and just take our word for it that employer encounters are likely to pay off for your students.

For those of you who are staying for this bit, we'd like to introduce you to the French social theorist Pierre Bourdieu.[29] Among other things, Bourdieu was interested in how power works in our society.[30] Like many others before him, he noticed that money (what he calls financial capital) talks. People with more money can get things done and rise to the top. But, he also noted that money wasn't everything and that sometimes people without a lot of money were still doing pretty well and that it wasn't purely on their merits.

This led Bourdieu to develop his theory of 'capitals'. In this he argues that money (financial capital) can be exchanged for better social networks (social capital) and for cultural refinement or educational knowledge (cultural capital). What is more, people with a lot of social or cultural capital can ultimately trade on this to gain access to money.

What this means is that if you are rich you hang around with other rich people (building your social capital) and learn to like the things that rich people like (building your cultural capital). If you lose your money you still know some rich and powerful people and so they give you opportunities because they know you, like you and like the things that you like. So, social and cultural capital serve as a safety net for advantaged people and also make it more difficult for disadvantaged people to penetrate the upper echelons of society ('they're just not the right sort!').

So, when you are organising employer engagement activities you are working with 'capital'. While you cannot give your students more money, you can introduce them to useful people who will tell them interesting things. It is particularly valuable if you can introduce your students to people who are different to the people that they know already. If you are going to be a successful lawyer, you are probably going to need to know other lawyers and to know what the social do's and don'ts are if you spend time with them. This is about acquiring social and cultural capital, and it is what you are helping your students to do every time you organise an encounter with an employer.

CASE STUDY

Dunchester is an old mining town where the mines and associated industries have long since closed down. Most of the parents of the students at Dunchester Progress Academy have family histories in the mines, but these days they work for the local authority, in retail or in one of the big call centres that have been set up on the old site of the pit. Less than 20% of them have been to university.

Although Rita finds the way that Dunchester is labelled as an 'area of deprivation' a bit patronising, it has given her a bit of funding to 'raise the aspirations' of the students at Dunchester Progress Academy. She uses the funding to organise an annual careers fair at the school. This allows her to bring together employers from Dunchester, but also to attract employers from the more affluent neighbouring town of Vanchester.

Before the careers fair she spends time with the students talking to them about what to wear on the day of the fair, preparing questions and talking about how to build a network that might be useful to their career.

She doesn't use the language of social and cultural capital with either the students or the employers, but she is aware that this is exactly what she is trying to build through this event.

Reflective questions: Which employers in your area would you consider it a priority for your students to engage with? What would you be aiming for students to get out of the encounters?

Different kinds of employer encounter

Employer encounters are a powerful source of career development, but some kinds of employer encounters are more likely to have an impact than others. The Gatsby Benchmarks talk about the importance of ensuring that encounters are 'meaningful', by which they mean that employer encounters should offer students the opportunity to learn about what work is like or what it takes to be successful in the workplace. This is clearly good advice and we'll return to this a little later on when we look at the issue of quality in employer encounters. But, the evidence also suggests that quantity is important, and if we are going to ensure that students have a lot of encounters with employers we are going to need to ensure that there is a wide range of different things to choose from.[31]

Below we are going to take you through some of the most common forms of employer encounters. We'd advise you to try to organise as many of these as possible, but to think carefully about how best to do this for your students. For example, you might want to run a programme of talks for your Year 8s, but get your Year 11s involved in some mock interviews. This links back to the idea that we covered in Chapter 2.1, that your careers programme should be progressive and allow students to develop across a number of years.

Key types of employer encounter

- **Business games and enterprise competitions.** These create an experiential learning opportunity which allows young people to have a simulated or real experience of running a business.
- **Careers carousels.** Also known as speed networking events. In a career carousel, a young person will speak individually or in a small group to an employee volunteer for a short period of time (commonly 5–15 minutes). At the end of the period, they will move on to another employee volunteer, circulating around a number of different volunteers over the duration of the event.
- **Careers fairs.** These usually take the form of a careers marketplace where 10 or more employers, training providers or universities are located around a large space and students walk round to talk to them about the job they do, the education and training routes they took and ask for advice on working in that sector or job.
- **Careers talks.** Such talks give students insights into a career by having an employee volunteer talk to them about their job, company and career. This may take place in an assembly, in a careers class or with a small group of students interested in a particular career.
- **Employer involvement in the curriculum.** This includes a range of activities where employers get involved in co-teaching a lesson or series of lessons with a teacher. This will often involve them talking about or demonstrating an aspect of their work that links to a topic which is covered in the curriculum.
- **Employer mentoring.** A sustained supportive relationship between an employer or working person and a young person. This relationship is usually one-to-one but can sometimes be organised between an employer and a pair or small group.
- **Transitions skills workshops.** Activities where an employer provides feedback on CVs and performance in a simulated job interview or assessment centre.

During the pandemic, many schools and colleges experimented with the provision of online or virtual encounters. These encounters can be really powerful and effective, and can also increase the efficiency of working with employers. But, they also pose some challenges in terms of monitoring and ensuring that encounters remain high quality. If they are going to be equivalent to face-to-face encounters, it is important that they have a clear learning outcome that is understood by the student and the employer, and that they involve a two-way interaction between a student and employer. For example, the provision of video case studies of employers can be valuable LMI (see Chapter 2.2), but it does not constitute an employer encounter – that requires genuine interaction between the student and the employer.

Link to Gatsby Benchmarks 2 and 4

There are lots of opportunities to link employer encounters to other Gatsby Benchmarks. In particular it is very common to make a link with the gathering of career and labour market information (Benchmark 2) and the curriculum (Benchmark 4).

Ensuring the required quantity of encounters

While there are a lot of different approaches to employer engagement, each of them takes time and energy to organise. The research tells us that the more encounters a young person gets, the more benefits that they receive from them.[32] To meet the standard set by the Gatsby Benchmarks you will need to ensure that all students get at least one encounter with an employer in every year that they are at school. However, we would recommend that you treat this as a minimum and try to move towards a situation where young people are routinely meeting employers as part of their experience of school.

Building up a network of employers is critical to your ability to offer a high volume of employer encounters. We are going to discuss effective networking in more detail in Chapter 3.4 of this book, but for now you just need to recognise that being an effective careers leader requires you to build up a thick address book of employer contacts. Once you have a strong network you will be able to call up employers and ask them to come in and help you with one of the employer encounters that you have got planned.

Thankfully, there is a shortcut to making direct contact with hundreds of employers. In most areas there are several organisations that exist to link you to businesses. These might be the local careers hub, bespoke education employer organisations, providers of a wider range of careers services or just local business networks like the Chambers of Commerce. Each of these organisations can serve as a *broker* for your relationship with employers.

Working with brokers is a very useful way for you to build up relationships with employers. It is far more efficient if there are one or two main organisations that provide the link between education and employment than if every single school and college in the country is working to build links with every employer. So, finding out who is your local broker (or brokers) is a really important part of your role as a careers leader.

> ### 💡 Resources: The Careers & Enterprise Company
>
> If you are in England, The Careers & Enterprise Company should be one of your main contacts as a careers leader. The Company has a network of local Enterprise Co-ordinators who can serve as brokers and advisers for your school (see www.careersandenterprise.co.uk/careers-hub/join-the-network/). The Company also hosts a provider directory (www.careersandenterprise.co.uk/find-activity-provider) which can help you find a range of brokers and providers of employer encounters locally.

Once you have decided what employer encounters you want to offer and have found employers who are willing to work with your school or college, you still need to find a way to fit these encounters into the day. There is a wide range of ways that schools and colleges typically do this, and you can use the following examples for inspiration.

Assembly talks. These are ideal, as they offer an opportunity for an employer encounter without asking too much of the employer or disrupting the school day. Ideally you will find a way to make this a regular encounter, perhaps taking place three or four times a term.

Arranging multiple encounters on the same day. Careers fairs and careers carousels are particularly effective ways to stack up multiple encounters.

Integrating encounters into existing provision. If you can find a way to use employers to deliver careers content or other parts of the curriculum, you can insert employer encounters into the school day without disrupting existing activities.

Extra-curricular opportunities. Many schools and colleges provide opportunities for students to engage with employers outside of the main curriculum, e.g. at lunchtime or after hours. This is particularly relevant where you have opportunities that are likely to appeal to a small but enthusiastic group, e.g. potential medics.

Setting employer engagement as homework. Although it is important to try to introduce young people to employers from outside of their existing networks, it is also valuable to make sure that they make the best use of the networks that they have. Encouraging them to interview a member of their family or a family friend as a homework task can be a way of increasing their employer encounters and strengthening their network at the same time.

This is not to say that you shouldn't be looking for opportunities to build employer encounters into the ordinary school day and into any time that you have allocated to the careers programme. Rather, it is a recognition that you should always be looking for opportunities to increase the number of employer encounters that are available to and taken up by your students.

Ensuring the required quality of encounters

While you should follow the broad principle of 'more is better' in relation to employer encounters, quantity is not the only thing that matters. It is equally important to focus on the quality of the encounter that you offer. You should expect that longer, more intense and better organised encounters such as sustained employer mentoring will have a greater impact than momentary interventions like a 15-minute assembly talk.

It is possible to draw out 10 key principles that should be considered when designing or delivering any employer encounters. If you follow these principles you will be delivering high-quality provision that will have the best chance of making a positive impact on your students.

Principles for effective employer encounters

#	Principle	Why it matters	Key question
1	Well designed	Employer engagement activities should be carefully designed with a clear idea about when they should be used, with whom and to achieve what outcome.	What do we want to achieve?
2	Learning focused	The provision of employer engagement alone will not necessarily result in career learning. Young people need to be prepared for activities, their learning scaffolded during participation and supported to reflect on what they are learning.	How will we maximise learning?
3	Context aware	Employer engagement activities are most effective when they are delivered as part of a broader programme rather than in isolation. The Gatsby Benchmarks provide an ideal example of what such a broader programme should look like and emphasise the importance of providing a range of activities across the whole of a young person's education.	How does this activity fit with everything else?
4	High volume	Activities have limited effects when they are brief and occasional. The evidence suggests that employer engagement needs to happen regularly so that learning is reinforced.	Are we doing this often enough?
5	Varied	Each type of employer engagement offers young people different learning opportunities. It is important that young people receive a varied diet of different employer engagement opportunities to support them to develop a wide range of career-relevant skills and knowledge.	Have we done this before?

6	Experiential	It is important for employer engagement to include a substantial element of 'learning by doing'. This should include giving students the opportunity to exercise autonomy, take risks, work in groups and undertake other tasks that are relevant to the workplace.	What will the students be *doing*?
7	Led and co-ordinated by professionals	Employer encounters are not just about turning your class over to an employer. The effectiveness of these activities relies on educational professionals to design and co-deliver provision.	Who is going to lead this activity?
8	Ensuring young people are prepared	Young people need to be ready for employer encounters. They need to understand who they are going to meet and why. They also need to have done some research and prepared questions to ask.	Are the students ready?
9	Recognising the diversity of learners	Young people are diverse and have a range of different career learning needs. Employer engagement should be organised to reflect the diversity of learners. It should also allow for differentiation and personalisation both by allowing young people to select encounters that interest them and by offering additional support and extension activities.	How can we adapt this for different needs?
10	Providing feedback and assessment	Young people need to receive feedback on their performance following meetings with employers. Formal and informal types of assessment can support learning and the utilisation of learning in career development.	How will we provide students with feedback?

The role of the careers leader

Careers leaders have a key role to play in building relationships with employers and with the various third-party brokers that exist to facilitate these relationships. Perhaps most importantly, once employers are engaged the careers leader is responsible for making sure that they are well used and that the relationship is effective.

The key jobs for a careers leader in relation to Benchmark 5 include:
- establishing and developing links with employers
- building a network of alumni who can help with the career guidance programme.

In a nutshell

Employer encounters are a key component of your careers programme. You should be building relationships with employers and working to ensure that your students have as many employer encounters as possible. To do this you will need to:

- develop an understanding of the different kinds of employers that are out there and work to build relationships with a wide range of them
- make connections with brokers and intermediaries who can help you to connect to employers
- design a range of different employer encounters which maximise both quantity and quality.

2.6 Work experience and other experiences of the workplace

We learn a lot about careers by watching others work, by talking to working people and, most importantly, by doing some work ourselves. It is important that at some point in your careers programme you offer young people the opportunity to get out of school or college and visit some workplaces. Ideally you should also make sure that they get the opportunity to do some work themselves.

In this chapter we are going to be looking at how you can ensure that your students get at least two experiences of the workplace before they leave school or college.

This chapter will cover:

- why it is important to give students experiences of the workplace
- different approaches to providing experiences of workplaces
- organising and managing experiences of the workplace
- ensuring that you maximise the opportunity for learning offered by these experiences of the workplace.

Introduction

In his comic novel *Three Men in a Boat*, Jerome K. Jerome wrote the immortal line '*I like work: it fascinates me. I can sit and look at it for hours.*'[33] If you are not careful there is a danger that your careers programme will echo this quote. You spend hours talking with students about work, encouraging them to think about work, to choose jobs and plan their careers, but at no point do they do anything that constitutes real work.

In the last chapter we looked at the importance of bringing in employers to your school. This is a big step in the right direction, but it is still a second-hand experience of work. For example, as the authors of this book and other books on careers, we love writing, reading and talking about careers all the time. If you asked us whether we enjoy our jobs we'd be enthusiastic and urge you to pursue a career in careers. But, if you don't share our interest you might find such a career very dull. Careers are personal, and you won't be sure whether you really like something until you have tried it.

CASE STUDY

Susan is a particularly charismatic Year 10 student at Dunchester Progress Academy. She has an encyclopaedic knowledge of fashion, hair and make-up and has built up over 10,000 followers on her YouTube channel. The channel mainly consists of her reviewing new make-up products and showing her viewers how to use them.

She has ALWAYS been certain that she is going to be a beautician and frequently informs her teachers that there is no point in her attending any careers activities. So when the opportunity for work experience comes up she is quick to organise herself a placement at a local beauty parlour ...

She absolutely hates it! She doesn't like having to stand up all day, listen to the problems of the customers, do what she is told or use standard products that she doesn't think are the right ones. The whole experience is a massive disappointment, but even more worryingly, it throws her career plans into serious doubt. Luckily, when she gets back to school she has an appointment booked with Raj, the careers adviser, who starts to pick up the pieces.

Reflective questions: What do you regard as the main purpose of work experience in your school or college? How do you communicate this to the students, their parents and the employers you work with?

As our case study shows, work experience can have a profound impact on people's careers. We hope it will confirm people in their aspirations, allow them to start building a network and open up a few doors, but in many ways it is just as useful if it helps you to rule out something that you have been thinking seriously about.

Susan's case study illustrates that work experience shouldn't ever just be a question of dropping students into a workplace and leaving them. Susan had a clear idea of the work experience she wanted to do, and the school had a plan in place to allow her to reflect on her experience with a careers adviser after the placement. These elements of preparation and follow-up are critical, and we'll return to them later on in this chapter.

One of the key benefits that experiences of the workplace offer young people is the opportunity to 'see behind the curtain' of a workplace. When you engage with businesses only as a customer or service user you only get the picture that they want to show you. Most businesses have a reception area which is well decorated and is staffed by their most skilled customer service operatives. But there is often a lot going on behind the reception area that you don't see. For example, when you are in a restaurant the table staff are employed to give the impression of calm poise. But behind the scenes this kind of work is fast and frantic and often replete with colourful language! Experiences of workplaces are designed to open some of these issues for students and help them to think about the distance between how organisations present themselves and what they are like to work for.

Given how long work experience has been a part of schools' careers programmes, it has received surprisingly little attention in the research literature. However, in a very useful paper Jonathan Buzzeo and Melissa Cifci have drawn together the research on work experience.[34] They argue that the evidence suggests that work experience can have a positive impact on students' motivation at school, their knowledge of the world of work, their career decision making and their employability skills. They also point out that there is a range of different kinds of experiences of the workplace and each can be expected to have different benefits.

Different types of experience of the workplace

There are eight main types of work experience that you can organise for your students. There is value in using all the different types of work experience and in thinking about which opportunities are right for which students. It is also important to try to offer a combination of different experiences in different workplaces to help young people to explore a range of possibilities.

The Gatsby Benchmarks say that students should have an experience of the workplace before they are 16 and then another one between 16 and 18. The Benchmarks aren't very specific on exactly how long these experiences should be, but we think that a total of 10 days would be good practice. So, before a young person is 16 they should have spent at least two weeks in a workplace and they should spend an additional two weeks once they are in the sixth form or at college. For some students a two-week placement with an employer may be the most appropriate provision, but for others the experiences might have been made up of several different activities, for example, visiting a factory for a day in Year 7, two days of shadowing a working friend or relative (e.g. 'take your daughter to work day') in Year 8 or 9, two days of volunteering and one week of work experience in an office in key stage 4. We'll be thinking more about how we can best slot the range of different experiences of the workplace together later in the chapter.

As we discussed in chapter 2.5, it is possible for all types of employer encounter to be delivered online. This is also true of work experience, although it is probably more challenging to do this well. The pandemic taught us that it is possible for a great many people to work from home using digital technologies to communicate and to manage their work. Given this, it is possible to deliver experiences of the workplace online.

In general, experiences of the workplace have a greater impact if they are face-to-face. The sights, sounds, smells and physical experience of visiting an employer offer powerful learning experiences. We suggest that online experiences of the workplace be reserved for those situations where there is little alternative, e.g. pandemics, very rural schools with few employers locally, and students who want to access specialist work that is not available in the locality.

If online experiences of the workplace are going to be high quality, they should be based on a clear and mutually understood set of aims, and provide students with an opportunity to interact with a range of people from the workplace and ideally to get involved in some actual work.

Types of experience of the workplace

1. School or college as a workplace
2. Workplace visits
3. Work shadowing
4. Short-term work experience
5. Extended work experience
6. Internships and holiday placements
7. Volunteering and social action
8. Part-time work

Type 1: The school or college as a workplace

Sometimes people talk about experiences of workplaces as being about taking your students into 'the real world'. We understand why people say this – young people often have very limited experience of anything outside of school and family, and will typically have little or no experience of formal paid work. In this sense, giving them experiences of the workplace is designed as a 'reality check' to help them to understand how adults spend their lives.

The problem with talk of workplaces as the 'real world' is that it suggests that life in school is in some way 'unreal'. This is a problem, as schools and colleges are actually workplaces and the education sector is a major employer in most developed countries.

This therefore suggests the first category of experiences of the workplace, which is considering *the school or college as a workplace*.

There is lots of value in helping students to recognise that their teachers are real people who come to work for a range of reasons, including earning money, and who also have lives outside of school. Just as important is helping students to recognise all of the other people who work in a school, from the cleaning staff to the business manager. In colleges the range of roles available is even greater and is also even more likely to include people who have worked in a wide range of sectors prior to coming into education.

Helping students to view their school or college as a workplace can be a very useful part of a careers programme. Whether this is through using school or college staff as careers speakers or whether it is through work shadowing or actual placements is for you to decide as you build your careers programme. For some students with particular special needs a placement in the school or college environment may be the most feasible form of work experience. However, while we believe that this is an important element to your careers programme, on its own it is not sufficient for most students. It is important that you also try to get students out of your institution and give them opportunities to see the rest of the world.

Type 2: Workplace visits

The second type of work experience is taking your students out for a visit to a workplace. Depending on the size of the employer you might be able to do this for a whole class or in small groups. The purpose of a workplace visit is to demystify what goes on in workplaces and to offer students an opportunity to meet a range of working people, to ask them questions and learn about the jobs that people do.

CASE STUDY

Aleksandra is responsible for employer relationships at Vanchester College. She notices that the college's main site backs onto a small business park filled with nondescript rectangular buildings. The College's students walk by these buildings every day but generally have no idea about what goes on in them. Aleksandra does some research and then makes contact with the businesses in this park. She then meets with the employers and asks if she can organise some visits. Six of the businesses are enthusiastic and agree.

Aleks talks to the different curriculum areas in the College. She proposes that they organise a 'workplace safari'. The day will begin with Aleks running a session on workplace etiquette and introducing the six employers. Tutors will then take students in small groups for a half-hour tour around each of the different workplaces. By the end of the day students will no longer see the buildings on the business park as concrete boxes, but will now know that they are studying alongside a series of interesting small business that may be future employers.

For Aleks this is a great opportunity to open up a new set of relationships with employers in a low-commitment way. She hopes that some of these employers will also get involved in her programme of talks and that they may offer more substantial experiences of the workplace in the future.

Reflective questions: How well do you know your local employers? How could you increase your knowledge and contacts through engaging students in a meaningful activity with the employers at the same time?

Type 3: Work shadowing

Work shadowing can be a very effective experience of the workplace. In work shadowing a student accompanies an employee throughout the course of one or two working days. The purpose of this kind of experience of the workplace is to give young people a realistic idea about how the working day is spent. For example, work shadowing reveals things like how much time is spent in meetings vs solo work, how often working people travel outside of their base and important things like how long you take for lunch.

Work shadowing is an excellent way for students to build up some 'cultural capital' by gaining an understanding of the unspoken and often unnoticed rules and priorities of a workplace. This includes gathering intelligence about what people wear, what they chat about and how people change their behaviour when the boss walks in. All of this stuff is just as important for a young person to learn as some of the more technical aspects of what people's jobs involve.

Observing workers can be a useful form of experience of the world of work for young pupils who are below the minimum age for work experience (Year 10), and for older students wanting to find out about jobs where it is less possible to undertake the actual tasks involved, e.g. surgeon or barrister. Work shadowing can be a very efficient way to give a young person a deep insight into a workplace. However, because it is typically a short encounter it is important to ensure that the student is well prepared and feels confident enough to ask questions while they are shadowing.

Type 4: Short-term work experience (one or two weeks)

The most common experience of the workplace is a concentrated one- or two-week placement. This often takes place at the end of Year 10 in many schools in England, but others have shifted the two-week block of work experience into Year 12, while others have developed new models or dispensed with work experience altogether.

An intensive block of work experience has several benefits. It gives students an opportunity to try out something that they are interested in. It is long enough to get a real insight into what it would be like to work in that environment, but not so long that students feel trapped. If it goes well, they can build up some useful contacts and potentially even use it as an 'extended interview' which might result in the offer of a part-time job, longer placement or apprenticeship.

As with all experiences of the workplace, short-term work experience requires good preparation and debriefing to ensure that the students' learning is maximised. It also requires that employers have thought about what they are hoping to achieve from the work experience placement and what they want the students to achieve. Is it essentially an extended work shadowing opportunity with the student being rotated through different business functions to gain an understanding of the business? Alternatively, do you want the student to have a real experience of work, perhaps with their own project to complete during the period that they are there? There is value in different models, but each takes some careful thinking and organisation on behalf of the employer. In general, we'd favour models which include some aspect of independent work for the student, but the opportunities and constraints will vary across different employers.

Type 5: Extended work experience

Another common model of work experience is to link a student with a company for an extended period of time. Typically, this is organised as a regular commitment, e.g. spending every Wednesday afternoon with the employer. This kind of approach has some benefits as it creates a sustained relationship between the young person and an employer. It is also potentially easier to fit around the school curriculum and may work particularly well in sixth forms and colleges where students often have more free periods.

One of the challenges with extended work experience placements is the danger of the student disengaging. Another is the difficulty for employers in finding meaningful work that can be done for a short period every week. One approach is to ask the student to complete a 'consultancy project' where they manage their own time and develop an output that is useful to an employer, e.g. a social media strategy. This kind of approach will work well for motivated and independent students but may be more challenging for other kinds of students.

Extended work experience placements need to be carefully discussed with the employer and the student and then monitored by the careers leader to ensure that they do not fizzle out. The careers leader might plan occasional visits to the workplace or meet with the student periodically to check that it is all going well.

Type 6: Internships and holiday placements

As the school year has got increasingly packed it can be difficult to find the time for work experience during school time. One option is to encourage students to take up work experience in their own time. The holidays, particularly Easter and the summer, offer good opportunities for this kind of work placement. In some cases, particularly in the longer placements, employers may even be willing to pay students who work for them.

These kinds of placement can often be quite competitive and require considerable planning on behalf of the student. Employers will need to be contacted well in advance of the holiday. The school is typically less directly involved in these kinds of placements, but you can support your students to identify and apply for opportunities as well as helping them to prepare and to reflect on what they have learned.

Type 7: Volunteering and social action

Another good approach to giving students work experience is to encourage them to get involved in volunteering or forms of community or social action. One of the advantages of this approach is that it can allow young people to follow their interests and devote their time to something they really care about. Some students might want to raise money for heart disease, others work with disabled children at the neighbouring special school, while still others might want to campaign for animal rights or even try to get their local Liberal Democrat candidate elected to parliament. Volunteering allows young people to think about their values, learn about the world and develop new skills. It is also particularly powerful as it involves young people in real work that has real consequences.

Many schools have charities or causes that they are particularly involved with. These offer a brilliant starting point for developing students' interest in volunteering. If students want to strike out and find out about other kinds of volunteering you can help them to do some of the research and make initial contacts. You may also have a local volunteering bureau in your community that you can refer them to or even bring into the school.

Type 8: Part-time work

Finally, it is worth noting that some students will already have jobs. Although fewer young people are working in Saturday jobs, paper rounds and other forms of part-time work than in the past, it is still common for a minority of young people at your school to have some part-time work experience.[35] This is particularly likely for young people who can work in family businesses.

Some schools are a bit nervous about young people working while they are at school. There are real concerns about students getting distracted from school and not having enough time to focus on their studies. Most of the research suggests that the negative impact of part-time working on performance at school is non-existent or small. Interestingly, some of the research finds that part-time working carries greater risks for girls than boys.[36] It also suggests that negative effects are not so much about the time that part-time work takes up as about the way that part-time working and the money that it provides enables young people to engage in more risky social behaviour such as smoking, drinking and going out to bars and clubs.

Despite these concerns, we're generally positive about part-time working. It can allow young people to gain skills and experiences that will be very useful to them, especially if the amount of part-time working is kept within reasonable limits (say no more than eight hours a week). We would encourage you to create opportunities for your students to talk about their experiences of part-time work, how they spend their money, whether it impacts on their studies and what they are getting out of it in addition to a regular pay cheque. It is important that this is framed positively, with teachers and careers staff being respectful about the work that students are doing and what they are learning from this; otherwise, there is a danger that students will view it as the school trying to 'muscle in' on their private lives.

Organising and managing experiences of the workplace

We have now talked through a range of different approaches to offering young people experiences of work and the workplace. One of the most challenging aspects of this is finding the opportunities. There are a few cases where one contact with an employer will result in multiple experiences (particularly in the case of workplace visits and with large employers). But, in general, experiences of the workplace should be individual and linked to a student's career aspirations – as a result you are going to need A LOT of experiences to offer to your students.

There are basically three ways that you can source experiences of the workplace.

Approaches to finding experiences of the workplace

Approach	Advantages	Disadvantages
Young people find their own experiences of the workplace. The school encourages or even sets the expectation that young people (and their parents) will source the experiences.	Less work for the school/college. Encourages young people to take responsibility and get involved in networking and applying, as well as doing the work experience.	Tends to result in young people accessing work experience from their own networks. This often doesn't expand their horizons.
The school sets up experiences of the workplace. You draw on your growing network of employer contacts to set up experiences of the workplace for your students.	You can offer a wide range of experiences and help slot young people into ones appropriate for them. Increases your confidence in the quality of the placement.	Setting up experiences is a lot of work! Your employer network is likely to be limited in size and diversity and may not meet the needs of all of your students.
The school contracts a broker to set up experiences of the workplace. You work with a local careers company, education business partnership or employer organisation to set up the experiences of the workplace.	Brokers will have a wide range of employer contacts. Less work for the school/college.	There is likely to be a cost for brokerage. This may be a charge for each experience of the workplace and so can become a major budget consideration.

Most schools and colleges use a mix of different approaches. As the table above shows, there are advantages and disadvantages to each approach. One thing to pay particular attention to is the equity of the opportunities that are made available to your students. It doesn't matter how a student gets a placement, but it does matter if you notice that all of the students with professional parents have higher quality placements than those whose parents work in manual or service jobs. The provision of work experience placements is one of the places where the school or college can really level the playing field and ensure that everyone gets high quality, aspirational placements. We recognise that achieving this outcome is challenging, but there is a very strong rationale to try!

Designing and managing your school's approach to experiences of the workplace is likely to be a major part of your work as a careers leader. This is one of the areas where it can be particularly useful to have some additional support. Many schools have a 'work experience co-ordinator' – a higher-level administrator who works to keep track of all of the school's employer contacts and to ensure that they are well used. During periods of active work experience they also keep track of where students are and provide a point of contact for both students and employers in case of any problems. We will be discussing this further in Chapter 3.2, where we look at the careers leader's management responsibilities.

In colleges it is common to have a department which has responsibility for managing the college's relationship with employers. Typically this department will be focused on developing apprenticeships and employer-funded vocational programmes, although they may also get involved in setting up extended placements that are required for certain vocational programmes. As careers leader it is important that you build a close relationship with this department and look at how its existing employer connections can be leveraged for your careers programme.

Permission, safeguarding and health and safety

Any experience of the workplace is designed to bring young people into a new environment and to give them a different experience than they would normally get within school. This raises several issues relating to permissions, safeguarding and health and safety. As a careers leader you have a duty of care to the young people whom you are involving in your careers programme.

The legal situation with respect to these issues of risk and safety is complex and ever changing, but there are some broad principles that you should adopt in relation to all of the experiences of the workplace that you organise.

Note: Most of these principles are essential for young people pre-16 but may be more flexible for those over 16.

- **Informed.** Young people should understand what they are going to experience and why it is in their interest to have this experience. They should have an idea about some of the potential risks that they might face and what to do about them if they encounter them.
- **Allowed.** Parents and carers should be informed about the experiences that young people are going to be having outside of school and their permission should be sought where appropriate. Parents should be aware of where their children are and why they are there.
- **Managed risk.** A risk assessment should be completed for each experience of the workplace that you are organising. This should set out any possible risks that you have identified and what you can do to prevent these risks (counter-measures) and to mitigate their impact if they happen (contingencies).
- **Supervised.** Young people should have clear supervision and mentoring while they are having an experience of a workplace. While they don't necessarily need to be watched at all times, they equally shouldn't be left to 'get on with it' without any oversight of their work.
- **Appropriate adults.** Young people should be in the care of appropriate adults while they are having experiences of the workplace. This means that you and the employer should go through a process of checking on the background of anyone who will be spending extended periods alone with a young person during their experience of the workplace, e.g. through a Disclosure and Barring Service (DBS) check in the UK.
- **Safe.** Young people should not be left in a situation where they have the potential to be harmed. Obviously, it is impossible to eliminate risk altogether, but both the school and the employer should attend carefully to issues of safety.
- **Legal.** You should be aware of key legislation that regulates experiences of the workplace. This legislation is frequently changing and so it is important that you keep up to date.

Tools: Item 2.6A. Risk assessment for experiences of the workplace. A sample risk assessment form is provided in the online resources accompanying this book: **https://indigo.careers/clh/.**

> ### 💡 Resources: Guidance on work experience
>
> 16–19 study programmes: work experience (guidance from the DfE) **www.gov. uk/guidance/16-to-19-funding-study-programmes-work-experience#funding-guidance**.
>
> Disclosure and Barring Service (DBS) **www.gov.uk/government/organisations/ disclosure-and-barring-service**.
>
> Health and Safety Executive (work experience resources) **www.hse.gov.uk/ youngpeople/workexperience/index.htm**.
>
> Not just making the tea: A guide to work experience **www.gov.uk/government/ publications/not-just-making-tea-a-guide-to-work-experience**.
>
> The Key, DBS checks: work experience providers **https://schoolleaders. thekeysupport.com/pupils-and-parents/safeguarding/safeguarding-checks-and-the-scr/dbs-checks-work-experience-providers/**.
>
> Work experience employer guide (Department for Work and Pensions) **www. gov.uk/government/publications/employers-could-you-offer-work-experience/ work-experience-employer-guide**.

Maximising learning through work experience

As the rest of this chapter has shown, providing young people with experiences of workplaces can be a time-consuming process. We believe that it is well worth the investment, but only if the experience of the workplace is well planned and designed to support the young person's career learning.

Before you start setting up experiences of the workplace you should stand back and review your careers programme. Where would it be most useful to slot experiences of the workplace into the programme to help you to facilitate your students' learning? What kinds of experience are most useful and connect most meaningfully with your programme?

Experiences of the workplace need to be progressive in line with the rest of your programme. This means that the kind of experience that is relevant for Year 7s is different to that for Year 11s. Ideally, each year's experience of the workplace should build on the last one and challenge students in new ways. Typically, as students get older they should spend longer periods out of school and take on work experience opportunities that require more skill and autonomy. As students move closer to the labour market they should have more choice about the workplace that they are going to experience and the link with their career aspirations should increase. So in Year 7 you might have a day where students shadow a parent around their workplace, in Year 8 you might take a whole class to see a local factory, but by Year 11 students should be choosing their own work experience placement.

Throughout this chapter we have emphasised that every student should have at least one experience of the workplace pre-16 and another post-16. You should try to avoid the second one simply being a repeat of the first. The experiences can differ in any of three ways: they may take the form of different types of experience; they may have different overall aims; they may be in different occupational sectors.

In colleges many students will already have some work experience built into the courses that they are doing. Such experiences will typically be designed to develop vocational skills in the field. These vocational placements offer you a good opportunity to build some career learning around the student's course. However, you should also try to provide them with at least one other experience of the workplace beyond their course. This may be with a different employer or with a different level of staff to help them to think about the way in which their career might develop.

> ### 💡 Resources: Making the most of work experience
>
> The OCR Guide to Best Practice in Work Experience www.ocr.org.uk/Images/168852-the-ocr-guide-to-best-practice-in-work-experience.pdf.

Possible aims for work experience

The activities listed earlier as different types of experiences in the workplace are all educational activities that use the world of work as a resource for learning. As with any educational activity, there should be clear overall aims and these should be shared both with your students and, in particular, with the employers providing the experiences so that they can arrange appropriate activities.

Miller, Watts and Jamieson[37] have identified ten different possible aims for work experience, not all of which relate directly to career learning. Some refer to enhancing learning in particular curriculum areas and others relate to developing knowledge and skills in vocational courses. The numbered list opposite provides a useful starting point for clarifying what you want to achieve through the experiences you set up. Some of the aims are more typically applicable to vocational education programmes, but the list gives you a range of possibilities to consider as you develop work experience opportunities for students. Aim 7 represents how work experience is used within programmes of technical and vocational education and applied learning, while aim 10 relates to individualised programmes of extended work experience.

Being clear about what you want students to achieve will help you to organise the right type of experience and will provide a focus to the preparation work with students. One experience may deliver more than one aim but cannot deliver all ten.

1. **Enhancing:** to enable students to deepen their understanding of concepts learned in classroom settings, and to apply skills learned in such settings.

2. **Motivational:** to make the curriculum more meaningful and significant to students and improve their levels of academic achievement.

3. **Maturational:** to facilitate students' personal and social development.

4. **Investigative:** to enable students to develop their knowledge and understanding of the world of work.

5. **Expansive:** to broaden the range of occupations that students are prepared to consider in terms of their personal career planning.

6. **Sampling:** to enable students to test their career preferences before committing themselves.

7. **Preparatory:** to help students to acquire skills and knowledge related to a particular occupational area, which they will be able to apply if they wish to enter employment in that area.

8. **Anticipatory:** to enable students to experience some of the strains of work so that they will be able to manage the transition to work more comfortably.

9. **Placing:** to enable students to establish a relationship with a particular employer which may lead to the offer of a full-time job.

10. **Custodial:** to transfer some of the responsibility for particular students for a period.

> **Link to Gatsby Benchmark 4**
>
> Aims 1 and 2 are linked to subject teaching aims, while aim 3 is linked to your PSHE programme. These show how the provision of experiences of the workplace can be aligned with the curriculum (Benchmark 4).

A model of effective work experience

There has been a lot of thinking about how people learn and develop through experiences. One of the most influential theories in this space is Kolb's Learning Cycle, which is a model of experiential learning.[38] We think that this cycle can offer a useful structure for thinking about career learning.

The cycle divides learning into four distinct stages: *active experimentation* (when we think about what we want to do and try it out); *concrete experience* (when we actually do things); *reflection and observation* (when we think about how an experience went); and *abstraction and conceptualisation* (when we think about what this experience means and consider how it might change the way that we see the world or behave in the future).

Kolb's Learning Cycle

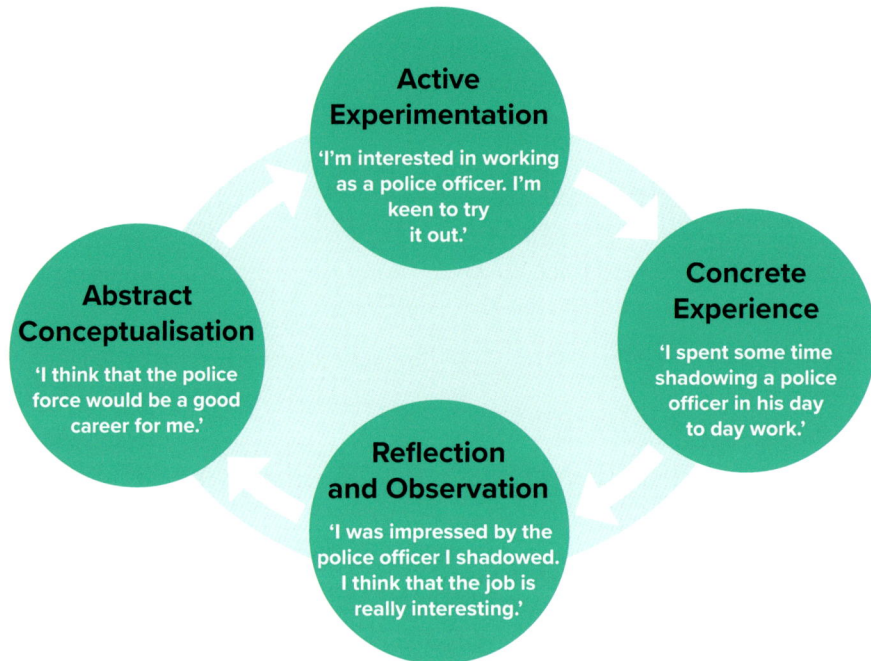

Active Experimentation
'I'm interested in working as a police officer. I'm keen to try it out.'

Concrete Experience
'I spent some time shadowing a police officer in his day to day work.'

Abstract Conceptualisation
'I think that the police force would be a good career for me.'

Reflection and Observation
'I was impressed by the police officer I shadowed. I think that the job is really interesting.'

You can see that in this model of learning the experiences that we have play a central role. Without the experience, the other stages don't make sense. This is why experiences of the workplace are such a critical part of career learning.

The other thing to note about this model of experiential learning is that it is a cycle. Career learning doesn't happen through just one experience of the workplace. Rather, each experience builds on the last, with students applying what they have learned from one experience to the next. This is why it is a better model to set up multiple shorter workplace experiences than just to offer one single opportunity pre-16 and one post-16.

Active experimentation

Your first job when you are organising experiences of the workplace is to inspire students to use the opportunity to experiment and try things out. A key part of the preparation for experiences of the workplace is to prepare your students to ask lots of questions. It is really important to spend some time encouraging them to think about the following issues.

- What experiences do they want to participate in? Why?
- What are they hoping to see?
- What are they hoping to do?
- Whom do they want to meet?
- What are the burning questions they want to ask?
- What do they hope to get out of it?

Spending time before they go on the work experience and helping them to think about these issues will encourage them to experiment more and get more out of the experience.

One way to ensure that the questions that young people have inform their experience of the workplace is by communicating some of these things to their host employer. It is possible to build this into wider career learning by getting students to write a letter to their host employer thanking them for offering the placement and outlining some of the key things that they are looking to get out of the encounter. This activity can also be an effective way to teach business letter writing.

Another approach is to draw up an informal contract between the employer and the young person. This can cover the things that the young people are hoping to get out of the experience and also raise some issues about workplace behaviour and employer expectations, e.g.:

Work experience contract
What I am hoping for from the experience

- *I would like to visit the control room and talk to some of the people responsible for managing the train network.*
- *…*
- *…*

What I will do while on placement

- *I will turn up on time.*
- *I will follow all safety instructions.*
- *…*
- *…*

Concrete experience
The most important stage of any experience of the workplace is actually having the experience. Experiences should, where possible, allow students:
- as much autonomy as possible
- to talk to and interact with employers, employees, customers and clients
- to see different roles within the same workplace
- to see the workplace and the environments within which work is undertaken
- to see other people working
- to do some work themselves.

While it is important to ensure that young people don't spend two weeks making the tea or operating the photocopier, it is also important not to try to sanitise the workplace and remove all difficult or undesirable elements from it. Work involves doing difficult things, repetitive things, boring things and things that may not strictly be in your job description. Work also hopefully involves doing interesting, inspiring, worthwhile and fun things as well! It is important for young people to see all of these elements of work. The whole point is to build up a real and substantial experience that they can learn from.

Reflection and observation

While students are experiencing workplaces they should be being encouraged to reflect on these experiences. Such reflection can take several forms. Students might be asked to keep a diary or blog, to jot down a list of questions that they have or even to take photos of things that interest or surprise them.

A very powerful way to aid students' reflection is to make sure that they have a mentor within the workplace. Employers should identify an employee who can serve as their mentor throughout the experience and provide them with someone who can push them to get involved and challenge them to think.

Even if it is not possible to offer students a mentor it is possible to support their reflection through regular visits and sending them texts and emails asking them how it is going. Visits by school staff to students in workplaces serve a range of purposes. They are a useful tool to check up that everything is going as you hope and that both students and employers are behaving as you hoped. However, they are also a part of the way that you can encourage students to get the most career learning out of their experience.

It is important to allocate time for reflection and debriefing after the experience has finished. Students need time to think about what has happened and what they learned from it. Some of this reflection can take place in class and can allow young people the opportunity to exchange what they have learned and learn from each other. There is also value in some individual reflection, perhaps facilitated by a careers interview following the work experience placement.

Abstract conceptualisation

Finally, you should make sure that students have the opportunity to think about what their work experience means for them long term. This is about linking their experience to their wider career aspirations and planning.

Again, this can happen in the classroom, but also has a strong individual element that students need to spend some time working through.

CASE STUDY

Anton has been volunteering in the local hospital every Wednesday afternoon throughout his A levels. He is really committed to the patients and loves the camaraderie and sense of purpose of the staff working in the health service. He's always wanted to be a doctor and his work experience has confirmed him in that ambition. However, at school things haven't been going quite as well. He's taking science A levels but his grades are middling at best. It isn't looking like he is going to get into medical school.

Anton spends time with his tutors and the staff at the hospital. He asks them for their feedback on what he is good at and not so good at and what they think he should do next. This raises a range of possibilities beyond medicine for him to think about. He realises that there are a huge number of roles in healthcare beyond being a doctor. He also realises that he is really good at the people side of working with patients and some of his colleagues at the hospital make suggestions like counselling, social care and social work.

He takes these ideas to the careers adviser and talks them through. He decides that there are a few other exciting options for him and resolves to try to get some more work experience to explore these further.

Reflective questions: What opportunities do your students have for talking about their experiences of work in groups and/or one-to-one settings?

As Anton's experience shows, the Kolb Learning Cycle is a cycle of continuous learning. Work experience should move your students forward in their career thinking. It should allow them to clarify their ideas, reject some things and move other ideas forward. One of the best ways to move forward is often to loop back round the cycle again and increasingly sharpen up your thinking.

International reflections: Work experience

Different countries have different histories of work experience and traditions of the way it is delivered. It is important to make a clear distinction between work experience and the vocational placements that are delivered as part of vocational education. Both have value, but the kind of experiences of the workplace that we are discussing here are more about career exploration and inspiration than the development of vocational skills.

Talk to educators, employers, parents and students, and consult the regulations and requirements in your country as you develop work experience opportunities for your school.

The role of the careers leader

The careers leader is responsible for ensuring that all young people get at least two experiences of the workplace. In fact, you should be trying to ensure that they get more experiences and that the experiences that they have are well organised and support their career learning.

The key jobs for a careers leader in relation to Benchmark 6 include:
- planning the programme of activity in career guidance
- managing the work of others, e.g. careers advisers and administrative and other staff involved in the delivery of career guidance
- co-ordinating encounters with employers and work experience
- communicating with pupils and their parents
- establishing and developing links with employers.

In a nutshell

Experiences of workplaces are a key element of your careers programme. Providing young people with a range of high-quality experiences can be a demanding and time-consuming activity, but it is well worth putting in the time. To deliver this Benchmark you will need to:

- ensure that young people have experiences of the workplace both before they are 16 and after they are 16
- choose the best types of experiences of the workplace for your learners
- engage employers and set up relevant experiences
- ensure that experiences are well run, that risk is managed and that students are safe
- design experiences of the workplace so that career learning is maximised.

2.7 Experiences of HE, FE and work-based training

An earlier section of this handbook covered the provision of career and labour market information to young people. It made clear that such information should include information on the full range of further study options available to young people. In England, partly as a result of raising the age of participation in learning to 18 and also as a consequence of both widening participation in higher education (HE) and increasing the number of apprenticeships, the immediate concern of most young people in schools and many in colleges is what courses and qualifications to pursue next and where to study. They should continue to explore different jobs and types of work but a major focus of careers programmes should also be in helping students to make informed choices about further study.

For this aspect of careers support to be effective, young people need to be given opportunities to find out about the options available through direct encounters with providers – universities, colleges and work-based training providers. This means hearing from both staff and students and gaining experience of the places where the courses and qualifications are offered.

This chapter will cover:

- working with universities
- working with colleges
- working with apprenticeship providers and other work-based training providers.

Introduction

Careers programmes in schools and colleges are concerned with more than thinking about future jobs. The more immediate concern for most young people leaving school or college is what to study next and where. This is why Gatsby Benchmark 7 focuses specifically on ensuring that young people have encounters with providers of further and higher education and of apprenticeships and other forms of work-based training.

They need to know and understand the full range of learning opportunities available to them, and the possible progression routes that follow.

Schools in England now have a statutory duty to ensure that they provide opportunities for a range of education and training providers to access all pupils in Years 8 to 13, in order to inform them about appropriate technical education qualifications and apprenticeships. This has become known as the 'Baker Clause'. Schools are required to have a policy on how this works in practice and to publish the statement on their website, so that education and training providers are able to easily see how they can have access to pupils. Recent legislation has strengthened this duty by specifying the number of such information sessions schools should arrange across years 8 to 13: schools are required to put on two encounters with providers of technical education and apprenticeships in years 8 and 9, and two more in years 10 and 11, that are mandatory for pupils to attend, plus a further two encounters in years 12 and 13, which are optional for sixth formers to attend.

The rationale behind the legal requirement is to ensure that young people become fully aware of all the opportunities open to them, not just those that are provided in their own school. It is part of a wider strategy to ensure parity of esteem between academic and technical/vocational pathways. In many ways, this enshrines good practice and may be something that you want to follow even if you are not in England. We would argue that a good careers programme should actually go beyond the legal duty, and ensure that young people are provided with information on all options at all points of transition. In practice, this means working in partnership with universities, colleges and providers of apprenticeships and other forms of work-based training, to organise encounters both in school and in the places of study.

The range of opportunities and providers

Young people have a range of opportunities available at three key points of transition.

At 13+/14+ most students will remain in their own school and continue on to key stage 4, where they will study GCSE courses and, possibly, vocational or applied learning programmes. However, if there is a university technical college (UTC) or studio school in the area, some students may move there to continue their education to age 16 or 18, opting for courses in line with the institution's specialisms. Similarly, a few students may progress onto 14–16 programmes at a local college, where such provision is available.

It is at age 16 that young people have a wider range of options. If the school has a sixth form, many of the students will choose to continue their studies within the school; but for some, the courses and programmes that best meet their interests and aspirations will be in a local college of further education or work-based training provider. If the school does not have a sixth form, then all students leaving Year 11 will progress to other institutions, including other schools with a sixth form and sixth form colleges. The courses and qualifications available at this age include general/academic studies such as A levels, technical education and vocational qualifications, apprenticeships and other forms of work-based training.

At age 18, a good proportion of students in schools and colleges will progress onto HE courses at universities or FE colleges that have HE provision, some will move on to courses of further education and others will embark on higher, or degree-level, apprenticeships or other forms of work-based or professional training. The range of providers, therefore, encompasses: universities; colleges of further education; apprenticeship providers and providers of other forms of work-based training.

Encounters and experiences

The careers programme should include opportunities for students to meet staff and students from universities, FE colleges and apprenticeship providers within the school or college, and for students to experience the places of study as well. Examples of the range of possible activities are explored in the sections that follow.

It is obvious that such encounters and experiences should be organised in the phase of education that immediately precedes the transition point, but schools could also introduce some opportunities at an earlier stage. For example, particularly in areas where there is not a high level of participation in HE, students may be encouraged to think about this as a possibility through a visit to a local university in Year 9 or earlier.

In all cases, it is important for the careers leader to plan activities that will prepare students to get the most from the experience or encounter, and then to follow up and debrief the activity.

Links to Gatsby Benchmark 2
Arranging experiences and encounters with universities, colleges and apprenticeship providers links with the importance of giving them good career and labour market information (Benchmark 2, see Chapter 2.2).

Resources: Meaningful encounters with learning providers

The Careers & Enterprise Company has published a useful practical guide to making the encounters and experiences with learning providers meaningful: **https://resources.careersandenterprise.co.uk/making-it-meaningful-benchmark-7**.

Advising on different options

As the careers leader, it isn't your job to advise individual students on what course or route to pursue. This stuff gets very technical very quickly and it is usually a good idea to pass detailed questions about different routes on to the careers adviser. However, you should feel sufficiently informed to be able to have a meaningful career conversation with all your students regardless of the route that they are thinking of taking.

This may mean that you have some professional development needs. If you have come through a typical route you will probably feel that you have a good idea about what university is like. But, it is always good to check that your memories of university still hold true. HE is changing and the world of student finance is changing amazingly quickly – so don't rely on your memories alone.

Depending on your own career history you may have less knowledge about other pathways. It is important that you actively develop your knowledge base on all of the options. Read up on them, talk to providers and to current students and if possible look for opportunities to go and observe provision. You will probably find the opportunity to watch teaching and learning in other sectors hugely interesting and informative for your own practice.

Becoming familiar with a range of post-secondary options is not about becoming an expert adviser. It is just designed to give you a good enough sense of what is going on to allow you to make sure that the careers programme informs students, and their parents, about the full range of future study options available, and to have meaningful career conversations with your students. When you are having these conversations it is important not to impose your opinion about what a student should do or, even worse, to spend time talking about what you would do if you were in their shoes. The conversation should stay focused on what is right for them.

Useful questions to ask include the following.
- What are they interested in?
- What are the pros and cons of different options?
- What do they think will make them … happiest, healthiest, wealthiest and so on?
- What do they think that they would be able to get into?
- How far are they choosing the easy option?
- How much do they really know about the different options? Have they visited any of them or talked to someone who is currently going through it?
- What do their family want them to do? How much are they just going along with what their parents want?
- What is the worst that can happen? And the best?
- What next after this choice? What progression does this route offer?

One of the things to remember is that, with a few exceptions, most choices that you make at 16 or 18 are not irreversible. It is also important to remember that there are multiple routes to different careers. Young people and their parents can tend to catastrophise, and so one of your most important roles is to offer some perspective.

Link to Gatsby Benchmark 8
Talking to young people about their choices has a close link with personal guidance (Benchmark 8, see Chapter 2.8). It is important that you work closely with the careers adviser and with other staff to think about when you should inform students about the options available.

Universities and other HE providers

In many schools, liaison with universities and preparation for university application may be the responsibility of a member of staff (e.g. the head of sixth form) other than the careers leader. We think that there is value in these roles being brought together, either by you taking this responsibility into your role or through close collaboration with the relevant member of staff.

Helping young people to learn about HE should begin in key stage 3 (or even earlier). One important thing to help young people to understand is that HE can take a range of forms. You can study for a degree at a university, a specialist institution like an art school or a music conservatoire, or at a college that mainly delivers FE but which also offers some HE. There is a growing range of Degree Apprenticeships, which allow you to combine work with studying for a degree. It is also possible to study for a degree abroad, and there may be some advantages in terms of fees in doing this. Opening young people's minds to the enormous range of possibilities is one of your main jobs.

All universities have schools liaison officers and outreach teams who will come into schools to work with students, not to promote particular courses but to introduce their university. In some cases, these outreach activities may include access to academic staff who come and work with your students around the curriculum – for example, by giving insights into their latest research. These opportunities can be motivating for students and help to strengthen the links between careers and the curriculum (see Chapter 2.4).

In-school activities may be followed by visits to a local university. Most universities will host visits by school and college groups to give students an insight into university life (and of course to promote their own institution). Visits of this kind can be great to 'demystify' what universities are about and give students real hands-on experience. They often include a campus tour, an opportunity to meet current students, talks on applications, student finance and university life and a 'taster' lecture of some kind.

Further activities and visits can be organised in key stage 4, particularly focusing on helping students make the right choice of post-16 studies to enable progression onto HE courses. Some universities arrange visits by groups of students that involve overnight stays in halls of residence.

Once students enter the sixth form, or advanced courses at a college, further activities, focused more on helping students to choose the right course and university for them, and helping them to prepare for application procedures and the transition to university life, will be organised. Schools liaison staff, admissions tutors and others might be invited into the school or college to speak to students, and perhaps their parents as well. Attendance at careers conventions and opportunities fairs at which universities are represented can be organised. Visits to HE open days and taster lectures can also be arranged, but at this stage it becomes increasingly important to focus these opportunities around the subjects that students are thinking of studying.

At this post-16 stage students should have opportunities to meet HE students as well as university staff. Many schools and colleges do this by organising networking events with alumni. One practical tip here: it is often more beneficial to invite second- or third-year students back to talk to current Year 12 or 13 students, than first-year students. A common reason for students dropping out of HE courses is transition problems, and students who have been at university for longer than a full year are more likely to give a realistic picture of university life, together with an insight into what comes next.

In England, just over 50% of students progress on to university,[39] but approximately 1 in 20 of those students drop out by the end of the first year.[40] The main reasons for drop-out are financial problems, academic difficulties, personal problems and mistaken choice of institution or course.[41] Enabling students to meet with staff and students from universities and to sample HE courses makes a significant contribution to helping students understand the options available. It is equally important that the information provided, both to students and their parents, includes the realities of student finance.

Resources: Choosing a university course

There are lots of resources available to help with choosing a university or course. The following offer some good starting points.

The Complete University Guide www.thecompleteuniversityguide.co.uk.

Discover Uni www.officeforstudents.org.uk/advice-and-guidance/student-information-and-data/discover-uni-and-unistats/.

UCAS (Universities and Colleges Admissions Service) www.ucas.com.

The Uni Guide www.theuniguide.co.uk.

What uni? www.whatuni.com.

In recent years the governments in England, other parts of the UK and several other European countries have introduced policies and programmes to attempt to increase not only the numbers of young people entering HE, but also the proportion from under-represented groups, including those from lower-income families or from families with no previous history of going to university. These widening participation initiatives represent a commitment to improving levels of social mobility and are likely to remain a feature of education policy and practice in the future. They attract significant levels of funding to support activities in schools and colleges to promote HE.

FE and sixth form colleges

In every area of the country there are general FE colleges which offer a wide range of technical education qualifications and vocational courses for 16- to 19-year-old students, alongside many full-time and part-time programmes for adults. Many also offer an alternative place to study A levels and other general/academic courses and some also offer 14–16 opportunities. In addition, there are specialist colleges offering courses in land-based subjects or the arts and, in areas where there are 11–16 secondary schools, there are sixth form colleges.

It is good practice for schools to work in partnership with all the colleges in the local area, to make students, and their parents, aware of the full range of study opportunities available. Indeed, as stated earlier, schools now have a statutory duty to enable providers to talk to students about these options. The most common approach is to invite representatives from the colleges, both staff and students, to present to students and parents at information evenings in the school and to take part in careers fairs and similar events. But the links with colleges can be extended by arranging visits to local colleges, encouraging attendance at open days and evenings, and organising taster classes.

Resources: Choosing FE courses

A useful place to look for information on FE courses and qualifications, and on possible sources of funding, in England is the government's website **www.gov.uk/further-education-courses**. This also includes a search facility that links you to local sites that give an overview of the provision in local authority areas.

The Association of Colleges website **www.aoc.co.uk** provides information on the different types of college and useful statistics.

If your school has a sixth form, don't assume that all students should progress into your sixth form. This can be difficult, as the financial viability of the school is likely to depend to some extent on its ability to retain or recruit students post-16. This may mean that your head teacher or the head of sixth form puts some pressure on you and the careers adviser to direct students towards your sixth form. However, your job as careers leader is to provide students with information about a range of post-16 options and to ensure that all young people make the choice that is right for them rather than for the school.

If you are a careers leader in a college you have all the same responsibilities as those in school. You need to ensure that your learners can think about how best to progress from their course to other education and training options. This may be about ensuring that there are good opportunities for learners to progress within your college, e.g. from a level 2 to level 3 qualification, but also being open to the possibility that they may want to pursue their next qualification at another college. You also need to ensure that you have good support in place for those students who want to transition to HE and that all learners understand that HE is a possibility that they may wish to access at some point.

In addition to supporting the progression of your current learners, colleges often offer pre-entry support for prospective learners. This may include information, talks and advice provided to young people in school, and pre-entry tasters and advice sessions for learners who are about to start. Often this focuses on whether people are choosing the right course for them, and helps them to understand a range of alternatives. As the careers leader, you may have some direct involvement in this pre-entry work, but usually it will be the responsibility of another department. One of the challenges is that there is often a tension between marketing the college and providing the best advice for individuals. As careers leader, you should be trying to make sure that the advice people get is in their interest – both for ethical reasons and because recruiting people for the wrong course or to the wrong institution generally just stores up problems for the future and leads to drop-out as well as to long-term career dissatisfaction.

CASE STUDY

Jenny is the associate principal at Vanchester College. She has over-arching responsibility for careers and has worked to develop the college's careers offer. However, she doesn't have any direct responsibility for recruitment and marketing, which is the responsibility of Winston, who is the deputy principal of the college. She arranges a meeting with Winston and they agree that the head of marketing and outreach should join the college's Careers and Employability Committee to help to join things up.

Reflective question: If you were to set up a Career Guidance Forum for your school or college, who would you want in the group?

Working with apprenticeship providers

In recent years there has been a growth in the number of apprenticeship programmes available to young people, both at 16 and at 18. Yet, for understandable reasons, these are opportunities that school staff often know least about.

The apprenticeships available to young people today are very different from those taken by previous generations but they still combine paid work-based experience and training with a minimum of 20% of time 'off-the-job' training to gain a technical or professional qualification. Apprentices receive a wage or a training allowance. In England there are four types or levels of apprenticeship:

- Intermediate Apprenticeships (level 2)
- Advanced Apprenticeships (level 3)
- Higher Apprenticeships (level 4 and above)
- Degree Apprenticeships (levels 6 and 7).

Intermediate and Advanced Apprenticeships are usually entered at age 16 and Higher and Degree Apprenticeships at age 18. All four levels are available in a wide range of occupational sectors.

The Higher and Degree Apprenticeships offer highly attractive and competitive alternatives to full-time study at university. Young people following these options gain valuable experience of work while studying at degree level and being paid a salary. As careers leader, you should work with the head of sixth form to make sure that students and their parents know about such opportunities.

For 16- to 24-year-old students who want to progress on to an apprenticeship but do not have the necessary skills or experience, Traineeships offer a way forward. These are programmes provided by colleges and private training providers and are designed around a high-quality work experience placement. They can be from six weeks to a year in length, although most last six months and include work preparation and further study of English and maths.

> ### 💡 Resources: Choosing apprenticeships and work-based learning programmes
>
> The following resources might be useful for students who are exploring apprenticeships and other work-based learning programmes.
>
> Apprenticeships **www.apprenticeships.gov.uk**.
>
> Apprenticeship Support and Knowledge (ASK) in schools and colleges **www.apprenticeships.gov.uk/influencers/ask-programme-resources**.
>
> Find an Apprenticeship **www.gov.uk/apply-apprenticeship**.
>
> Not Going to Uni **www.notgoingtouni.co.uk**.
>
> School leaver jobs **www.allaboutschoolleavers.co.uk**.

In the same way that colleges can be invited into school, and experiences at college can be arranged for students, apprenticeship providers should be invited to talk to students and to parents, and visits to providers should be arranged. There would be benefit also in staff from the school, particularly those delivering the careers programme to students in Years 11, 12 and 13, visiting an apprenticeship provider and gaining first-hand experience of the work-based training they offer.

CASE STUDY

At Dunchester Progress Academy, the careers leader, Rita, worked with apprenticeship providers in the town to enable all the Year 11 tutors to work-shadow an apprentice on one of the school's professional development days.
  This raised their awareness of the training provided and gave them some good contacts whom they could then invite in to speak to their class.

Reflective questions: Would an activity like this be seen as valuable CPD in your school or college? What placements for staff colleagues would you like to set up to benefit your careers programme?

Supporting transitions for learners with special needs

Transitions to further learning can be particularly worrying for learners with SEND. Whether you are a special school or a mainstream school with some SEND learners you will have been working to provide your SEND learners with a supportive environment where their needs are well understood and appropriate adjustments made. Moving into college or university is an important step towards independence, and for some learners and their parents this may raise concerns.

Young people with SEND are very diverse, so how to approach this is likely to vary enormously. In some cases, supporting them to make choices about further learning might be very similar to any other learner; in other cases it might require careful liaison with the institution that they are moving to, including meetings involving the student and their parents and the sharing of detailed notes and experiences.

In general, when dealing with transitions for young people with SEND it is important to start early and to ensure that there is sufficient time to support them. For a careers leader in a special school this will be a major focus of your job. If you are a careers leader in a mainstream school or college, in most cases it won't be your role to lead this process directly, but you should be involved in it and ensure that it is happening. This is likely to mean that you meet with the SENCO in a school or with learner support services in a college.

Some key questions that you should be asking include the following.
- Do I have any learners with SEND?
- What additional needs are they likely to have when transitioning to the next stage of their education?
- Is there any specialist or bespoke provision that they should be considering?
- What issues are they likely to experience during the application process? Have we talked to them about when and how to disclose their special need or disability?
- What issues are they likely to experience if they are successful in their application? Has the college or university that they are going to already got adjustments in place?
- Are there any additional resources or support that they can get access to?
- How should we involve their family in the transition?
- What records should we be passing over? How should we manage this?
- Does the college or university offer any form of contact over the long summer holiday between leaving school and starting the college or university course?

The role of the careers leader

The careers leader should be working with all staff in the school to make sure that all educational and training routes are portrayed positively. The school's careers provision shouldn't be about retaining students in school or promoting HE. Rather it should be about opening up the full range of possibilities.

Careers leaders should take the lead on establishing links with learning providers and ensuring that the school is not only meeting its statutory duty but also enabling all students to gain an understanding of the full range of study options available at each point of transition. Although you will have oversight of the partnerships, and may well organise some of the encounters and experiences yourself, many of the activities may be organised by other colleagues, including key stage directors and head of sixth form.

Key tasks for the careers leader include:
- understanding the implications of a changing education landscape for career guidance, e.g. technical education reform
- ensuring compliance with the legal requirements to provide independent career guidance and give access to providers of technical education or apprenticeships to pupils in schools, including the publication of the policy statement of provider access on their website
- establishing and developing links with FE colleges, apprenticeship providers, UTCs and universities.

In a nutshell

As the careers leader you are responsible for ensuring that students, and their parents, have as much information as possible on further study options. You will need to:

- ensure that there are opportunities for all students to meet with representatives, staff and students from HE, FE and apprenticeship programmes
- provide opportunities for students to visit universities, colleges and apprenticeship providers.

2.8 Personal guidance

Personal guidance describes the one-to-one support that is given to an individual by a careers professional. It is probably what most people think of first when they think about 'career guidance'. But as we have seen in the rest of this section 'good career guidance' is much broader than this. However, personal guidance has a critical role in providing personalised support and in helping students to link together the learning that they have done in the other Benchmarks.

As a careers leader it isn't your job to deliver personal guidance (although if you have a background in personal guidance you may continue to do this alongside your responsibilities as a careers leader). Your job is to ensure that young people receive career guidance from a professional careers adviser before they are 16 and then again between 16 and 18. This may involve you in commissioning career guidance from an external provider or in managing an internal career guidance person.

This chapter will cover:

- defining personal guidance and looking at common models
- when to have a career conversation and when to refer to a careers professional
- the ethical and professional standards that guidance professionals work to
- how to procure, appoint and manage guidance services
- linking guidance to wider pastoral and student support services.

Introduction

We've already said that careers are highly individual. No two people will have the same aspirations or follow the same career. Two of your students might both want to become ambulance drivers, but their reasons for wanting this, their chance of success and the way that this occupational choice connects to their wider life ambitions will all be different. Therefore, it is important to talk one-to-one with them to provide personalised support.

So far we've emphasised the importance of differentiating activities and allowing students space to follow their own interests. We've also argued that it is important that young people get the opportunity to have as many career conversations as possible. At some point they are likely to want to sit down and have a deep conversation about their interests, ambitions and options with someone. Ideally that person will be skilled at having such conversations, will understand psychology and have a knowledge of the labour market. Thankfully, there are professionals who are skilled at doing this. These people are variously known as careers advisers, careers professionals, careers coaches, careers consultants and careers counsellors. You need to make sure that you have at least one of them attached to your school, and probably a whole team of them within your college.

You have probably realised by now that there are two key professional roles that are distinct but complementary: the careers leader, who is responsible for leading and managing the overall programme of career guidance in the school or college; and the careers adviser, who provides independent, personal guidance to students, usually in one-to-one settings. This handbook has been written to support the training and professional development of careers leaders. Later in this chapter we look at professional qualifications for careers advisers. While some schools and colleges choose to combine the roles of careers leader and careers adviser in one person, it is important that they remember these are two separate jobs.

💡 Resources: The role of the careers adviser

The Career Development Institute has produced a short briefing explaining the work of a careers adviser:

Understanding the role of the Careers Adviser in 'Personal Guidance' (July 2021); **www.thecdi.net/write/Documents/CDI_119-Role_of_a_Careers_Adviser-2021-FINAL_v_to_use.pdf**.

What is personal guidance?

The term 'personal guidance' was invented by the Gatsby Charitable Foundation to distinguish between what it calls 'career guidance', which encompasses everything that we have been discussing in this section of the book, and the one-to-one encounters that take place between a careers professional and a young person. Gatsby describes personal guidance as usually taking the form of a 'one-to-one interview with a careers adviser (who may or may not be a member of school staff)'. The staff responsible for delivering career guidance should be 'trained to an appropriate level', which we'll discuss in more detail below.

In as much as the person in the street thinks about 'career guidance' they are probably thinking about what we are calling personal guidance. The use of the term personal guidance is therefore helpful because it makes this distinction, but it may need to be explained to people so that everyone is clear what you are talking about.

There are lots of alternative terms that are used to mean essentially the same thing. In England people often talk about 'information, advice and guidance' or 'IAG'. We're not particularly keen on turning things into acronyms as it can be confusing, but you will certainly hear people discussing IAG. This term has come about because some people argue that there are three distinct activities that take place as part of personal guidance: (1) the giving of factual information; (2) the provision of advice or recommendations about what to do; and (3) a deeper interaction (guidance) which explores why clients are asking particular questions and challenges their thinking. We're not so sure that these are all distinct activities (rather than interrelated ones), but it is useful to notice that a lot of different things can go on in a one-to-one conversation and that it takes some skill to decide what is the best way to support a particular individual in developing their career.

In other countries it is more common to refer to this activity as 'guidance counselling' or 'career counselling' and there has been a recent move to change the terminology to 'career coaching'. There are different academic and professional tribes and factions which make the case for each of these terms and argue that they each constitute a radical break with the existing terminology. For an outsider much of this debate is a bit baffling and it is reasonable to conclude that all these terms mean pretty much the same thing in practice, but to notice that there are some different flavours in the way that people do it.

Models of personal guidance

So, what do careers professionals actually *do* when they are *doing personal guidance*? One of the most popular approaches was defined by Gerard Egan in his book *The Skilled Helper* and is often known as the three-stage model.[42] The three-stage model provides a structure for the conversation that careers professionals have with their clients.

1. **Exploring the current scenario.** Asking 'What is going on?' Finding out what the client's life is like and what has brought them to seek personal guidance. This might include thinking about what they are interested in, good at and what their values are. This stage is about building up a picture of the client which can provide the careers adviser and the client themselves with clues about what might be possible for them.

2. **Understanding the preferred scenario.** Asking 'What do you want instead?' or in the case of young people both 'What do you want to do next?' and 'What do you want to do eventually?' In this stage the careers adviser can sometimes be trying to stimulate and inspire ideas about the future or they can be helping to shape and clarify pre-existing ideas. So, it is very common for young people to say 'I have no idea what I want to do with my life', but other young people may start from a very different place, perhaps asking 'How can I become a civil engineer?' The careers adviser needs to be able to deal with all of these different possibilities.

3. **Supporting the taking of action.** Asking 'What can you do to make this happen?' This stage is all about exploring strategies and actions that the client can take to move towards the career outcomes that they have identified. This commonly includes coming up with lists of possible actions, weighing up the suitability of them and making plans to start implementing them. Sometimes these will be about further exploration – for example, doing some further research or participating in work experience. At other times they might be very focused on achieving a particular outcome – for example producing a draft of a UCAS personal statement to get onto a particular course.

CASE STUDY

Raj opens the door and invites Chloe into his office. He explains to her that they've got about 20 minutes to talk at this appointment, but if she needs more time she can book another appointment. Chloe's a bit nervous and blurts out 'I've not got any idea about careers, sir. I mean I don't think that I can go to university, because I'm too thick, but what should I do?'

STAGE 1 Raj says 'OK, we'll talk about your career next, but let's find out a bit about you first … For now, forget work or school, what do you like, what are you interested in?' Chloe starts to loosen up and talks about her family, her passion for animals and her secret enthusiasm for collecting and cataloguing Sylvanian Families toys – 'I say it is for my little sister, but it isn't!'

STAGE 2 Raj encourages Chloe to think about the things that they talked about in stage 1. He asks her what sort of things she enjoys most and whether she might like to do any of those in her career. Chloe isn't very sure, but Raj reminds her of some of the things that she's been talking about and points out that she seems to really like working with people and that she is also very neat, detail focused and keen on helping to bring order to the world. Chloe agrees and shows him her meticulously laid out revision timetable. Raj comments that he's impressed and encourages Chloe to be more positive about her abilities.

STAGE 3 They are running out of time, but Raj is happy because they've identified some clear interests for Chloe to explore. He sets her some homework to think about possible future careers and look at some information about these careers. He advises her to do some more thinking and talk to friends and family about her ideas. She can then book another appointment when they can spend more time working on her next steps and considering whether university is right for her or whether there are some other options.

Reflective questions: Who provides personal career guidance for your students? When do you talk to them about their work?

Egan's three-stage model is just one approach to organising a careers interview. Another popular approach is taken from coaching and is known as the GROW model.[43] In this model the careers adviser asks clients to focus on the **G**oal, to consider the **R**eality of their current situation, to explore their **O**ptions and to determine a **W**ay forward. Beyond this there are many other approaches to careers interviews. Some encourage clients to focus on telling their story, others on preparing for chance events, still others on self-reflection or on visualising success.

> 💡 **Resources: The theory and practice of personal guidance**
>
> If you want to find out more about the theory and practice that informs personal guidance we'd recommend one of the following books.
>
> Liane Hambly and Ciara Bomford, *Creative Career Coaching* (2018). Routledge.
>
> Hazel Reid, *Introduction to Career Counselling and Coaching* (2015). Sage.
>
> Julia Yates, *The Career Coaching Toolkit* (2018). Routledge.

As a careers leader you don't necessarily have to understand everything about the theory of personal guidance. Nor do you necessarily need to pick a favourite approach or theory. There is merit in all these different approaches, and skilled practitioners will often make use of more than one approach. The key point is to pick a competent professional who knows what they are doing and why, and can explain their approach to guidance.

Understanding the careers profession

We have already highlighted that there are a lot of different terms that are used to describe career professionals. Research conducted by the University of Derby a few years ago revealed 103 different job titles that were in use to describe careers professionals of one kind or another.[44] What is more, none of these terms is legally protected, which means that pretty much anyone can turn up at your school or college and tell you that they are a qualified careers adviser. As a careers leader it is your job to figure out the competent professionals from those who are still training, who are unqualified or who are not fit to practise. You should try to make sure that your students benefit from the professionalism of people who know what they are doing.

> ### 💡 Resources: The Career Development Institute
>
> In the UK the Career Development Institute (CDI) is the professional association for people working in careers. It represents careers leaders as well as careers advisers, so you should think about joining yourself. It provides a wide range of resources which will be useful to you in your role as careers leader and especially in relation to working with careers advisers. Key resources include:
>
> Getting qualified (**www.thecdi.net/GettingQualified**) – information on careers qualifications, including a full list of training providers.
>
> Professional register (**www.thecdi.net/Professional-Register-**) – information about professional registration and the expectations of registered professionals. You can also search the register to find careers advisers available for work in your locality.
>
> Code of ethics (**www.thecdi.net/Code-of-Ethics**) – the ethical standards that all careers professionals have to sign up to.

One of the first things to look for is the right *qualifications*. In England, Wales and Northern Ireland qualifications are described by levels. These range from *entry level* (level 0) to *doctoral level* (level 8). Careers-relevant qualifications exist at almost all the available levels. But ever since the Careers Profession Task Force published its recommendations in 2010, a qualified careers adviser has generally been seen as someone who has either a level 6 qualification (degree level) or level 7 (masters level).[45] In other countries the qualifications will vary, but it is usual for someone who is practising at the professional level to hold a careers-specific qualification to at least degree level.

This doesn't mean that people who hold other careers qualifications (typically at level 3 or 4) don't know what they are doing. But, level 3 and 4 qualifications are designed for para-professional staff who are working with, and supporting, a fully qualified careers professional. In many cases such staff will be keen to upskill and you should encourage them to do so. Some schools or colleges will pay for the training and qualification of staff to ensure that everyone is up to the level 6 standard.

Having the right qualifications is an important start, but ideally as a careers leader you will be able to see that the careers adviser that you are working with is keeping up to date with developments in the education system and labour market, and paying attention to their continuing professional development. It is reasonable for you to ask staff that you manage or commission about this and to favour people in recruitment processes who can convincingly answer questions about keeping up to date. One way to feel confident about the careers adviser that you are working with is to ensure that they are signed up as a *registered professional* on the UK Register of Career Development Professionals which is maintained by the CDI.

International reflections: IAEVG

The exact role and qualifications of careers professionals vary from country to country. Obviously, it is important to research the profession in your own country to aid you in working with these professionals.

You may also be interested to look at the International Association of Educational and Vocational Guidance (**https://iaevg.com/**), which brings together careers professionals from across the world.

Professional ethics

One of the most important aspects about employing a career development professional is that they should know about, understand and make use of the CDI's code of ethics. Ethics are critical to professional practice in any field. Ethics are a collectively agreed upon set of answers to some of the most difficult problems that we experience when we are in practice. The CDI's ethical framework is made up of 11 key principles. We have listed them here because they should underpin both your work as a careers leader and the work of any careers advisers that you manage or contract in.

Career Development Institute Code of Ethics

1. **Accessibility.** Members must promote access to career development activities and services in a range of ways that are appropriate and ensure inclusion.

2. **Accountability.** Members are accountable for their career development activities and services, and must submit themselves to whatever scrutiny is appropriate to their role, including the CDI Discipline and Complaints Procedure. Members must act in the interest of society and at all times exercise integrity, honesty and diligence. Members must in all circumstances endeavour to enhance the standing and good name of the career development profession and the Career Development Institute.

3. **Autonomy.** Members must encourage individual autonomy in making decisions and always act in the individual's best interests.

4. **Competence.** Members must monitor and maintain their fitness to practise at a level that enables them to provide an effective service. Members must represent their professional competencies, training and experience accurately and function within the boundaries of their training and experience.

5. **Confidentiality.** Members must respect the privacy of individuals. Personal guidance interaction or interviews should be conducted in an agreed and suitably private environment. Clients must be informed of the limits of confidentiality and data sharing at the outset. Disclosure of confidential information should only be made with informed consent or when required by law.

6. **Continuous Professional Development.** Members must maintain their professional competence, knowledge and skills through participation in continuous professional development informed by reflective practice and the National Occupational Standards: Career Development.

7. **Duty of Care – to Clients, Colleagues, Organisations and Self.** Members have a duty of care and are expected always to act in the best interests of their clients. Members must develop and maintain professional and supportive working relationships with colleagues both inside and external to their own organisation and respect the contributions of other career development professionals to the activities and services on offer. Members must fulfil their obligations and duties to their employer (where applicable), except where to do so would compromise the best interests of clients. Members have a duty of care to themselves, in terms of their personal integrity, personal safety and their capacity to practise, in order to provide an effective service to clients.

8. **Equality.** Members must actively promote equality and diversity and work towards the removal of barriers to personal achievement resulting from prejudice, stereotyping and discrimination.

9. **Impartiality.** Members must ensure that professional judgement is objective and takes precedence over any external pressures or factors that may compromise the impartiality of career development activities and services. In doing so, members must ensure that advice is based solely on the best interests of and potential benefits to the client. Where impartiality is not possible this must be declared to the client at the outset.

10. **Transparency.** Members must provide career development services and activities in an open and transparent manner.

11. **Trustworthiness.** Members must act in accordance with the trust placed in them, ensure that the clients' expectations are ones that have reasonable expectations of being met and honour agreements and promises.

All of these principles are important, but the principle of *impartiality* is particularly central to careers advisers. Impartiality means acting in the best interests of the young person and not favouring or promoting particular options, nor deliberately omitting other options. It is acceptable to suggest opportunities that the individual has not previously considered, but the overall aim should be to help the young person to make the best choice for them. Sometimes this will be in conflict with the needs of the school or college to recruit and retain students, which is why careers advisers, and careers leaders, can find themselves conflicted between their professional practice and the demands of their employers. Where such situations arise they should be discussed between the careers leader and the senior leadership.

In England schools were given a new statutory duty in 2012 to secure access to independent career guidance. In this context 'independent' is defined as 'provided by people not employed by the school'. This is an attempt to ensure impartiality, but it is only a crude proxy. Externally commissioned careers advisers could still find themselves under pressure to present only certain options. We believe that the guiding principle should be impartiality: the careers adviser should be professionally competent; work to a code of ethics; and be allowed to present the full range of options. Whether they are employed by the school or by another organisation is less critical.

As a careers leader you have a duty to ensure that careers work is being practised ethically. This requires you to have a good understanding of the ethics and to be able to explain it (ideally before a crisis flares up) to key staff in your institution. You may find that you experience situations where these ethical principles are tested or challenged. In these situations, the CDI code of ethics should serve as a guide as to how best to resolve the situation.

When to talk and when to refer

Career conversations are too important just to be left to professionals. Students in your school or college should be being challenged all the time to think about and talk about their careers. This means that you need to feel comfortable having career conversations, but that you also need to make sure that all teaching and support staff in your school also feel comfortable. You should offer some training and support for this (see Chapter 4.3 for more on this). It is helpful to involve your careers adviser in this training, both to help clarify what their role is and to pass on some of their experience and tips about how to have career conversations.

There are lots of ways to have effective career conversations with young people. The kinds of conversations that teachers and other staff have will often have a number of these features.

Informal, unplanned and unstructured. Students will often come up to you at the end of a lesson or even during a lesson and ask something. It might be 'Sir, do you think that I could do chemistry at university?' or 'Miss, I'm thinking about taking a gap year'. These kinds of conversations are really important and your staff should be ready for them. One of the keys is to recognise that you are not going to answer these kinds of questions quickly or alone. But, you can help to move your student forward in their thinking.

In context. One of the key advantages that teachers and other staff have with respect to having career conversations is that they operate in context. A teacher can point out to a student that they are good at something and ask whether they've thought about pursuing this area in the future.

Based on a pre-existing relationship. Students will normally approach adults whom they know well before they seek out help from strangers. This means that as a teacher or lecturer you are likely to get students asking you for help a lot. This pre-existing relationship gives you many advantages as you have much to draw on in understanding that young person and what might be useful or possible for them to do to move their career forward.

Not always labelled as a 'career conversation'. Many students don't think about their careers very much and some are even scared to talk about them. Both of these things make them less likely to engage with a careers adviser. A conversation that you have might not be labelled as a career conversation, but it might raise several career-related issues. For example, students might talk to you about whether they can leave the area because one of their parents is sick. This kind of conversation quickly turns into a conversation about educational and career options and allows you to discuss something that a student might be very concerned about.

BUT, it is also important to be clear with all of the staff in your school or college that you are not asking them to become careers advisers. There is an important distinction between the kind of career conversation that a teacher or other member of school or college staff might have and the kind of conversations that are had by careers professionals. Key to managing this is knowing your professional boundaries and referring on to more specialist help when you reach those boundaries.

One of the key issues that all professionals have to be aware of is what are the boundaries of their experience, knowledge, skills and indeed of their whole profession. Members of staff at a school or college usually have some responsibility to have pastoral conversations with students and to help them to deal with issues, particularly where they impact on their academic performance and their participation in school. As most personal issues have some impact on this, this can be challenging to draw a boundary round. But, there are some key questions that you should always be asking yourself when you are talking to a student.

- Can I actually help this young person?
- Do I have the knowledge to answer this question?
- Do I have the skill to help this young person?
- Will me helping them raise any safety or safeguarding issues?
- How will their family feel about the help that I am giving?
- Should I inform anyone in the school/college about the help that I am giving?
- What information should I record?
- Can anyone else help?
- Can anyone else help more than me?

Asking yourself these questions will help you to figure out where the boundaries of your role sit. Obviously, these kinds of situations often take you into grey areas where things may be technically out of your responsibility, but there is no one else who can help. In such cases, you have to do your best, but you should also make sure that you inform your line manager about what you are doing and keep good records.

CASE STUDY

Sandra is a lecturer in business studies at Vanchester College. After a class, Robert comes up to her and is visibly upset. He confesses that although he is studying business studies he is desperate to pursue a career in musical theatre. He thinks that Sandra's lectures are great – but it just isn't what he wants to do. Sandra starts to talk to him and quickly discovers that this is part of ongoing tensions between Robert and his father. 'He's always wanted me to follow in his footsteps and take over the family accountancy firm.' Sandra realises that this is a very complex issue which is bound up with career, family, talent and Robert's identity.

She is happy to talk to Robert, but isn't sure that she should get involved in mediating between him and his family. She also has no idea whether a career in musical theatre is possible for Robert or how he would go about it. She thinks about it and refers him to Sheena, the head of the drama department, for a conversation, and suggests that he book a meeting with a careers adviser. In the meantime, she tells him to keep coming to business studies and they'll meet again in a week to see how he is getting on.

Robert is pleased that he's been listened to and has got a way forward.

Reflective questions: How well do your staff colleagues know the referral systems for personal career guidance? How could you better inform them?

As Sandra and Robert's case study shows, you can achieve a lot by referring someone to the right person (or people).

Managing referrals

Once you've decided that you need to refer a student to someone else there are several things that you should try to do to make sure that the referral goes smoothly. It can be useful to work through the following questions.

- **What is the issue that the young person is dealing with?** Having a clear understanding of what they are experiencing is important to allow you to refer to the right person.
- **Who is available to help them?** In this book we're focused on careers issues, but that doesn't mean that the careers adviser will always be the best person to refer a young person to. In some cases, the nature of the issue they are experiencing may mean that they should be referred to a social worker, youth worker or SENCO. It is also important to check that the person or service that you are referring to has the availability to see the student in a timely fashion.

- **How should the referral be recorded and what records should be passed over?** Keeping good records is an important part of careers leadership (see Chapter 2.3). Such records can support effective inter-professional working but also raise a host of data-sharing issues that you need to be careful about, particularly if you are referring a student to people who do not work for the school.
- **What is your ongoing role in the referral?** Referring to someone else is not simply offloading the problem. Whether you are the careers leader or a form tutor you are likely to have an ongoing relationship with that young person. In some cases, once you refer to another professional the young person may wish to keep what they are talking about with that person confidential. In other cases, you might continue to be involved, perhaps even accompanying them to meet other professionals and helping them to put things into practice.
- **How are you reviewing referral processes to ensure that they are working well?** As the careers leader you should talk to both teachers and careers advisers to find out how referral processes are working from both sides. It is your job to spot problems and to try to figure out how to put them right.

Referral systems for personal career guidance in schools and colleges should enable both referrals from tutors and teaching staff and self-referrals by students. As discussed in Chapter 2.3, many referrals will come via tutoring and mentoring conversations and, as careers leader, you should be part of any forum for reviewing and developing the school's or college's overall approach to supporting individual students.

> **Tools: Item 2.8A. Bringing coherence to personal guidance.**
> A template for reviewing all the one-to-one interviews that students might have and the associated documentary records is provided in the online resources accompanying this book: **https://indigo.careers/clh**. The aim is to bring coherence to all the personal advice and guidance support, and enable efficient and effective referrals between the various aspects.

How much personal guidance do students need?

Key questions related to the provision of personal guidance include: who should get personal guidance; how much of it they should get; and how often should they get it? The Gatsby research gives us a clear minimum to start from. Every young person should have had access to at least one personal guidance interview before they are 16. They should then get access to another interview between the ages of 16 and 18. Such an interview should be with a careers professional (qualified to at least level 6) and normally be one-to-one and face-to-face.

Gatsby does not specify how long each of these appointments should be, but the evidence tells us that an effective personal guidance interview is likely to last at least 30 minutes, and possibly up to an hour.[46] While some schools may be tempted to try and meet this Benchmark by squeezing the length of interviews down to 10–15 minutes, such interviews are unlikely to be particularly effective. The whole point of these interviews is to give young people a chance to talk, reflect and get expert feedback. Given this, it is important to set some quality thresholds when you are commissioning personal guidance. The case studies in this chapter show how personal guidance can often take the form of a series of appointments rather than a single appointment. They also show that the need for personal guidance is not uniform; some students are likely to need personal guidance more than others.

This means that as a careers leader you've got some difficult resource planning to do. On the one hand, you've got to ensure sufficient resources to allow every student to be seen once before the age of 16, and then again during the post-16 phase of their education. On the other hand, you need to ensure that there is some flexibility built into your system. Students should be able to seek additional help, teachers and other staff should be able to refer and careers advisers should be able to recommend repeat appointments where this makes sense.

Managing guidance services

Delivering personal guidance for all your students is relatively resource intensive and requires access to specialist resources. There are two main ways in which you can achieve this: firstly, by appointing a careers professional (or number of them) to the staff of the school or college; and secondly, by procuring services from an external body or individual.

If you **appoint a careers professional** or, in the case of colleges, **establish an internal careers service**, you will need to develop a job description, run a recruitment process, figure out where they are going to sit in your management structures and performance-manage them. We discuss management in more detail in Chapter 3.2. This approach has many advantages, but it is also likely to take up more of your time. As the careers leader there is a strong argument for you having line-management responsibility for any careers advisers in your organisation (although this is not the only model). If you do line-manage the careers adviser or anyone else, it is important for you to get clear recognition for the time that you are spending on this.

As we indicated earlier, some schools and colleges are choosing to combine the roles of careers leader and careers adviser in one person, either by appointing a careers adviser to the role of careers leader or through supporting the careers leader to complete further training to become a professionally qualified careers adviser. In such arrangements, it is important that senior leadership remember that these are two distinct roles and that the person appointed needs the appropriate amount of time and support to fulfil both roles.

> **Resources: The matrix Standard**
>
> **The matrix Standard** (http://matrixstandard.com) is a quality standard that helps organisations to assess and measure their advice and support services. Colleges are expected to use it to quality-assure their personal guidance provision. Schools are recommended to use the standard when deciding upon organisations from which to commission career guidance services.

If you choose to **commission guidance services** from another organisation or individual outside of your school or college you will need to go through a procurement process. The CDI provides a useful guide to this process which breaks it down into the following 10 steps.

1. Determine whether you want to commission personal guidance services (rather than appointing internally).

2. Decide whether to commission on your own or with other schools and colleges as part of a multi-academy trust (MAT) or other grouping.

3. Identify who will lead on the commissioning process (usually the careers leader, but often with support from more senior staff and finance officers).

4. Review your existing personal guidance provision.

5. Identify the services that need to be commissioned. Is it just personal guidance or is it linked to other career development activities that you want to procure? Draft a specification for the service to be commissioned.

6. Confirm the budget for personal guidance.

7. Identify possible providers.

8. Research potential providers.

9. Draw up a shortlist, invite bids, decide between them and appoint a favoured provider.

10. Monitor and keep under review the delivery of the service.

> **Resources: Guide to commissioning career guidance services**
>
> The Career Development Institute has produced Career Guidance in Schools and Colleges: A Guide to Best Practice and Commissioning Career Guidance Services, which includes templates to support the steps outlined above, www.thecdi.net/write/Documents/CDI_120_Career_Guidance_in_Schools-2021-FINAL.pdf.

If you commission an external careers adviser working as a sole trader or employed by an organisation providing career guidance services, you will need to manage the contract and the day-to-day work of the adviser when they are in the school or college. You will not line-manage them but, as the careers leader, you should be responsible for: ensuring that they provide the personal guidance and any other services agreed; managing the referrals; and quality-assuring their contributions to your careers programme.

International reflections: Working with providers of personal career guidance

Very few other countries have a policy for career guidance for young people based on schools and colleges being expected to commission the personal guidance (or career counselling) from an external provider. In almost every other country, there is either an external careers service funded by the government or schools employ their own guidance counsellors.

Where there is an external service, and the careers advisers (or guidance counsellors) go into schools to provide the personal guidance, the careers leader should ideally negotiate a partnership agreement with the service, to determine what services are to be provided and how they relate to the overall careers programme. This agreement should be kept under review at least annually.

Where the school employs a guidance counsellor, the careers leader will either manage their work or agree a working arrangement that integrates their work into the careers programme.

Personal career guidance for young people with SEND

When the UK government transferred responsibility for providing independent career guidance for young people in England to individual schools and colleges in 2012, local authorities retained responsibility for providing support for young people deemed 'vulnerable and disadvantaged'. This definition includes students with SEND, but the level of career guidance that is provided in practice varies across different local authorities, depending on budgets and how the statutory duty is interpreted. Careers leaders in special schools are advised to check with their local authority about the support available for their pupils, and you may find that you need to supplement the service with further personal career guidance that you commission from an external provider.

The role of the careers leader

The careers leader has an important role in overseeing personal guidance activity. They should develop an approach to delivering personal guidance and then work with the wider staff body to ensure that referrals are smooth and that personal guidance integrates well with other forms of pastoral support and advice and guidance services.

The careers leader does not have to be a careers adviser, but they do need to understand careers advice and engage closely with the ethical standards which inform the work of careers professionals. It is very likely that as the careers leader you will be involved in managing or supervising the work of careers advisers and, as such, it is important that you have a good understanding of their work.

Key roles for the careers leader include:
- supporting tutors, providing initial information and advice
- managing the work of others, e.g. careers advisers and administrative and other staff involved in the delivery of career guidance
- monitoring access to, and take-up of, guidance
- managing the careers budget as appropriate
- managing their own CPD and supporting the ongoing CPD of colleagues in the careers team
- liaising with tutors, mentors, SENCO and heads of year to identify pupils needing guidance
- referring pupils to careers advisers
- commissioning career guidance services where appropriate.

In a nutshell

As a careers leader you are responsible for ensuring that pupils have access to at least two personal guidance interviews during the time that they are at school. You will need to:

- ensure that you understand the professional practice of careers advisers
- manage the links between careers advisers and other school or college staff to ensure that referrals work well
- develop a delivery approach through managing key staff or commissioning external services.

Section 3:
The role of the careers leader

Introduction

The previous section of this handbook examined the components of an effective careers programme. We organised it around the framework of the eight Gatsby Benchmarks. Towards the end of each chapter the specific responsibilities for the careers leader relating to that element of the careers programme were identified.

But, what exactly is a careers leader?

We'll start with some definitions, provide a brief history of the role, discuss some of the different ways in which the role can be organised within schools and colleges, and then go on to spend most of this section looking at the four main jobs that a careers leader does (leadership, management, co-ordination and networking).

In the previous section we drew extensively from the Gatsby Benchmarks to help us to define what an outstanding careers programme looks like. Again, we'd like to start this section by drawing your attention to a couple of useful papers that will help you to understand the basis of the careers leader role.

💡 Resources: Understanding the role of the careers leader

Firstly, The Careers & Enterprise Company and Gatsby Charitable Foundation (yes, them again!) have produced a couple of useful booklets called *Understanding the Role of the Careers Leader* – one for schools[1] and another for colleges.[2] These guides set out the official version of what a careers leader is. They also offer some key principles that underpin careers leadership and a range of case studies to show how this works in practice. We would strongly recommend that you download one of the guides (**https://resources.careersandenterprise.co.uk/resources/understanding-role-careers-leader-guide-secondary-schools** or **https://resources.careersandenterprise.co.uk/resources/understanding-role-careers-leader-guide-colleges**) and read it alongside this book.

Secondly, we will also be drawing on a couple of academic articles that we wrote entitled "*... and now it's over to you': recognising and supporting the role of the careers leaders in schools in England*'[3] and '*Careers leadership in practice*'[4]. In the first of these articles, we looked at the history of the careers leader role, describe the role and set out some of the key challenges and opportunities that those in the role faced. In the second article, we looked at how the role works in schools.

Defining the careers leader

Careers leaders are people who have been given the responsibility and accountability for the delivery of a school's or college's careers programme. The role is described as follows in *Understanding the Role of the Careers Leader*:

> *Careers leadership involves: planning, implementing and quality assuring a careers programme for the school; managing the delivery of career guidance; networking with external partners, including employers; coordinating the contributions of careers teachers, subject teachers, tutors and SENCO.*

We think that this is a pretty good definition as it captures the wide range of activities that a careers leader is involved in as well as the wide range of people that they must work with. It is possible to add quite a lot to this definition – for example, by highlighting the role that the careers leader has in managing upwards and involving senior leaders, head teachers or college principals and governors in supporting the careers programme. We could also talk about the wider range of skills that a careers leader needs to put the careers programme into practice. However, we'll get into the detail as we move through this section.

The careers leader is a leadership role responsible for the important area of careers in the school or college. While they are responsible for leading this activity, they shouldn't be responsible for delivering all of it. They are variously a commissioner, a line manager and a persuader of others but should avoid the temptation to do everything. As they are leading their school's or college's careers programme, they should expect to be able to access the resources and support needed to make this a success.

Other important roles (What a careers leader isn't)

The terminology around careers leadership can be confusing. There are lots of jobs with the word 'careers' in them. If you are not careful you might find that all of these get heaped onto your plate. So it is important that you understand the various other roles that exist and make sure that you think about how you interact with all of them.

Other careers roles

Careers Co-ordinator	Co-ordinating a careers programme.	*Historically the role of careers co-ordinator was often filled by a fairly junior member of staff. The shift to careers leader is a signal that there is a need to upskill people in these roles or replace them with someone more senior. Consequently, we anticipate that in most schools and colleges the role of careers co-ordinator will be replaced by that of careers leader.*
Careers Adviser	Providing information, advice and guidance to students one-to-one and in groups.	*The careers leader works with the careers adviser and may manage or commission them. In some cases the two roles can be combined, but it is important that enough time is preserved for careers leadership.*
Careers Administrator	Supporting the careers leader by undertaking a range of administrative and logistical tasks.	*The careers leader will typically be line-managing the careers administrator.*
Enterprise Adviser	A volunteer from business who will work with the careers leader and the SLT to drive improvements in the school or college's careers provision.	*The careers leader should normally be involved in recruiting the Enterprise Adviser and in being the lead point of contact with them.*
Enterprise Co-ordinator	Providing schools and colleges with a local source of expertise and support for their careers provision.	*The Enterprise Co-ordinator should be a key contact for the careers leader, helping to connect him or her to employers and other careers leaders in the locality.*
Careers Hub Lead and Trust Lead for Careers	Facilitating a network of schools and colleges to work collaboratively on developing the careers programmes in their schools and colleges and to share practice.	*The careers leader will represent their school or college in the network and take the opportunity to learn from colleagues in similar roles.*

A brief history of careers leadership

We are great believers that it is helpful to know where you have been if you want to know where you are going. Consequently, we are going to present a brief history lesson here.[5] If you aren't interested in the history, feel free to skip ahead.

Up until 2012 careers programmes in schools were organised through a partnership between the school and an external careers service (known as the Careers Service from the 1970s to 2000 and Connexions from 2000 to 2012). Responsibilities for careers were shared between the partner organisation and the school. The arrangements in colleges were slightly different. Although the external service did work with students in FE, many colleges had established their own internal careers service, often located within a wider student services department.

Originally the person who led careers activities in a school was known as the *careers teacher*, but gradually other titles were introduced such as *head of careers* or *careers co-ordinator*. One driver for this change was the increasing likelihood that the person doing the job may not be a teacher. Another was the steady increase in the complexity of the role. In the early days the careers teacher was probably just managing a careers library, arranging a schedule of interviews for the careers adviser and teaching a few careers lessons. As we have shown in Section 2, the role is considerably more demanding than that these days. As more members of staff have become involved, as tutors providing initial information and advice and as teachers delivering programmes of careers education, the role has evolved into one of leading and managing the work of others.

In colleges the person who led careers activities was most often the student services manager or the leader of the team of careers advisers. But, again as the role has evolved, becoming more central to the curriculum, careers leadership has typically moved up the hierarchy of the college and spread out, with more departments and curriculum areas having an active interest in careers.

Just as the role of the school was becoming increasingly complex, the role of the external partner also evolved. The Careers Service and Connexions no longer just provided advice and guidance, but increasingly got involved in brokering relationships with employers, providing guidance on curriculum and offering specialist support services, e.g. for young people with special educational needs.

This partnership came to an end in 2012 when the responsibility for career guidance was transferred from the local authorities which ran Connexions to schools and colleges. At this point, all of the complex tasks that had been done by both the school or college and Connexions were left at the door of whoever had responsibility for careers in the school or college.

This new situation put schools and colleges at the heart of the delivery of careers, but it didn't mean that the idea of partnership had disappeared forever. In fact, schools now had to build multiple partnerships with The Careers & Enterprise Company, Jobcentre Plus, university outreach organisations and so on. Colleges had already begun to develop similar partnerships. We'll be looking at these relationships in more detail in Chapter 3.4.

Initially schools struggled to deal with these new responsibilities (colleges arguably managed the transition more easily). More responsibilities meant that schools needed more capacity to deliver them, and this ultimately resulted in a consensus around the need for careers leadership.

> ## 💡 Resources: The history of careers education
>
> If you want to know more about the history of this area you might find David's *Careers Education in Schools*[6] an interesting read.

Models of careers leadership (schools)

One of the questions that new careers leaders are often keen to have answered is what grade or pay scale they should be on and where they should sit in the hierarchy. Unfortunately, it is not easy to answer this as careers leaders come from a range of backgrounds and schools manage them in at least five main ways. The different approaches to careers leadership that we have seen are set out in the table below.

Models of careers leadership

Model of careers leadership	Descripton
1. Middle leader	A single middle leader takes responsibility for all the tasks, and reports to a senior leader with overall responsibility for careers. In some 11–18 schools, the role may be split between the careers leader, who takes responsibility for the careers programme in key stages 3 and 4, and the head of sixth, who looks after careers in Years 12 and 13.
2. Senior leader	A single senior leader, usually an assistant head or, in small schools, a deputy head, takes on responsibility not only for the strategic overview but also for the day-to-day operational leadership and management of careers.

Model of careers leadership	Descripton
3. **Outsourcing**	The school commissions an individual, often a careers adviser, either from a careers organisation or as a sole trader, to not only provide a career guidance service but also to lead the school's careers programme.
4. **Distributed leadership**	The tasks of careers leadership are shared among a small team of senior and middle leaders. In such examples, a senior leader usually takes on the strategic leadership and then leads a team of two or three middle leaders who take on different aspects of operational management, co-ordination and networking.
5. **Multi-school leadership**	One individual, either a senior leader or a middle leader, is responsible for leading careers in more than one school, often within the same multi-academy trust.

Of these different models in schools, the first two are by far the most common, i.e. having a single careers leader. The advantage of having a middle leader in the role is that he or she can devote time to the tasks, whereas a senior leader will have many competing demands on their time, some of which may take them away from the careers leadership job at short notice. However, a middle leader can be truly effective in the role only if he or she has active support from a link senior leader.

Conversely, the advantage of having a senior leader doing the job is that they have a greater amount of authority in the school to drive change. If they can really devote the time to careers leadership this model can work well, especially if they have an 'assistant' or 'deputy' careers leader who can work with them to implement their vision. Sometimes it can be useful to have a senior leader doing the job when it is first created and then pass it on to someone at a middle leadership level once the programme is established.

A word of warning here. Some schools have combined the roles of careers leader and careers adviser. This arrangement can work, but it is important that both the post-holder and the senior leadership understand that these are two distinct roles for which both need appropriate training and sufficient time and resources.

The other three models all have some benefits but they bring potential risks as well. Outsourcing, for example, offers the opportunity to bring in careers expertise but it is not always easy to locate the individual within the school's management structures to enable them to be properly effective in the role. Similarly, although having a careers leader shared across two schools brings efficiencies, the person concerned is not able to be on site in both schools all the time. A few schools have developed distributed leadership approaches and these can build capacity, provided that attention is paid to ensuring coherence and good communication between the members of the careers leadership team.

Although not many schools have chosen to go down the route of sharing a careers leader, an increasing number of multi-academy trusts (MATs) are establishing Trust-level roles, to provide strategic leadership support to the careers leaders within their individual schools. Each school retains its own arrangements for careers leadership and the trust-wide role is located either in one of the schools, as an experienced careers leader, or within the trust's central team. Such posts provide strategic support and can fulfil more of the outward-facing aspects of the role, linking with various external partners and organisations.

Models of careers leadership (colleges)

Turning to colleges, here careers leadership is much more likely to be shared among a team of managers than vested in one individual. This is partly because of the sheer size of a college, but also because many colleges have several different campuses. Clarity of roles and efficient communications become vital, and the team does need to be led by a senior member of staff at assistant or vice principal level.

College careers programmes typically comprise elements of: career advice and guidance, usually as part of wider student services; employability programmes and other links with employers, often delivered through curriculum areas; career learning within personal development programmes delivered by tutors; pre-entry and at-admission guidance. Each element can be led and managed by a different operational leader. How these responsibilities are divided up depends on a variety of factors but the work of the different operational leaders needs to be co-ordinated by a strategic leader who operates at a sufficiently senior level and either line-manages the operational leaders or brings them together for regular meetings of the college's careers leadership team.

Although many colleges now have a careers leadership team some of the smaller FE colleges and most sixth form colleges adopt a model similar to that employed by the majority of schools, namely a single careers leader, at the level of either a senior leader or a middle leader.

Position and pay

To return for a moment to the questions of salary and position in the leadership and management structure, it is not possible to prescribe precise pay, conditions or reporting arrangements. This is because there is such a diverse range of models in schools and colleges, along with a wide range of professional backgrounds for careers leaders. Nonetheless, it is possible to set out some broad principles for thinking about managing and resourcing careers leaders.

The job of careers leader involves more than simply co-ordinating a programme of activities and networking with a few external partners. Those remain important parts of the work, but the role also involves preparing and implementing a careers strategy, planning and quality-assuring the programme, and managing the delivery across the school or college. These are leadership and management tasks.

Leading means setting out the vision and getting people to follow that vision; managing means working with people to make sure that all the elements happen correctly and at the right time. Careers leaders combine the roles of leader and manager. The job of careers leader is at least a middle leadership role, and in many schools and colleges it is a senior leadership position.

To enable careers leaders to fulfil their responsibilities effectively they need to be positioned appropriately within the leadership and management structure. In practice this means, firstly, that the careers leader should have regularly scheduled one-to-one planning and review meetings with a nominated member of the senior leadership team, or be a member of that team. Secondly, the careers leader should attend middle leadership meetings so that they are able to work with heads of subject departments and leaders of tutor teams.

These principles apply equally to careers leaders who are qualified teachers and to those from a different professional background, such as qualified careers adviser, teaching assistant or HR manager. The jobs they have been given are the same, and they need to be positioned appropriately to undertake the role successfully.

This brings us to the issue of pay. The guiding principle here is that the job of careers leader is a post of responsibility and should be assigned a salary level commensurate with that responsibility. Many careers leaders in schools are middle leaders with Qualified Teacher Status (QTS) and, as such, should be paid on the main teacher pay scale plus a Teaching and Learning Responsibility (TLR) payment to recognise their specific responsibility for careers. Careers leaders who are not teachers should be paid an equivalent salary, i.e. the main salary grade for the other part of their work plus an allowance equivalent to the TLR. They are, after all, doing the same job as someone who happens to be a teacher. Traditionally, schools have seen themselves as having three groups of staff: leaders, teachers and support staff. Careers leaders who are not teachers are not support staff either: they are part of growing number of professional staff working in schools who do not have QTS. Their pay should reflect their status. Similar principles should apply to careers leaders in colleges. Their salary should reflect the fact that they have a professional post of responsibility.

> ### International reflections: Pay and position
>
> Issues related to pay and position within the school or college hierarchy will vary by country. It would be possible to point to a number of countries – such as Finland or Canada – where the role is respected and professionalised, and pay is relatively high. However, it is not possible to make any general pronouncements on what careers leaders should earn or how they should be positioned with the school. In each country, these issues will have to be discussed and debated.
>
> What we *are* sure of is that the careers leader role is one that (a) takes time, (b) requires authority within the school, and (c) develops a range of skills that are relevant for wider forms of school leadership. Given this, it is important that careers leaders have the time and resources that they need to do their job, and that their work is recognised in their pay and promotion prospects.
>
> We would recommend that all careers leaders discuss these issues with school leaders, with employer bodies responsible for teachers' and school staff pay and with relevant trade unions.

Careers leadership tasks

Over recent years, a consensus has been established about the nature of the tasks involved in being a careers leader. The language may differ slightly from one setting to another, but there is broad agreement on what the role involves. The role combines elements of strategic leadership and operational management, together with co-ordinating the contributions of a range of internal colleagues and networking with external partners. The careers leader has delegated responsibility for the school's or college's careers provision and is accountable to the head teacher or principal and the governing body. It is a senior leader or middle leader role.

We can summarise the key tasks that a careers leader has to perform under the headings of leadership, management, co-ordination and networking.

Leadership
- Leading the team of teachers, administrators, external partners and others who deliver career guidance.
- Advising the SLT on policy, strategy and resources for career guidance and showing how they meet the Gatsby Benchmarks.
- Reporting to senior leaders and governors.
- Reviewing and evaluating career guidance and providing information for school/college development planning, Ofsted and other purposes.
- Creating a vision for career guidance in the school or college, and getting this endorsed by the senior leadership and governors.

- Preparing, and leading the implementation of, a career guidance development plan (sometimes called a strategic careers plan).
- Ensuring that details of the careers programme are published on the school's or college's website, along with relevant contact details.
- Understanding the implications of a changing education landscape for career guidance, e.g. technical education reform.
- Ensuring compliance with the legal requirements to provide independent career guidance and, in schools, give access to pupils to the providers of technical education or apprenticeships, including the publication of the policy statement of provider access on their website.

Management

- Planning the programme of activity in career guidance.
- Briefing and supporting teachers and tutors involved in career guidance.
- Monitoring delivery of career guidance across the eight Gatsby Benchmarks, using the Compass review tool.
- Supporting tutors, providing initial information and advice.
- Managing the work of others, e.g. careers advisers and administrative and other staff involved in the delivery of career guidance.
- Monitoring access to, and take-up of, personal career guidance.
- Ensuring that universities, colleges and apprenticeship providers have access to students to share information on opportunities.
- Managing the careers budget as appropriate.
- Managing their own CPD and supporting the ongoing CPD of colleagues in the careers team.

Co-ordination

- Managing the provision of careers and labour market information.
- Managing the careers section of the school's or college's website, ensuring that information is accurate and up to date.
- Liaising with the PSHE/Personal Development Programme leader and other subject/course leaders to plan their contributions to career guidance.
- Liaising with tutors, mentors, SENCO/head of learner support and heads of year/department to identify students needing personal career guidance.
- Referring students to careers advisers.
- Co-ordinating encounters with employers and work experience.
- Communicating with students and their parents.

Networking

- Establishing and developing links with FE colleges, apprenticeship providers, UTCs and universities.
- Establishing and developing links with employers.

- Negotiating a service level agreement with the local authority for support for vulnerable young people, as appropriate.
- Commissioning career guidance services where appropriate.
- Managing links with the Local Enterprise Partnership (LEP), Careers Hub and other external organisations.
- Securing funding for careers-related projects.
- Building a network of alumni who can help with the career guidance programme.

The list of tasks can be used as the basis for preparing or reviewing job descriptions, not only for the careers leader but also for the careers administrator.

There are some variations to these jobs in colleges. A more detailed discussion of this can be found in the document *Understanding the Role of the Careers Leader: A Guide for Colleges* (see the Resources box on page 138).

Tools: Item 3.0A. Reviewing the organisation of the careers leadership responsibilities.
A grid which enables you to identify which members of staff take responsibility for each of the key responsibilities of careers leadership tasks is provided in the online resources accompanying this book: https://indigo.careers/clh. This will enable you to determine how the role is organised and to review what model might suit your school or college best.

We will now move on to look at each of the four areas of responsibilities in turn.

3.1 Leading

The first responsibility of a careers leader is to lead. Leadership is about inspiring people and getting them to buy in to your vision about the purpose and value of the careers programme and how it should be organised. People should want to follow leaders rather than feeling that they must because they have some power over them. Leadership is not confined by the hierarchy of the school or college. It can take place upwards, horizontally or downwards.

This chapter will cover:

- the tasks involved in *leading* careers programmes
- what makes a good leader
- conditions for successful careers leadership
- working with senior leaders and with governors
- quality assurance and leading staff development.

Introduction

This chapter will explore the elements of running a careers programme that require leadership and ask you to think about what kind of leader you want to be and how you can be good at it.

Leadership is the central responsibility of the careers leader (the clue's in the name). As a careers leader you will be weaving a compelling narrative in your school or college that will bring everyone together around the idea of careers and engage everyone in delivering it.

You may feel that this kind of inspirational leadership is beyond you and that leaders are born rather than chosen, but in this section of the book we are going to try to show you that there is a huge number of tricks of the trade that will enable you to lead people in your organisation around the development of your careers programme.

There are lots of different ways to lead and it is important that you choose one that works for you. But it is also important that you are positive and ambitious and commit to the idea that you are leading an important part of the school's or college's activity.

The tasks associated with leadership focus on setting a clear direction for your careers programme, creating strategy and working with senior staff and stakeholders to implement your vision.

The art of good leadership

Leadership is about being able to create a vision and bring people around your vision. It is not linked directly to where you sit in the hierarchy. It is possible for very junior staff to lead others if they have the vision and personal qualities to do so – this is called 'leading upwards'.

Obviously, leadership does have some relationship to where you sit in the hierarchy. We expect more senior members of staff to lead more and ask more junior members of staff to follow them. This is one of the reasons why it is important that as careers leader you have clear recognition as part of the school's or college's leadership team. But, the point remains that leadership is something that you do, and that others perceive you as doing, rather than the position that you hold.

Leaders can create a narrative about the value of the careers programme which can draw people together, motivate them and create change. This rarely happens through a single 'great leader' taking a command and control approach. Effective careers leaders are able to work with other leaders in the school or college, empower those whom they work with and distribute authority across the school/college. Careers leadership is first and foremost an exercise in communication and co-operation.

Jeremy Sutcliffe interviewed lots of school leaders for his book *8 Qualities of Successful School Leaders*.[7] He found that effective leaders have the following qualities.

1. **Vision.** Effective school leaders are able to create a clear sense of what needs to be done and to instil a sense of moral purpose in those around them. For careers leaders this is about getting everyone in the school to believe that careers is an important part of what the school does and enthusing them to engage with it.

2. **Courage.** Successful school leaders are determined and able to see things through. As a careers leader you are likely to find that there are obstacles in your way. You will need to push through these and make things happen even when others say that it can't be done.

3. **Passion.** You have to believe in what you are doing and to believe that it is important that it be done properly. We think that it is easy to be passionate about careers work because it is about being passionate about the futures of the young people that you work with. This is about people's lives, it is not just a question of ticking boxes. It is important that you show other people that you are passionate and that you encourage them to share in your passion.

4. **Emotional intelligence.** Leaders have a good understanding of what others are thinking and feeling. While it is important to be passionate about careers, you also need to understand that other members of staff have other priorities and

demands on their time. You need to think about how they are feeling and use that to inform the way that you engage them in the careers programme.

5. **Judgement.** As a leader you will be required to make judgement calls. Sometimes this might be about when to compromise and when to stick fast. At other times it might be about deciding on questions of emphasis, e.g. how much resource should you focus on Oxbridge applications over other opportunities? It is important to be decisive, but also to listen to others and reflect on decisions after you have made them.

6. **Resilience.** We wish we could tell you that leading careers in a school or college is going to be easy. But, you are bound to face frustrations and setbacks. Many things won't go as you hope and, if you do it for a while, you will see the level of interest in careers in your school or college (and in the government) wax and wane. Building anything worthwhile is always a marathon rather than a sprint, so you will need to pace yourself – but keep on going, no matter what.

7. **Persuasion.** The ability to bring others around to your way of thinking and to get them to do what you want them to is probably your most important attribute as a careers leader. As a careers leader you don't normally have a lot of formal power in the school or college, and so what you do has to be achieved through careful persuasion and bringing people on side. This is why co-ordination (Chapter 3.3) and networking (Chapter 3.4) are just as important as management (Chapter 3.2).

8. **Curiosity.** Finally, it is important for you to be curious. Careers opens up all sorts of fascinating subjects about how people learn and put their learning into practice, what is going on in the labour market and how young people make transitions to their future. The more you read, think and talk to other people, the better you will be at doing your job.

Resources: Leadership and school leadership

There are lots of books and articles about leadership in general and school leadership in particular. Some useful starting points include the following.

Seven strong claims about successful school leadership: https://dera.ioe. ac.uk//6967/1/download%3Fid%3D17387%26filename%3Dseven-claims-about-successful- school-leadership.pdf.

Successful school leadership: www.educationdevelopmenttrust.com/our-research-and-insights/research/successful-school-leadership.

Mindtools – core leadership theories: www.mindtools.com/pages/article/leadership-theories.htm.

John Adair's website on effective leadership and management: www.johnadair. co.uk.

We are also convinced by Barbara Kellerman's argument that 'followership' is just as important to think about as leadership.[8] To find out more about this idea, the Wikipedia page is a good place to start: https://en.wikipedia.org/wiki/Followership.

We'd really encourage you to read widely about leadership, especially if this is your first leadership position. We'd also encourage you to talk to other people who have been careers leaders or who have experience of leading schools or other organisations. One really good idea is to take up the opportunity to shadow another careers leader in a different school or college or to spend some time in an industrial placement thinking about how leadership works in other contexts.

Conditions for successful careers leadership

For a careers leader to be effective in their role, certain conditions need to be in place. Firstly, the senior leadership should have agreed your role and approved what you are trying to achieve; this should also be known to all other members of staff in the school or college. In England, schools and colleges are required to give the name and contact details of their careers leader on their websites. It would be good practice to also include a summary of the role.

Secondly, once the role has been clarified, the individual needs to be given sufficient authority and power to fulfil all the tasks. This means being placed in the right position in the school's or college's management structures and having a direct link to a nominated member of the SLT.

Thirdly, although the role of careers leader is time consuming, careers leaders rarely have the role as a full-time job. Given this, it is critical that as a careers leader you argue for enough time to do the job properly. It is difficult to say exactly how much time you should have as a careers leader, but we are sure that it should be measured in days rather than periods. We also think that as the role develops you are likely to want to make the case to increase your hours.

As we say in the introduction to Section 3, careers leadership involves a lot of different roles. If you are going to lead and manage effectively, you will need some help, particularly with the more routine organisational tasks. If you can identify some administrative support (a careers administrator) you can delegate some of these tasks and make better use of the time that you have available to lead the careers programme.

And lastly, any individual taking on the role of careers leader needs expertise in understanding young people, careers and career guidance, as well as having the skills and qualities to lead and manage colleagues, and to build working relationships with external partners. Not everyone will have everything they need from the outset. Access to appropriate training and professional development for the role is therefore a crucial factor. It is likely that you are working through this handbook to develop your expertise in careers leadership, and in Chapter 4.2 we will look at CPD in more detail, including some free courses currently available to careers leaders in England.

Creating the vision

In Chapter 2.1 we talked about planning your careers programme by breaking it down into the Gatsby Benchmarks and year groups and figuring out how it all fits together. This approach is hugely valuable but it doesn't create a big vision or story that everyone can rally around and believe in. As a careers leader you must have a strong grip on the detail, but you also need to inspire people with the big vision.

In order to crystallise your vision you should create a *vision statement* and a *strapline* which set out what you are trying to achieve and communicate it in an inspiring and easy-to-access way for everyone to read. This is the first thing that people should encounter when they visit your website and it should provide the context for all of the detail about what is happening when.

A vision statement should answer the following questions.
- Why is your school or college committed to delivering a careers programme?
- What values underpin it?
- What will young people get out of it?
- How will you ensure that it is great?

The strapline should then summarise this in a sentence or less.

CASE STUDY

Rita is keen to define a vision for Dunchester's careers programme. She spends some time reading about careers and prints out a number of other schools' visions from their websites. She also looks at the school's official mission statement and thinks about how she can pick up some of the language from that. Finally, she calls a meeting with her line manager (assistant head), the head of PSHE, the school's careers adviser and the head of sixth form. They spend an hour brainstorming words and phrases that describe the vision they are trying to create. Rita then goes away and comes up with the following ...

Career describes the way that every individual moves through their life, learning and work. Dunchester Progress Academy is committed to every student going on to a fulfilling career. The ability to make use of the knowledge and skills learned at school and apply them across the rest of your life is a key measure of the success of the school. It is only through ensuring that young people can successfully transition to their lives after school and establish themselves in work and in society that we will succeed in our aim to transform the lives of young people. We want all Dunchesterians to leave school as ambassadors for the school's values, to live their dreams and to make a positive impact on the world. It is through building successful careers that this will be achieved. Dunchester's alumni are skilled, capable, positive and ambitious and in high demand by educational institutions and employers.

She then stands back and comes up with a strapline.

Fulfilling lives, transformational careers

She quickly gets the school webmaster to create a new web page and uses the strapline as the title of the page. The vision is now out there!

Reflective questions: How would you sum up your vision for careers in the school or college in a single sentence? How does this correlate to your school or college's overall mission statement?

Getting the team on board

As we've already pointed out, the careers leader needs to have an influence way beyond the power that they have in the school or college. If you are lucky you might be managing a small team, but you will be trying to lead pretty much everyone in the school/college to engage with your vision. This isn't easy, but there are a few steps that you can take to get people to buy in to your vision.

Tell them about it. The first thing to do is to make sure that you talk about the careers programme, both one-to-one and in staff meetings. Explaining to people what you are doing and why is the first step to involving them.

Lead by example. There is nothing like showing people what you mean by putting it into practice yourself. For example, if you want other teachers to link careers to their subjects, make sure that you are doing it yourself.

Celebrate success. You are likely to have some early successes. Tell everyone about them! Perhaps you've organised an employer talk and Year 8 really impressed you with the questions they asked. Make sure you tell the head of year about what happened. Or perhaps you have run a series of mock interviews and one of your employers has offered a student an apprenticeship place. Again, shout this from the rooftops! The programme is working! Everyone will want to be part of something new and successful.

Make it easy for them. Teachers and other staff who work in schools and colleges are busy people. Unfortunately, your new-found enthusiasm for careers can easily be seen as just another thing to do. You need to devise some simple, entry-level ways that people can help, so that you can start to bring people on board without making major demands on their time.

Change the context. Remember that you can't do it all alone. You will need the head or principal to make it clear that this is important and get the rest of the SLT to back you up. We will go on to look at managing upwards in the next section.

Ask for their feedback (and take their ideas on board). Finally, it is important to listen to people's feedback and to create opportunities for other staff (and students) to influence the careers programme. The more that people feel that they have a stake in it, the more they will want to be involved.

Leading in-house staff development

One of the most powerful ways that you can engage the wider staff in your careers programme is to provide them with access to training and development opportunities. This may be about sourcing specialist training from outside or about you taking on the role of delivering training to your colleagues. We will be looking at this in more detail in Chapter 4.3 of this book, but it is important to consider it briefly here, as providing training and development is such an important part of leadership.

Although careers leaders deliver some aspects of the careers programme themselves, many elements are delivered by other teachers and tutors, most of whom are not careers specialists. In order to ensure that this broader careers activity aligns with your overall vision it is helpful to lead staff development sessions for teams of colleagues. Such sessions are most likely to be held on the school or college premises and may take only part of the day.

Leading a staff development session is not very different from teaching a lesson to students, except of course the students in this case are both adults and your colleagues. Thought should be given to preparation and explaining how the knowledge and understanding and skills being developed will be applied, as well as the activity during the session itself. You might also consider working with a colleague to lead the session, either another member of staff or an external partner where relevant.

Leading upwards

A lot of the key leadership roles undertaken by a careers leader are about leading and managing upwards. You have the job of advising the SLT on policy and strategy relating to careers and being accountable to them and to the governors.

Working with senior leaders

The SLT has overall responsibility for all aspects of the school's or college's work and the careers provision is an important subset of this. They have an overview of requirements, resources and priorities. Nothing can happen in the school or college without their authorisation, but they cannot lead and manage every aspect of the school's or college's work. That is why they delegate responsibility for different parts of the operation to middle leaders.

The careers leader is accountable to the SLT for the careers programme. As careers leader, therefore, you need to establish a working relationship with the SLT. There are elements of the role that you can get on with on your own, but there will be others where you will need a decision from a senior leader or their support.

Let's consider a couple of examples. As careers leader, you will have a view about what career guidance services the school or college should be providing, what support students need and where such services could be purchased from. However, the final decision will be taken by the senior leaders. The job of the careers leader here is to present costed proposals to the senior leader, to explain and advocate for the solution that you propose and then to implement what is agreed.

To take another example, you will know where careers education should best be placed in the curriculum and who should teach it, but only the senior leader responsible for curriculum will have an oversight of competing requests for curriculum time and teaching staff. Again, your role is to present your proposals to the senior leadership and then to work with them to implement what is decided.

Ideally, you will either be on the SLT or report to someone who is. If you are a middle leader, make sure that you schedule regular review meetings with your line manager and spend time talking about your progress on the careers programme. Ideally you will also make sure that you have some regular time addressing the whole SLT directly about the careers programme (perhaps one meeting a month or one a term depending on how your SLT is organised).

It is important to make sure that you present what is being achieved in the careers programme positively to your senior team. You don't want to become the bad news person, nor the person who turns up only when they want something.

When you are leading an area it can be easy to focus on the frustrations and on what is not being achieved in the way that you hoped. It is always important to remember that there are also a lot of things that are going well, and where careers provision is being successfully delivered, your students are learning and your programme is better than it was last year. Make sure that you tell these things to your senior leaders as well as the areas where you need some improvement.

Working with governors

As well as working with your SLT you also need to work with the governors. It is the governors that are ultimately responsible for the work of the school or college. They set the overall direction and then provide appropriate support and challenge.

Provide regular reports to governors, at least once a year, if not more often, e.g. termly. Every governing body is interested to receive information on destinations, and you can use this as an opportunity to inform the governors about developments in your support for students. Make your reports to the governing body short and to the point; governors are sitting in the middle of a blizzard of information, acronyms and data, so if you want to cut through you need to try and get your message across in one to two pages. If you interest them, they will ask you for more detail.

Ideally you will get some time to present directly to the governing body and set out your vision. If you can't get this you will need to work closely with your head or principal to brief them on what they need to be saying to the governors about the careers programme.

It is really useful to identify a 'link governor for careers' whom you might be able to work with more closely than you are likely to be able to with the whole governing body. A link governor should be someone on the governing body with an interest in careers (perhaps a local employer) who can provide you with some support and advocate for the careers programme at the governors' meetings. You can meet with them more regularly and use them as a sounding board for your more strategic ideas.

Leading a quality programme

The foundation of a high-quality careers programme is being sure that you are meeting all the legal requirements, government expectations and key drivers that you need to address. We've already discussed the drivers that are important in Chapter 2.1 of this book. But you need to keep your eyes open. The education and training system is changing all of the time and the labour market is even more dynamic. As the careers leader you need to be watching for change and making sure that your programme is developing in line with it.

As well as ensuring that you are compliant with the law and responsive to changes in the economy and policy, you are also responsible for leading the broader development of your programme. The careers leader should be monitoring, reviewing and evaluating the school's or college's careers programme every year. This element of the work will be covered in more detail in Chapter 4.1 of this book. However, it is worth a mention here because the issue of self-review and continuous improvement links to external accountability assessments within the overall quality assurance process. Schools and colleges are both subject to regular inspections by Ofsted, during which the careers provision will be scrutinised. The careers leader has a role to play in leading the preparations for inspections and drawing up plans of action in response to the findings, all in consultation with the senior leaders and governors.

Additionally, the school or college may choose to seek external accreditation for its careers provision through the Quality in Careers Standard. This is the national quality award for careers in England. It is a voluntary award which schools and colleges use to review and improve their careers programmes and to gain recognition for good practice. There are several different awarding bodies that schools and colleges can choose from, which differ slightly in how they operate, what support they offer and how much they charge. Once a school or college gains the standard, it is valid for three years (with one exception of two years) before the school or college would need to apply for re-assessment. Details can be found at **www.qualityincareers.org.uk**.

The other form of external quality assurance that careers leaders in colleges are likely to get involved in is the matrix Standard, which is the UK's quality standard for all organisations providing advice and guidance services. In England all FE colleges are required to be matrix accredited, as part of their funding agreements, but this is usually waived for sixth form colleges. Schools do not normally seek matrix accreditation.

In a nutshell

This chapter has looked at how you can be an effective leader of careers programmes. Key things to keep in mind include the following.

- Spend time thinking and learning about leadership.
- Make sure that you set out a clear vision of what you want to do, and seek to involve others in delivering it.
- Spend time engaging with your colleagues and working to get them to engage with the careers programme.
- 'Managing upwards' to engage the SLT, head or principal and the governors is a critical part of your job.
- Think about how you can ensure that your programme is high quality and that you make use of all available tools and feedback.

3.2 Managing

The previous chapter focused on the leadership responsibilities of the careers leader role: creating a vision and strategy for career guidance in the school or college and inspiring people, particularly senior staff and governors, to buy in to that vision. This chapter concentrates on the management aspects of the role: making sure that the day-to-day things that need to be delivered happen as they should.

This chapter will cover:

- the tasks involved in *managing* a careers programme
- the distinction between line management and project management
- practical approaches to the management tasks
- the effective use of administrative support and information systems.

Introduction

Too often the terms 'leadership' and 'management' are used interchangeably. Indeed, it was not that long ago when schools had senior management teams, but now they have SLTs (and probably not much has changed except the terminology). However, we believe that the distinction between leadership and management is an important one. All organisations need **both** leaders **and** managers. *Leaders* set out the vision and get people to follow them towards achieving that vision; *managers* work with members of staff to make sure all the elements that should be delivered happen correctly and at the right time. As the careers leader you need to combine both sets of responsibilities.

The term 'management' is often used to describe activities that relate to directing the work of people who sit below you in an organisational hierarchy. This is *line management*, which is a very important activity – but it is unlikely to be the most important for you in your role as careers leader. While you may line-manage a small number of people, you are more likely to be involved in the management of projects, tasks and activities. Both project management and line management have key skills and approaches that we will introduce you to through an examination of the key tasks involved in managing the delivery of the careers programme; directing, supporting and monitoring the contributions of your colleagues.

CASE STUDY

Adrian is the careers leader at Dunville Special School. At the beginning of the year he puts together a brilliant plan and publishes it on the school's website. The plan sets out how the school is going to meet all of the Gatsby Benchmarks over the course of the next year or two.

At the start of the year Adrian calls a meeting of all of the school's staff and takes them through the programme and provides them with clear descriptions of what they should be doing, resources and advice about some additional online training that they can access. He convinces the head to appoint a dedicated careers adviser and to allocate a decent amount of resources to the careers budget to allow him to organise trips to specialist colleges and events for employers.

Everything is going brilliantly until Ofsted comes knocking. Adrian gets completely distracted in the preparation for Ofsted and the recriminations that follow. The careers programme slides down everyone's priorities and Adrian gets pulled into a working group to look at some of the issues raised by Ofsted.

Without clear management from a careers leader things start to slide. Some things go on as planned, some happen in a half-hearted way, others don't take place when they should and others don't happen at all. What is more, Adrian doesn't really pick anyone up on the things that have gone wrong. Without any ongoing management the programme all but fizzles out and when Adrian reviews progress at the end of the year he is very disappointed to see that it is patchy, at best.

Next year will be different!

Reflective questions: Have the arrangements for careers leadership in your school or college been set up in such a way that you are in a position to be able to manage the programme effectively? How often do you and your senior leader line manager review these arrangements?

Tasks associated with management

As careers leader you are responsible for ensuring that all the elements of your careers programme are delivered correctly and at the right time. This means working with several different groups of staff and individual colleagues to direct and support their contributions and to monitor delivery. This chapter will examine each of these tasks. The nature of your role is that very little of this will be achieved through direct line management. Unlike the leader for a traditional school subject such as English or science or a vocational programme in a college, you will not be the line manager of the teachers or tutors delivering your careers programme. Having said that, they will have different line managers, but you will be project-managing the work that they deliver on the careers programme. If the school or college has appointed a careers administrator, the careers leader is most likely to be the line manager. Similarly, if the school employs its own careers adviser, the careers leader could be their line manager.

Within colleges, careers leaders are more likely to have more direct reporting relationships, although the nature of these will vary, depending on where you sit in the college.

Principles of effective management

There are numerous books, papers, websites and blogs offering insights and advice on management. One of the key points that is made by much of this literature is that, while there are some basic principles that you should follow, a lot of what constitutes effective management is highly context specific. So, the best way to manage a branch of McDonalds, or an office full of consultants, will be different from the best way to manage in a school or college. Even more importantly, every school and college is different and the way that you manage in each of them will have to respond to the context you are in.

In this sense management is essentially thinking about the question '*how do I get things done around here?*' But there are a number of typical processes and principles that all managers use. In this chapter we will introduce you to some of these.

> ### 💡 Resources: Management
>
> There are lots of general books on management that you might find useful. A couple of useful examples are: James McGrath and Bob Bates' *The Little Book of Big Management Theories and How to Use Them*, published by Pearson; and Bob Nelson and Peter Economy's *Managing for Dummies*. But you'll be able to find lots more useful books with a quick search on Amazon.
>
> Even more useful are some books which look specifically at the process of management in education. These include Tony Bush and David Middlewood's *Leading and Managing People in Education* and Megan Crawford's *Developing as an Educational Leader and Manager*, both published by Sage.

In the rest of this chapter we are going to discuss the careers leader's management tasks under six key headings that you will find in the management literature. We are going to look at each of these areas in the context of the work of the careers leader, but it is also worth thinking about what you are learning through this process that you might apply to managing other activities.

The six key activities of management are:

1. planning
2. budgeting
3. briefing, directing and supporting colleagues
4. project management
5. line management
6. monitoring and reporting.

Planning

In Chapter 2.1 we discussed the process of planning a careers programme. In that section we encouraged you to get specific and to say what students should be doing every year to meet each of the Gatsby Benchmarks. We then built on that through the rest of Section 2, looking at some of the other key things that you need to plan and organise. So, in Chapter 2.4 we looked at writing a scheme of work and preparing lessons for the discrete element of careers education and in Chapter 2.7 at arranging encounters with places of further study to meet the statutory duty to ensure that colleges and apprenticeship providers have access to pupils from Year 8 to age 18.

Through all this work you will have created a careers programme for your school or college. You should have gone a stage further and published this programme online so that all your stakeholders can see what you are doing and think about how they might get involved in it. For example, schools in England now have a requirement to publish their policy on access for technical education providers. It is very likely that writing this policy and planning the opportunities for providers to come into school will form part of your job as the careers leader.

Getting to the stage of having a published programme on your website is an important first step, but planning goes a lot deeper than that. You will be writing schemes of work, scheduling activities such as talks, encounters with employers, visits to colleges and universities, curriculum days etc. This requires you to get even more specific. So, your published plan will say that you are organising visits to university open days for Year 12 students. But, when you get into planning these in detail you are going to have to answer the following questions (and a host of other ones as well).

- What universities are we going to visit?
- Will all students go to the same universities?
- Will they be accompanied or supervised in any way?
- What transport will be provided?
- What kind of preparation and debriefing will we organise?

Each activity is likely to require some documentation detailing the objectives, key decisions that you have made, setting out a project plan and likely risks and addressing resourcing implications and so on. In some cases, the amount of planning involved in an activity will be minimal, but for others it might be more involved, especially if you are taking students outside of school or college or if you are involving external stakeholders.

Resources: Tracker

The Tracker tool provided by The Careers & Enterprise Company can be a helpful way to plan your careers activities **www.careersandenterprise.co.uk/careers-leaders/tools-resources**.

There is a strong overlap between management and administration. As a manager you should be making key decisions and setting up systems and processes to ensure that careers activities happen. Often this will involve you getting into a lot of the details of administration such as checking opening times, booking minibuses or rooms and sending notes to students and parents about arrangements. Ideally you will be able to make the case for some administrative support. We will explore this issue in greater depth later in this chapter.

Budgeting

Closely related to issues of planning are questions of budgeting. Depending on how your school's or college's budget is organised you might have more or less responsibility for the budget. But, regardless of exactly how much formal responsibility you have, it is important that you understand budgeting. Budgeting is the process by which resources (including staff time, space and money) are allocated to your careers programme. It includes both the allocation of existing resources and the decision to invest new resources.

A budget begins as a prediction of what is likely to happen over a particular period (usually the next year). After that you need to manage how events unfold and ensure that you are working within the planned budget while being ready to make the case for adjustments to the budget where necessary.

Budgeting for a careers programme involves a lot more than planning what things are going to cost. As the careers leader you should start by proactively submitting a proposal for the budget that you will require to deliver a good-quality careers programme. You should also seek opportunities to secure additional funding from careers-specific funds or as part of other initiatives that the school or college may be engaged in.

Once you have secured a budget, you will need to oversee its use during the year and account for the expenditure at the end of the year. It would be simplest if you spent exactly what you predicted that you would spend at the start of the year, but in the real world this rarely happens. So you need to understand what processes exist for you to ask for more money or to inform people if you are going to underspend. Underspending can be potentially as big a problem from a budgetary point of view as overspending, so it is important to keep your line manager up to date with any major variations from your initial budget.

Typically, you will have a fairly puny budget in terms of spendable money. Schools and colleges have multi-million-pound budgets, although most of that money is spent on staffing and premises. It is useful to remember this both because it reminds you to be ambitious when you are making a case for your budget, and also because it is important to remember that money, staff and space costs are to some extent interchangeable. So, you could contract with an external organisation to provide your school with personal guidance or you could appoint a careers adviser as a member of staff. These two options will both cost money, but contracting external providers is likely to come out of your running budget while staffing costs may not.

The fact that schools and colleges have multi-million-pound budgets also means that you are not alone when you are thinking about your budget. You are likely to have a bursar, business manager or even a whole accounts and finance department who are thinking about these issues. Try to build an effective working relationship with these people, as they will be able to teach you a lot about budgetary management.

Briefing, directing and supporting colleagues

Once you have planned and organised activities you will usually need to engage your colleagues in delivering them. Generally, you will not have direct line management responsibility for most of these staff, but you are expected to direct their activities within the context of the careers programme.

All staff involved in the careers programme will need to be briefed and supported so that they are confident to deliver what you have spent many hours planning. This will apply both to the team of teachers or tutors who will be delivering the careers education lessons and to teams of tutors involved in providing the initial information and advice to students at key times when they approach option choices.

You will need to work with the line managers of these teachers and tutors to identify convenient times when you can meet with them, to take them through the activities you have planned. It is good practice for the line manager to remain present when you are providing this briefing, to reinforce the importance of the activity and, if possible, you should be available when the activity is being delivered, to offer support where needed.

There may be occasions when colleagues may need more than a simple briefing. You may want to arrange to lead some form of in-house CPD or even suggest attendance on an external course. We look at the whole area of CPD in Section 4 of the handbook, but this will involve speaking not only to the colleagues for whom you think the CPD would be relevant, but also their line managers and the senior leader with overall responsibility for CPD in the school or college.

Once projects are underway you also need to take responsibility for checking on the progress that staff are making and providing them with additional support and advice if they get stuck or drift off course.

Project management

The tasks described so far are all examples of project management. Most of the work you are likely to undertake when managing your careers programme comes into this category. You will be applying your knowledge and skills, and different tools and techniques, to a broad range of activities to deliver a programme for your students. Much of this work will involve working with colleagues within the school or college, and external partners. Only in a small minority of cases will you line-manage those colleagues. For most of your colleagues their contribution to the careers programme will represent only a small proportion of their work and they will be line-managed by other middle and senior leaders, but for their work on the careers programme you will be their project manager.

While a lot of project management involves dealing with people, as we describe in the preceding paragraphs, it extends beyond people management to include planning, budgeting and monitoring. The Project Management Institute (**www.pmi.org**) sets out five phases of project management:

1. **Conception and initiation.** This is where you come up with the idea to undertake a project and establish its broad aims. This phase also includes thinking about who should be involved and what overall resources, including time, are needed. You should discuss these ideas with your line manager before you get into the detailed planning that constitutes the second phase.

2. **Definition and planning.** This involves creating a detailed roadmap for the project. It begins with setting clear objectives and continues with identifying resources and a realistic timescale. It is good practice at this stage to also establish some interim outcomes or performance measures for the project. Roles and responsibilities should be clearly defined so that everyone knows what is expected of them. Communication with your colleagues and any external partners is particularly crucial at this stage.

3. **Launch and execution.** This describes the phase in which the activities actually take place. Your role here is to ensure that everything happens when planned and that colleagues are given the support they need.

4. **Performance and control.** This element will take place simultaneously with phase 3 but focuses on monitoring the activities and measuring whether or you are achieving your objectives. By monitoring your project throughout you get the information you need to make adjustments to the activities where things aren't working out as you hoped.

5. **Project close.** This is when you bring the project to an end and review what happened. Schools and colleges are busy places and this stage can too easily be overlooked, but it is important that you make time not only to identify what didn't go so well and what needs to be changed next time, but also to acknowledge what went well and to thank your colleagues and external partners.

This project lifecycle can be applied to the management of your careers programme as a whole or, equally, to the management of a set of activities that constitute one element of your programme, such as a module of eight lessons in the Year 9 PSHE programme or a work shadowing programme for all post-16 students on level 1 and 2 courses.

The five-phase process provides a useful framework for thinking about how to approach the management of your careers programme. As you get further into your role of careers leader you will find that you no longer consider each stage as a separate step, but it still gives you a useful checklist for effective management.

Line management

Careers is a complex activity which should involve all staff in the school or college to a greater or lesser extent. Because of this you are unlikely to line-manage many of the colleagues who will be contributing to the careers programme. In a school the most likely line management relationships that you will have will be with the careers administrator and the careers adviser. In a college, you are more likely to have a greater number of direct reports, but these will vary depending on the nature of your role. Whatever your context, there is almost always going to be a strong case for having some administrative support for the careers leader.

If you were to review your role description you would quickly identify several areas that involve a considerable amount of logistical and organisational tasks that could be accomplished more cost-effectively by an efficient administrator. This would release you to spend more time on the leadership and management tasks. If you succeed in securing a careers administrator you should meet with that person at least once a week to direct and support their work and review progress.

> **Tools: Item 3.2A. Careers administrator responsibilities.**
> A template to help you identify the key responsibilities to include in the job description for a careers administrator is provided in the online resources accompanying this handbook: https://indigo.careers/clh.

In Chapter 2.8 we discussed the different approaches to providing career guidance now that responsibility for securing access to guidance has been devolved to individual schools and colleges in England. Many schools commission services from an external provider, but a significant minority of schools, and almost all colleges, have appointed their own internal careers advisers. In such situations it is common for the careers leader to line-manage one or more careers advisers.

Whoever you are managing, you will have to find your style as a line manager. There are many different ways to manage people but the workplace relations organisation Acas suggests the following five tips for all line managers.[9]

1. **Check how your team are doing and support them to shine.** Ask them 'how are you?' and listen to their concerns. Make sure they have access to training and development to ensure that they can live up to their potential.

2. **Be clear in what you want.** Make sure that you set goals and give clear feedback on performance.

3. **Ask your team for feedback and suggestions on how things could work better.** Remember that you don't have all the answers and make space for everyone to input.

4. **Deal with problems quickly.** When things go wrong and relationships aren't working properly make sure you prioritise trying to put things right. If you don't focus on the people you will only make more work for yourself.

5. **Be a good role model.** Nothing beats leading by example. If you demonstrate positive behaviours, your team are likely to follow suit. In previous roles, and indeed in your current job, you will have been managed. It is worth reflecting on this experience to identify what you think makes for effective management.

Monitoring and reporting

As the careers leader you need to monitor that your plans are working, that the projects are running smoothly and that your colleagues and team are happy and effective. You ultimately have the responsibility and accountability that the careers programme has taken place and that it has worked in the way that you hoped.

There is a strong tradition of monitoring teaching and learning in schools and colleges, and this should extend to all areas of the curriculum, including the careers programme. You should use the school's or college's established processes to monitor the delivery of any careers education lessons and make sure that you review them with the staff who taught the sessions. This can often be combined with briefing the team for the next batch of lessons.

You should also monitor other elements of the programme, particularly the provision of personal career guidance. You should maintain records of which students have attended guidance interviews. It would also be good practice to note what encounters with employers the students have experienced, as this can help you to target future opportunities (see Chapter 2.3).

Compass provides a useful tool for reviewing the school's or college's overall careers programme against the Gatsby Benchmarks, leading to the generation of a report bespoke to the school or college. You should use this to keep your programme under review, and there are advantages in inviting others to join you as you complete the self-review questions, in particular the head of sixth, the SENCO and the careers adviser.

We discussed the process of record keeping in Chapter 2.3 from the perspective of ensuring that each student is able to access the support that they need. Record keeping on individual students is also a critical part of management, as it allows you to see who is getting what, who is being left out and where some of the operational problems might lie. To aid you in this, you might want to use a bespoke careers system like Compass+, but other schools make use of facilities within their existing school- or college-wide systems.

Finally, you will be expected to report on the delivery of the careers programme to your line manager, the head or principal and the governors. Making sure that you have good data and are able to access it, summarise it and present it in a variety of formats is critical (see also Chapter 4.1).

In a nutshell

This chapter has looked at the management aspects of the careers leader role. Key points to bear in mind include the following.

- The foundation of effective management is good planning.
- You should keep a close eye on everything that is happening across the careers programme to ensure that your plans are being followed.
- Build working relationships with colleagues whom you do not necessarily line-manage.
- Link monitoring and review activities to ongoing support.
- Establish a careers administrator role.
- Invest in appropriate monitoring systems.

3.3 Co-ordinating

In addition to the leadership and management responsibilities of the role, a careers leader spends a lot of time linking with staff within the school or college, and with external partners. To distinguish between the internal links and the external relationships the responsibilities are separated into, respectively, co-ordinating and networking. This chapter deals with the various aspects of internal co-ordination.

Co-ordination is one of the subtlest elements of being a careers leader. In essence it is about getting people to do things even though you have no power over them. It is also about standing back and thinking about how the careers programme is working as a system. Are the right people collaborating, communicating and sharing work appropriately? As the careers leader it is your job to think about all of this and to intervene to make everything work more effectively.

This chapter will cover:

- the tasks involved in co-ordinating a careers programme
- working with key members of staff
- managing referrals for personal career guidance
- maintaining communications with young people and their parents/ carers.

Introduction

This chapter will examine the tasks involved in co-ordinating the careers programme. It will explore how the careers leader should work with colleagues within the school or college to deliver the careers programme. Co-ordination could also be described as team working or co-operation and is essentially non-hierarchical in nature. In other words, co-ordination is about getting people to work together around a common aim, even if what you are asking them to do isn't strictly part of their job. As we discussed in Chapter 3.2, careers leaders rarely have all the staffing resource that they need, and so learning to co-ordinate others is a key skill.

People who choose to work in the education system are generally positive, co-operative and want the best for the young people that they work with. However, they are also busy, and pulled in several different directions. Careers is only ever one among many priorities, and so as a co-ordinator you will need to be respectful and understanding as well as persuasive.

One of the privileges of being a careers leader is that you get to work with staff right across the school or college. This work can give you insights into how the school or college works as a system and what other people in the organisation do. As a careers leader you should expect to work with at least the following people:

- administrator
- bursars or finance manager
- careers adviser
- head teacher/college principal
- librarian
- SENCO/head of learner support
- head of sixth form
- website manager
- subject teachers/course lecturers
- tutors and pastoral managers.

It is useful for you to draw up a list of all the people that you currently work with on the careers programme and then to consider who else it might be useful to engage.

Tools: Item 3.3A. Who am I working with?

To gain an overview of all the people within the school or college that you need to work with to deliver the careers programme, try completing the following activity, using the proforma provided in the online resources accompanying this book: **https://indigo.careers/clh.**

Column 1: Gatsby Benchmarks	Column 2: What do I do directly with students and parents?	Column 3: Who else do I work with within the school or college?	Column 4: What is their role/ contribution to careers?	Column 5: What are my leadership and management tasks?

Column 1 lists all of the Gatsby Benchmarks and provides you with a structure for reviewing the activities that you are co-ordinating.

In **column 2** of the proforma, make a note, against each of the benchmarks, of activities that you personally deliver to students and/or their parents.

Next, in **column 3**, write the name or role of all the members of staff who either deliver an element of your careers programme or with whom you work in order to plan or organise an element of the programme. The range of people who may feature in column 3 could include: tutors, subject/course leaders, PSHE teachers, personal development tutors, SENCO/head of learner support, head of sixth, librarian, IT network manager, heads of department, heads of year, mentors, careers advisers, etc.

In **column 4** indicate what is the role of each of the people that you are co-ordinating in the careers programme.

In **column 5** describe your role in relation to their contribution. Phrases that could feature in column 5 include: 'liaise with'; 'jointly plan with'; 'negotiate with'; 'report to'; 'secure support from'; 'brief and support'; 'monitor'; etc.

Once you have completed the proforma as fully as you can you should have a good idea about whom you need to work with. You might then want to reflect on how best to achieve this – for example, through formally arranged meetings, one-to-one conversations or, most likely, a combination of the two approaches.

Principles of effective co-ordination

There is a lot of research which looks at how organisations work (and how they can work better). It highlights the limitations associated with top-down 'command and control' ways of organising things. If everyone is waiting for the boss to tell them what to do, then things only move as fast as the boss can make decisions. If, on the other hand, everyone feels trusted to do their job, then they can all be making progress.

The problem with devolved management is that if everyone is just left to get on with it they can sometimes get under each other's feet and at other times they can wander off on tangents. Ultimately, managers have a key role in providing direction and managing performance, but often these kinds of problems can be headed off with effective co-ordination.

A co-ordinator is a key part of a team. One of the features of effective teamwork is the recognition that people have different roles within the team. A co-ordinator's role is to keep their eyes on the team's objective, to check that the team is making progress towards these objectives and to support members of the team to work effectively together. Many of the principles of effective co-ordination echo those of effective leadership and management, but a co-ordinator is working with their colleagues and their authority comes as much from the respect of the group as it does from authority that has been given to them from above.

> ### 💡 Resources: Effective co-ordination and teamwork
>
> There are lots of useful resources that help you to think about how teams work and how you can maximise co-operation. A quick Google will probably find you thousands of team-building books, websites and resources.
>
> We often start from the BusinessBalls website (**www.businessballs.com**), which gathers together a lot of resources that will help you to think about the skills you need to build teams and influence your colleagues.
>
> If you are looking to get into this more deeply there are a few books that might be useful. Elena Aguilar's *The Art of Coaching Teams*, published by Jossey-Bass, looks at how you can foster team work within schools. Another useful book is Mario Martinez's *Teachers Working Together for School Success*, published by Corwin, which looks at effective inter-personal relationships in schools.

Key principles for effective co-ordination could include the following.

- **Engaging colleagues.** Spending time with colleagues helping them to see why it would be worth their time getting involved in the careers programme.
- **Agreeing common objectives and a common sense of purpose.** Helping your colleagues to understand the value of the careers programme and to see what needs to be done to make it happen.
- **Fostering mutual respect among your colleagues.** Valuing and celebrating everyone's contributions and encouraging people to see that all staff have something useful to contribute to the delivery of the careers programme.
- **Encouraging the sharing of knowledge and experience.** As a co-ordinator you should notice which members of the team are good at particular tasks and which are not so good. By pairing people up and encouraging those who are more experienced and expert to share, you can increase the capacity of the whole team.
- **Building a community of practice.** As the careers leader you ideally want the staff who work on the careers programme to become a community of practice. If you can create the right mix of training, meetings, informal get-together and socials you will find that the team takes on a life of its own and provides mutual aid and support.
- **Helping to allocate and organise work tasks.** Ideally by taking into account the strengths and interests of your colleagues and trying to ensure that people get jobs that they are interested in and able to do.
- **Gathering and sharing information on how things are going.** Thinking about what is working well and what needs to be changed. The provision of information about what is going on is a powerful tool. As the careers leader you should be thinking about what communication channels you have at your disposal and how you use them to communicate to all stakeholders.

- **Spotting gaps and problems.** Noticing when things aren't working well, bringing this to the attention of the group and helping to solve problems.
- **Listening, encouraging and supporting.** Providing people with an opportunity to discuss their concerns and frustrations and helping them to address these issues.

Co-ordination can often be an almost invisible job. Sometimes you may have a formal and acknowledged role in delivering some aspect of your careers programme. However, at other times you will be playing a key role in the team that others might not even spot. Everyone notices when things go wrong, but no one notices when you have taken pre-emptive actions to stop things going wrong. Co-ordinators are always trying to make sure that the careers programme works well by connecting people, attending to the resources available, keeping their eyes on the objective and providing everyone with useful feedback.

CASE STUDY

Rita has built an impressive careers programme, but she's the first to admit that it is too dependent on her activities, and she is running around doing everything. She resolves to get more of her colleagues involved in the programme.

She begins by arranging a series of meetings with some of the key people that she is working with. This includes the careers adviser, the SENCO, the librarian and the head of PSHE. Rita recognises that all of them are critical to the effective running of the careers programme, but that none of them has much awareness of the bigger strategy. She spends time explaining what she is trying to do and listens to their concerns about workload and their lack of knowledge about the rest of the programme.

She decides that these meetings have been really useful and resolves to meet with these staff regularly. Through these meetings she is able to engage all of them more effectively in the careers programme, to better understand some of the difficulties that people are having and help them to solve some of these problems (often by putting two of the key people together). After a term of regular one-to-one meetings she suggests that they all have a regular 'careers coffee' together, on the grounds that a problem shared is a problem solved.

Increasingly Rita doesn't feel so alone. She has created informal structures that allow the careers programme to be co-ordinated. Her colleagues are just happy to be drinking coffee and solving their problems together.

Reflective questions: Who are the key individuals in your school that you need to link with? What arrangements would you like to set up in order to work with them?

Tasks associated with co-ordination

Co-ordination is all about working with other people and building positive relationships. In the remainder of this chapter the careers leader's co-ordination tasks are considered in further detail, under five broad headings: managing information; linking with curriculum areas; referring young people for guidance; co-ordinating links with employers; communicating with young people and their parents/carers.

Managing information

Having available, comprehensive and up-to-date information on the options available and the progression opportunities that follow from those options is the foundation of career decision making. Assembling and disseminating this information to pupils and students involves establishing working links with several members of staff.

Link to Gatsby Benchmark 2
The provision of good-quality career and labour market information is the basis of Benchmark 2. It is discussed in depth in Chapter 2.2.

A lot of career and labour market information will arrive at the school or college from a wide range of sources. As the careers leader you will need to work with the careers administrator and librarian to catalogue and display the information for young people. You will also work with the same colleagues to order relevant publications and to maintain the school's or college's careers information base.

Some careers and labour market information relates to particular subject areas. Distributing this to subject teachers will help to foster links with the curriculum areas and promote the careers programme within the school or college. As careers leader you will also work with subject departments to produce information for pupils and students on the options and qualifications available at key points of transition. This may be in the form of booklets or material for the school's or college's website.

Increasingly, career and labour market information is mainly made available digitally. This requires you to think carefully about how such information can be managed and brought to the attention of students. In many cases this will require you to work closely with the member of staff who is responsible for the school or college website. Schools and colleges in England are required to publish details of their careers programmes, and the name and contact details of the careers leader. In addition, schools must publish a policy on enabling access for apprenticeship and technical education providers. Ideally you will go beyond the minimum requirement and use your website as a hub for online information sources and other careers resources.

Linking with curriculum areas

Working with teaching staff is one of the key aspects of co-ordination. As a careers leader you will rarely have any formal authority over teachers working in other departments. However, you will be trying to influence their practice and to co-ordinate activities across all subjects that support the careers programme. Developing a series of learning outcomes associated with your programme (or making use of the Career Development Framework discussed in Chapter 2.4) is an important starting point for these negotiations with the curriculum. Once you are clear about the learning that you are trying to achieve through your programme, you will be in a much better position to look for overlaps and cross-fertilisation with other curriculum areas.

In schools the most common location for delivering the discrete element of careers education is as part of the PSHE programme, while in colleges, and indeed in school sixth forms, it is more usually organised as part of the personal development or tutorial programme. It follows that you will need to negotiate with the PSHE leader, and with the tutorial programme leader, to identify where the careers education element might best fit into the overall programme, to plan these sessions and to brief the team of PSHE teachers or personal tutors delivering the programme. You will probably work with this key member of staff quite a lot, so it might be useful to timetable a schedule of regular meetings throughout the year.

In Chapter 2.4 we also looked at establishing links with different subject areas. You will need to create your own strategy for how to approach this, but it is likely to involve attending, at least occasionally, the heads of department meeting (if you are not already part of that meeting) to discuss your overall plans, and then individual meetings with subject representatives to plan particular links. Several schools have reported that it is sometimes more effective for each subject department to nominate a link person for careers, rather than direct everything through the head of department.

Link to Gatsby Benchmark 4

Benchmark 4 encourages you to embed careers content into the curriculum. In Chapter 2.4 we explored the careers leader's role in planning and ensuring the delivery of careers education.

Co-ordinating referrals

An important feature of any careers programme is that young people should have access to personal career guidance whenever they need it. This was covered in Chapter 2.8. The practical implications are that pupils and students should be able to self-refer for guidance interviews, but there should also be a system for schools and colleges to be able to identify when a young person might need guidance and to refer them to a qualified careers adviser. The members of staff who are likely to know the pupils and students best are those who have the most frequent contact with them: their tutors, mentors and, in the case of young people with SEN, the SENCO/head of learner support.

As careers leader you will need to work with the tutorial and pastoral managers, including, in a school setting, heads of year, and the SENCO/head of learner support, to establish mechanisms for tutors and mentors to proactively identify when one of their pupils or students might need access to personal career guidance and then to refer them to the careers adviser, either directly or through you or the careers administrator.

You might find it useful to attend pastoral team meetings when appropriate and to timetable regular meetings with the SENCO/head of learner support.

Co-ordinating links with employers

Establishing, developing and maintaining links with employers clearly involves building relationships with external partners, and this is covered in the next chapter, on networking, but the work with employers also involves a certain amount of internal co-ordination. As well as building lots of external links you will need to keep careful records of which young people have had what encounters and to encourage other teachers to consider engaging with employers and keeping records on the kinds of engagements they build.

Many teachers bring outside speakers into schools for a range of reasons associated with their subjects. This is even more common for lecturers in colleges. However, not all of these will be thought of as part of the careers programme. As a careers leader you should be interested in these activities and try to co-ordinate them with other forms of employer encounter that are going on in the school. Perhaps a teacher brings in an employer from a pharmaceutical company as part of a chemistry or biology lesson. You may be able to encourage them to also talk about their career as part of this encounter. But you will be able to co-ordinate only if you are able to gather information about what is going on.

This highlights the importance of having good record keeping as part of your careers programme. You should think about how you can ensure that you are capturing the kinds of information that you need. This will require you to work closely with all staff to highlight the importance of keeping records and to oversee the work of any administrators who are involved in data entry and data management. The data that you gather will help to determine how future opportunities for encounters with employers should be targeted and what gaps may need to be filled by sourcing new contacts.

> **Link to Gatsby Benchmarks 3 and 5**
> Benchmark 3 highlights the importance of keeping records on students' participation in your careers programme. Good record keeping provides you with the information that you need to co-ordinate provision. See Chapter 2.3 for more detail.
> Benchmark 5 sets a high expectation that each and every pupil and student will have at least one meaningful encounter with an employer each year. We discuss this in more detail in Chapter 2.5.

Communicating with young people and their parents/carers

Young people will need to be kept up to date with a variety of different activities that have been planned for them, for example: careers talks; opportunities to meet employers and representatives of universities, colleges and apprenticeship providers; personal career guidance interviews; vacancies in employment; etc. Notices via tutors and display boards have limited impact; increasingly schools and colleges are using social media, emails and text messaging to communicate with pupils and students. An efficient careers administrator can be a real benefit here, but the content of the messages and their timing will need to be co-ordinated by the careers leader.

Research shows that parents and carers are highly influential with regard to their sons' and daughters' career plans.[10] They will be providing lots of informal advice and it will be important that they are kept informed about the careers support that is provided by the school or college. Regular updates should be made available via newsletters, emails and website updates. You can also explore other ways to engage with parents on careers as part of parents' evenings or even through special careers-focused events.

CASE STUDY

Adrian, the careers leader at Dunville Special School, is keen to involve parents in the school's careers programme. He worries that the parents of young people with SEND often underestimate what their children are capable of.

He arranges a short series of twilight careers sessions for parents. Parents are asked to come in for an hour after school every week for four weeks to hear about how they can help their children to make an effective transition to further learning or work.

In the sessions Adrian brings in some former pupils to talk about their experience and some employers who regularly employ young people with SEND. Most importantly, he works with the careers adviser to provide parents with a guide to having career conversations with their children.

At the end of the four weeks, the parents who attended regularly feel much more optimistic about their children's futures. They also feel empowered to help their children and to reinforce the messages that are being communicated through the careers programme at school.

Reflective question: What sort of arrangements would you like to set up for engaging with parents?

In a nutshell

This chapter has looked at the co-ordination aspects of the careers leader role. Key points to bear in mind include the following.

- Remember that as the careers leader you are dependent on the goodwill of a lot of your colleagues.
- Co-ordination is a subtle part of your role as a careers leader – sometimes when you are being really effective, people won't even know that you are doing anything.
- You should draw up a list of all the members of staff that you currently work with and think about all of those that you need to work with.
- Schedule regular meetings with those that you need to speak to most frequently.
- Talk to your line manager about which team meetings it would be helpful for you to attend.

3.4 Networking

The previous chapters in this section have mainly explored the careers leader's role in working with staff within the school or college. However, we have also repeatedly stressed that an excellent careers programme is one that builds a strong connection between your students and the world beyond education. Careers work needs to bring the world to your students and open doors to allow your students to move into the world. Because of this you will need to build connections with a wide range of external partners.

This chapter looks at the careers leader's responsibility to build a network around the school or college that can support the career learning of your students. No matter how brilliant you and the teachers and careers advisers in your school or college are, you cannot go it alone. Good careers work requires you to network with external organisations and help to build a bridge between your school/college and the wider world. As the careers leader you are trying to connect the work of your internal colleagues with the contributions made by external partners and to fuse all of these into a coherent whole.

In this chapter we will be looking at the role of the careers leader in networking with people and organisations beyond the school/college.

This chapter will cover:

- the principles of effective networking
- the tasks involved in networking
- identifying organisations and individuals who can add value to your careers programme
- managing relationships with careers providers and suppliers
- managing relationships with external partners
- thinking about different approaches to partnership.

Introduction

Careers work, by its nature, requires you to look beyond your school or college. When you are thinking about how to support your students' careers you need to think about how to expose them to how life is lived and how work and study are conducted after they have left school or college. To do this effectively you need to build relationships beyond the school or college and to bring your students into contact with new people.

Networking with external organisations can be challenging for teachers and other education professionals. For most of your career you will have been focused on working within the school or college. You probably feel that your most valuable working time is when you are in front of a class or talking to a student one-to-one. As a careers leader you are likely to spend less time at the chalkface and more time leading, managing and co-ordinating within your school or college. But, networking changes the nature of your working life even more. You will often be working outside of your institution and spending more time in strategic conversations with adults than in conversations directly with young people. Building these kinds of relationships can be very rewarding. Research with careers leaders has found that this opportunity to work with the wider community and build links with people and organisations beyond schools and colleges is one of the main things that attracts them to the role.[11]

Becoming a careers leader, particularly if you have been a classroom teacher previously, can be quite a shift in the nature of your working life and in your professional identity. Such a shift isn't for everyone, but while you will be spending less of your time directly with young people you can still make a huge difference to young people by helping to change the relationship between education and employment. This ability to network, to represent the school or college and to build strategic relationships is likely to stand you in good stead for your future career (see Chapter 4.4).

Principles of effective networking

Networking describes a process of making, maintaining and managing professional connections. Effective networkers are able to meet new people and keep in touch with them. As a careers leader you will be networking with a wide range of people and seeking to engage them in your careers programme in one way or another.

You can sometimes feel like you are cold-calling a succession of people and trying to get them to do something for nothing. However, there are three key principles that should make you feel more positive about networking.

1. **Reciprocity.** Effective networkers need to give as much as they take. As a careers leader you need to think about what the individuals and organisations will get out of working with you. For example, businesses need to recruit people, raise awareness of the skills that they will need and improve the way that their organisation is seen in the

community. When you are talking to people, don't just focus on what you need, also ask them what they need from the relationship.

2. **Equity.** Effective networkers treat people equally and don't just talk to the most important person in the room. When you meet new people and talk to them about your school or college and your careers programme you need to be interested in them and to treat them with respect even if they weren't the person that you came to meet. You might have travelled across the country to attend an event with the idea of getting a Russell Group university to run a programme at your school. But, when you get there you find yourself talking to someone from the local FE college. Use the opportunity to network anyway; they may have more to offer than you think. It is also always worth remembering that you never know who the person you are talking to knows and may be able to introduce you to.

3. **Authenticity.** Effective networkers keep it real! Honesty is always the best policy. Don't pretend that you are an outstanding school if you are not, or that your careers programme is brilliant, if it isn't. Of course, you want to show your school or college in the best light but, be truthful. People are amazingly good at spotting a fake and will often punish you for your attempted deception.

Being honest, generous and decent will help you to form deep and enduring relationships and help you to engage external organisations in your careers programme. But being nice is only part of it. You also need to be well organised and clear about what you are trying to achieve. The next three principles of networking highlight this.

4. **Strategy.** Effective networkers think about whom they are trying to network with and why. When you are networking, you aren't just doing it for fun. You should have a clear set of ideas about what role you want external organisations to play in your careers programme. These objectives should be related to your strategy and should inform your thinking about whom you are trying to meet and to bring into your network. Your time is limited, so you need to make sure that you are spending it wisely, going to the right events and following the right people online.

5. **Tenacity.** Effective networkers make sure that they maintain relationships (that is why reciprocity is so important). As a careers leader the amount of time that you are likely to have for networking is going to be limited. Ideally you will make a contact, lock them into your careers programme and keep them coming back year on year. This requires you to be both tenacious and organised. So, if you meet an employer or useful contact try to follow up the next day with an email and then keep in regular touch with them.

6. **Evaluation.** Effective networkers review their approach to networking and think about how they could do it better. You may find that you've been attending events with employers but you haven't been able to get them to actually commit to getting involved in your programme. Even worse, you may have been attracting a lot of external speakers to your school, but the students have hated them all. It is important to spend time evaluating your network and your networking approach to check that it is working for your school or college.

All six of these principles[12] of networking are important. You will need to keep them in mind, whether you are networking face-to-face or online.

Tasks associated with networking

Networking involves: working with providers of opportunities in education, training and employment who can contribute directly to your careers programme by giving young people insights into future options; contracting with agencies that can provide services such as personal career guidance; forging relationships with organisations that have a role in supporting the development and delivery of careers programmes in schools and colleges; harnessing the active involvement of former students to contribute to your careers programme. It also increasingly involves building a profile online and making connections with stakeholders through social media.

As this list shows, you are going to be working with a wide range of different individuals and organisations. It is very easy to lose track of these organisations and relationships and so it is vital that you develop a system for recording your relationships with all of these organisations.

In the rest of the chapter, the careers leader's tasks of networking are considered in the following areas:
- working with employers and working people
- working with education and training providers
- working with careers providers and suppliers
- building a network of alumni
- building a network online.

The chapter then finishes by asking you to consider whether you should move from a series of networked relationships to a more formal kind of partnership with some or all of the organisations that you are working with.

Working with employers and working people

Building up relationships with a network of employers is a critical part of developing your careers programme. It can also be a fairly daunting aspect of the role, as many careers leaders don't have particularly strong links with local businesses. One way to start is to make contact with local business networks and with organisations that exist to connect education and employment.

> ### 💡 Resources: Networking with employers and working people
>
> There are lots of local and national business networks that you can tap into to get some advice and open up new connections that might be useful to your careers programme. The following offer some useful starting points.
>
> Association of Education Business Professionals (http://theaebp.co.uk) is a network of 80 local organisations dedicated to connecting education with business.
>
> British Chambers of Commerce (www.britishchambers.org.uk) brings together the 53 Chambers that exist across the country to allow local businesses to network with each other. It includes links to all of the local chambers.
>
> Professional associations (https://en.wikipedia.org/wiki/List_of_professional_associations_in_the_United_Kingdom). Wikipedia provides an impressive list of professional associations in the UK. Many professional associations will be willing to provide you with a speaker or advice on how to find someone.
>
> Unions in Schools (www.tuc.org.uk/union-reps/organising-and-bargaining/unions-schools) is the Trade Union Congress's campaign to build understanding of trade unionism in schools. It includes resources and information about how to invite a speaker to your school or college.
>
> And, of course, in England there is the Enterprise Adviser Network (EAN) established by The Careers & Enterprise Company.

Exploring these local and national organisations can be useful, but it is worth remembering that most networking connections come from informal relationships and friends of friends. Start by thinking about whom you and the other people involved in delivering the careers programme know already. Perhaps someone you were at university with, play football with on a Saturday or know socially would make a good speaker for your students? If they aren't right for it, they might know someone else who would be. This kind of organic networking is powerful. Husbands, wives, partners and other family members and friends of your staffroom colleagues could be a further source of useful contacts for contributors to your careers programme. Many schools also survey parents when their children start in Year 7 to ask if they would be willing to talk to students or to be part of events such as mock interviews and 'career speed dating'. In these ways you can soon build an extensive database of potential contacts.

> ### 💡 Link to Gatsby Benchmarks 5 and 6
> Chapters 2.5 and 2.6 focused on the important contribution of encounters with employers, both in school or college and on the employers' premises.

Working with education and training providers

As the careers leader you need to develop working relationships with any UTC or studio school in the area, schools with sixth forms, local FE colleges, apprenticeship providers and universities.

It is usually easier to contact education and training providers than employers. Many of them will be keen to connect with you, as they will need to recruit students for their programmes. Most will have a formalised recruitment and outreach department that you can work with.

💡 Resources: Learning provider organisations

In addition to making direct contact with your local or target colleges, universities and apprenticeship providers it can also be useful to be aware of some of the national organisations that exist to support these institutions.

Association of Colleges (AoC) (www.aoc.co.uk) represents the UK's further education colleges and includes links to all of its member colleges.

Association of Education and Learning Providers (AELP) (www.aelp.org.uk) is a network of over 800 organisations involved in delivering apprenticeships, employability programmes and vocational learning.

HELOA (www.heloa.ac.uk) is the professional association for HE staff involved in admissions and outreach.

NEON (www.educationopportunities.co.uk) is a national network of practitioners involved in widening access to HE.

All education and training providers can give young people information on the opportunities they offer and, where appropriate, advice on how to get into those opportunities. They can also help young people to prepare for the transition from school or college into the next stage of their progression through learning and into work, both through talks and attendance at careers fairs in school or college and by hosting visits and taster sessions on their campuses.

Link to Gatsby Benchmark 7
Chapter 2.7 focused on the importance of including universities, colleges and other post-secondary providers in your programme.

Working with careers providers and suppliers

Over recent years in England, as schools and colleges have been given greater responsibilities for career guidance, there has been a growth in the number of organisations offering help and support to schools.

Some of these organisations are commercial enterprises, offering priced products and services, and as a careers leader you will make your own judgements on how you want to spend such budget as you have available and you will decide where you need additional help. Schools and colleges do not receive any dedicated funding for careers, so as careers leader you will be on the lookout for sources of additional money. The Careers & Enterprise Company, some LEPs and some local authorities make funds available from time to time, as do some other organisations. As careers leader you will need to search out such opportunities and develop the skills of writing proposals and submitting bids.

Other organisations are government funded or do not charge schools and colleges for their services. The Careers & Enterprise Company in England offers a range of support across all eight Gatsby Benchmarks. Jobcentre Plus offers school advisers who can come into schools and colleges to talk to young people, parents/carers and staff about apprenticeships and the local labour market. In England there is a national network of LEPs which have as a prime objective the creation of local jobs and driving economic growth. The LEPs can be a source of local labour market information, but they may also offer some funded initiatives to support the development of careers programmes in schools and colleges. Some local authorities also provide support and particular projects to their schools.

As careers leader you should find out what is available in your area, and a useful first point of call is your local Enterprise Co-ordinator based in the LEP. He or she should be able to signpost you to services and projects available in the locality.

> ## 💡 Resources: Finding careers providers
>
> Careers activity providers database (**www.careersandenterprise.co.uk/delivery**) offers you a tool to find careers providers in your area.
>
> CDI professional register (**www.thecdi.net/Professional-Register-**) is a searchable database of registered careers professionals.
>
> CDI guide to commissioning guidance services (**www.thecdi.net/write/CDI_120-Career_Guidance_in_Schools-2021-FINAL.pdf**) offers advice on best practice and useful templates for commissioning independent career guidance services.

An important subset of careers providers is those who are involved in delivering personal guidance (see Chapter 2.8). For many years personal career guidance for young people in England was provided by a locally delivered national service. This is still the model that exists in the rest of the UK and in many other countries. However, in England responsibility for securing access to career guidance has now been devolved to individual schools and colleges. Some schools, and most colleges, have opted to provide career guidance to their pupils and students through internally appointed careers advisers. Many schools, and a few colleges, however, work with external expert services.

There are two different types of arrangement which meet the needs of different groups of young people. Your school or college may need to make use of both of these types. As careers leader you will have a major role in establishing these arrangements but you will also need to work with other colleagues.

The first type of arrangement concerns support for the transition at 16 for young people who are deemed to be vulnerable and disadvantaged. In England local authorities have retained responsibility for supporting such young people and each school and college needs to negotiate an annual service level agreement with the local authority for this support. In some schools and colleges this negotiation is led by the careers leader, in others by the SENCO or head of learner support. This service is provided free of charge to the school or college, but the precise details of the arrangement may vary from year to year.

The other type of arrangement concerns the provision of impartial career guidance to all pupils or students. As discussed in Chapter 2.8, there is a range of options available, including employing a careers adviser directly. However, if schools or colleges decide to contract services in, they may: contract with a local authority careers service operating on a traded basis, or buy in the services from a private careers company, a social enterprise or a sole trader. In each case the arrangement is a client–provider contract. The school commissions the service. As the careers leader you will undertake all of the research on the options available and make recommendations to the SLT, but the final decision will probably be made by the senior leadership and the governing body.

Building a network of alumni

Former students of the school or college are a particularly rich resource for your careers programme. Current pupils and students can be inspired by hearing about the careers of former students and, as many jobs are never advertised, it is important that young people develop the skills of networking.

Independent schools have always made good use of their alumni networks, and state-funded schools and colleges are now seeing the benefit of investing in establishing similar networks.

> ### 💡 Resources: Future First
>
> Future First (**https://futurefirst.org.uk**) is a charity which helps state-funded schools and colleges to build an alumni community.

Responsibility for establishing and maintaining the network may be given to another member of staff, but as careers leader you should work with that colleague to plan how to make good use of the wide range of contacts to contribute to your careers programme.

Networking online

The traditional approaches to network building discussed so far are important and can't be replaced with social media, but increasingly careers leaders are turning to a range of online tools to build their profile and the profile of their school or college. We've already talked about the importance of you keeping your school's or college's website up to date, but social media can take your online networking to the next level.

The world of social media is ever changing, but if you are going to start anywhere we'd advise you to set up accounts on LinkedIn (**www.linkedin.com**) and Twitter (**https://twitter.com**). You can use these accounts both to network with other careers leaders and to share hints and tips and to reach out to new contacts. If you are on Facebook, you will probably want to join the Careers Leaders UK group (**www.facebook.com/groups/CareersLeaders**) and, if you are a member of the CDI, the CDI Career Development Professionals Community of Practice (**www.facebook.com/groups/CDPCoP**), as both of these groups are full of engaged careers leaders and careers advisers sharing resources and discussing the issues of the day.

> ### 💡 Resources: Social media
>
> There are lots of resources online explaining how you can use LinkedIn, such as Open Colleges' Beginners Guide to LinkedIn (**www.opencolleges.edu.au/blog/2020/05/25/beginners-guide-to-linkedin**). Once on LinkedIn, search for some of the key movers and shakers in the careers world and join relevant groups like the CEIAG and Children and Young People Workforce Group (**www.linkedin.com/groups/3841751**), the Career Development Institute Group (**www.linkedin.com/groups/4676148**) and any local groups.
>
> There are also lots of good resources explaining how to use Twitter, including the site's own guide (**https://help.twitter.com/en/twitter-guide**). Once on, follow a few key accounts like Tristram's (@pigironjoe), the CDI (@TheCDI), Janet Colledge (@careersdefender) and National Careers Week (@CareersWeek) as well as a few key hashtags, such as #careers, #careerschat and #careersleader.

Moving from a network to a partnership

In this chapter we have been discussing how you can build relationships with external organisations and get them to engage with your school or college. But it is worth thinking about whether this kind of networked relationship serves all your needs.

Some of the relationships that you have with individuals and organisations are likely to be deep, enduring and supportive of mutual aims. In such cases you are moving from having a networked relationship to a partnership.

There is a range of levels of formality that you can use to create a partnership. In some cases, you may want to create a formal contract (e.g. with a provider of personal career guidance or an organisation providing work experience placements) or a service level agreement (e.g. with the local authority for support for vulnerable young people), and even make a public announcement celebrating your partnership; in others you might be happy to keep the relationship more informal.

> **Tools: Item 3.4A. Who am I networking with?**
> To gain an overview of all the organisations and individuals external to the school or college that you are working with to deliver the careers programme, try completing the proforma provided in the online resources accompanying this book: https://indigo.careers/clh.

As you develop new partnerships, you should be able to answer the following questions.

- What are the aims of the partnership? What can both organisations achieve through working more closely together?
- Is the partnership designed to be enduring or time limited?
- Who is part of the partnership? Some partnerships are between two organisations, but it is also possible to build partnerships between larger groups of organisations.
- What are the risks of going into partnership? Where are there tensions between your organisations and where could things go wrong?
- What are the responsibilities associated with the partnership? What have you both agreed to do? Are any money or other resources going to change hands?
- How are you going to manage this partnership? How will problems and tensions be resolved? This may just require you to establish a pattern of meetings or it may require a more complex form of governance being established, e.g. involving the heads of your respective organisations.
- When and how will you review and evaluate the partnership?

CASE STUDY

Dunchester Progress Academy sends around 15% of its students to Vanchester College every year. Until recently this relationship has been fractious, with the Head of Dunchester often muttering about the College 'poaching our students'. However, since Rita has taken over as careers leader at Dunchester, and in the light of the legal changes giving colleges access to school students, there has been a concerted effort to improve the relationship.

Rita decides to set up a regular meeting with Aldous, who leads on recruitment and outreach for the College. They get on well and realise that they are both trying to achieve similar things but often end up duplicating effort. They start to explore a new kind of partnership which will give the College much greater access to Dunchester students and in return will see them making a more substantial contribution to the school's careers programme, including providing some qualified careers advisers who will visit the school regularly.

Rita and Aldous sketch out the details of a new kind of partnership and then convene a meeting with the head teacher and the assistant principal with responsibility for careers provision. Negotiating this partnership will not be easy, but they are both convinced that it is in the interests of all of their students.

Reflective questions: How would you describe the working relationships with your local FE colleges and other post-16 centres? Is there scope for greater cooperation and collaboration?

In a nutshell

This chapter has looked at the networking aspects of the careers leader role. Key points to bear in mind include the following.

- You have a responsibility to look outside of the school or college and build relationships with a wide range of stakeholders.
- Maintain an up-to-date database of your contacts with education and training providers and employers.
- Talk to your line manager and the link governor for careers about the school or college's policy on securing careers providers and career guidance services.
- Make contact with your Enterprise Co-ordinator.
- Establish regular meetings with the co-ordinator of your school's or college's alumni network.
- Consider where the relationships that you are building would be better managed by being turned into more formal partnerships.

Section 4:
Ensuring continuous improvement

Introduction

Becoming a careers leader is an important step in your own career. It may not be a step that you planned or even wanted, but we hope that the rest of this book has shown you that it can be interesting and fulfilling as a role.

When you start your role, there is so much to think about, learn and get straight, that it is difficult to consider the future. As you start to relax into the role you will be able to start planning and thinking ahead. In this section we are going to help you to take a longer view and to think about how you can continue to improve your programme and how your role as careers leader fits into your career, into the careers of others around you and into the wider development of the school or college.

By the time you are reading this section you have probably set up your careers programme and been doing the job of careers leader for a while. Even if you've managed to do everything that we've recommended (and **we realise that it is a lot easier to write it than to do it!**) you will probably have a lot of plans for next year, frustrations about things that you haven't been able to do (yet) and dreams of what you might do if you only had the time, resource or know-how. In this section we are going to ask you to think more about these things and turn them into a plan for development.

You will probably have reassured yourself on the long nights when you are preparing career lessons or sending emails out to employers that it will be easier 'once you've got it all set up'. This is right: you now know what you are doing, have good systems in place and hopefully have a network of supporters in your school or college. However, this doesn't mean that you will never have to think about your careers programme again. You should always be thinking about what is working and not working, about what new ideas and innovations are out there and about what has changed in the school, college or wider world.

To do this, you need to commit to a cycle of continuous improvement. A cycle of continuous improvement asks you to think carefully about what you are doing and how you are going to do it (plan), to put your plan into action (do), to make sure that things worked out as you planned (check) and then to make some changes and develop what you are doing (act).

The cycle of continuous improvement

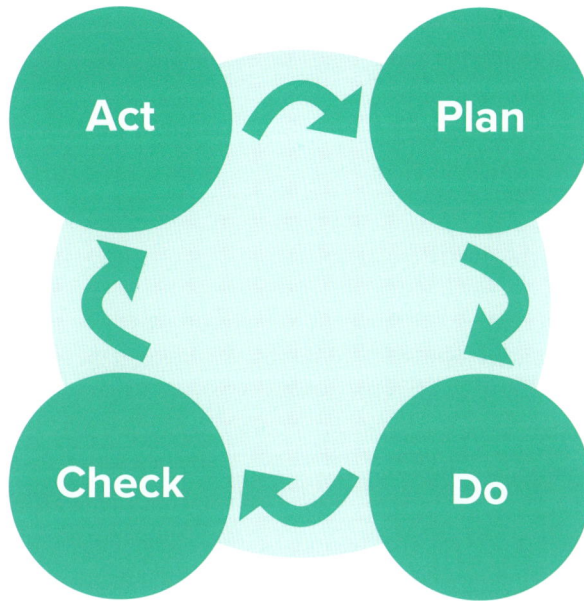

You will probably recognise that this cycle is similar to Kolb's Learning Cycle from Chapter 2.6. In Chapter 4.1, we'll develop this cycle and turn it into a framework for evaluating your programme. These cycles are similar because they are essentially all about how we learn as individuals, as professionals and as organisations.

Before we dive into section 4 we'd like to ask you to reflect on the following questions.

1. What do you feel that you still need to learn or do to be a better careers leader?

2. How does being a careers leader fit into your own career?

3. What knowledge would you like to pass along to other people in your school or college to help them to be more effective in delivering your careers programme?

4. What would you like to change or develop about your careers programme? How do you know that these are the right things to focus on?

5. How are you going to ensure that your programme continues even after you leave the school?

Section 4 is going to focus on these questions and provide you with some tools to help you to move forward.

Your own development

To help you to think about yourself, your learning and how you want to progress we are going to look at your CPD and your career. In Chapter 4.2 we look at how you can become a better careers leader by developing your capability in the role. In Chapter 4.4 we look beyond your immediate role and ask you to think about how being a careers leader fits in with your longer-term career goals.

The development of others

No one is an island, least of all the careers leader. Throughout this book we've argued that you need to manage upwards and downward, co-operate with your colleagues and network with people outside of the school. A careers leader is only ever as good as the careers team that he or she builds. As a leader, one of the roles that you will need to take on is developing others through mentoring, advising and running in-house training and CPD. We look at your role in developing others in Chapter 4.3. Perhaps the most important aspect of working with others is thinking about who is going to replace you and making sure that the programme that you build outlasts you. We look at the issue of succession planning in Chapter 4.4.

The development of your programme

All of the chapters in this section are relevant to thinking about how you develop your programme and ensure continuous improvement. But, the idea of evaluation lies at the heart of this process. It is only by knowing what is going well, and what is going not so well, that you will be able to improve your programme. Because this is so important, this is where we will start in Chapter 4.1.

4.1 Evaluating and developing your programme

It is important that you learn from your mistakes and build on your successes. Evaluation is about trying to figure out what has worked, why it has worked and what you can do about it. Perhaps even more importantly it is about figuring out what has gone wrong and what you can do about this in the future.

Evaluation is not something to leave until the end of the year. Rather, it should be built into everything that you do and used to support the design and delivery of your programme.

This chapter will introduce you to an approach for evaluating your programme and help you to see that evaluation is not an optional extra.

This chapter will cover:

- understanding what evaluation is and why it is important
- the evaluation cycle
- developing a theory of change
- differences between monitoring and evaluation
- a range of tools and approaches that will help you to evaluate your programme.

Introduction

Evaluation is about thinking about what you have done, whether it has gone well and what you might do differently in the future. Pretty much everyone would agree that this is a good idea. No one wants to keep doing the same things even if they don't work. But in practice it isn't always that simple. Firstly, you need to think about *why* you are doing what you are doing, and secondly, you need to think about *whether you really know* if you are achieving your aims.

It is important to understand that evaluation is ultimately about the impact that your programme has on students and on other key beneficiaries of the programme, such as employers. Sometimes people use the terms monitoring, review and evaluation as though they are interchangeable and together describe a single process, whereas they are in fact three interlinked activities. Monitoring is about whether what you have planned takes place; review is about how you, and other contributors to your programme, think the activities went; evaluation is about what happened because of the programme. The idea of the 'counterfactual' (what would have happened differently if you had done nothing) is key to evaluation.

As the careers leader you will need to oversee all three processes. Ideally you should monitor and keep under review everything that you do but, as evaluation is a deeper process, we suggest you focus your energy on aspects of your programme that you wish to examine in greater detail. Evaluation involves reviewing what you did, measuring the outcomes and analysing the relationship between the two.

In the introduction to this section we talked about continuous improvement and suggested that you view the development of your programme as a cycle where you plan, act, check and do. Evaluation is an evolution of this cycle and can be set out like this.

The evaluation cycle

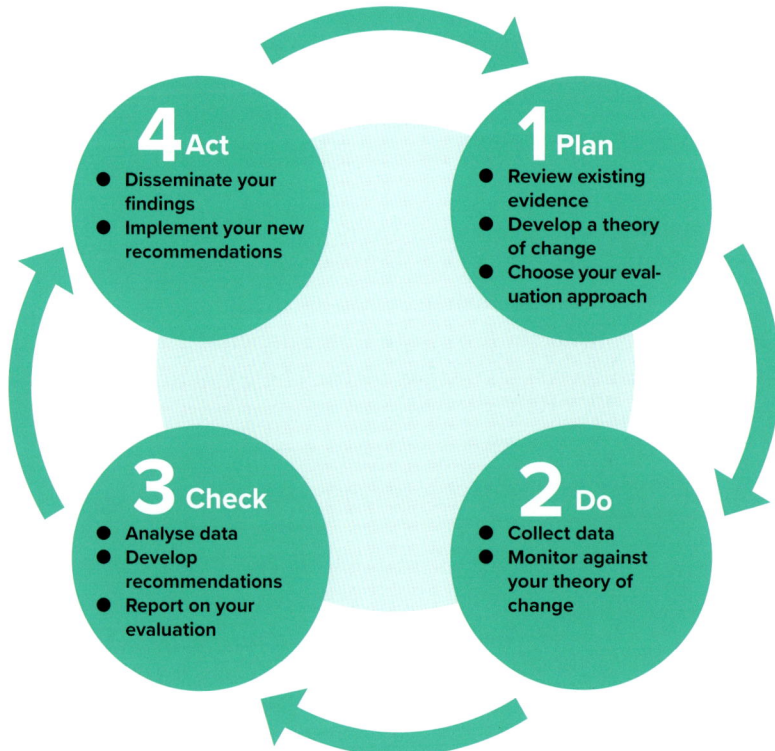

4 Act
- Disseminate your findings
- Implement your new recommendations

1 Plan
- Review existing evidence
- Develop a theory of change
- Choose your evaluation approach

3 Check
- Analyse data
- Develop recommendations
- Report on your evaluation

2 Do
- Collect data
- Monitor against your theory of change

We'll be using this version of the evaluation cycle to structure this chapter. Let's start by looking at how you plan your evaluation.

> ## 💡 Resources: Approaches to evaluation
>
> There are lots of useful books and resources that you can access to help you with evaluation. The following are particularly useful.
>
> Lena Dahlberg and Colin McCraig's (2010) book *Practical Research and Evaluation: A Start-to-Finish Guide for Practitioners*, published by Sage, offers an accessible introduction to evaluation.
>
> Rob Coe, Stuart Kime, Camilla Nevill and Robbie Coleman (2013) have produced *The DIY Evaluation Guide* for the Educational Endowment Foundation, which is available to download for free from **https://educationendowmentfoundation.org. uk/public/files/Evaluation_Guide/EEF_Evaluation_DIY_Evaluation_Guide.pdf**.

Stage 1: Plan

Reviewing existing evidence

We have drawn on a lot of evidence throughout this book. We've done this because we believe that evidence is critical to ensuring that careers interventions are effective and because it offers a shortcut to the collective wisdom of generations. Bernard of Chartres' famous maxim, often misattributed to Isaac Newton, that '*if I have seen further than others it is by standing on the shoulders of giants*' is well worth remembering.[1] Evidence allows us to stand on the shoulders of those who have gone before us to create better careers programmes.

Before you start any evaluation, you should look for existing evidence that might inform what you do and ask yourself the following questions.

- Has anyone already evaluated a similar programme anywhere else in the world?
- Does any of the existing literature give you any ideas about how best to deliver the programme or activity?
- Does any of the existing literature give you any ideas about how to approach your evaluation?
- Has any research been done that might underpin your thinking about what should work or why it should work?
- Can you use any existing research to give you baseline data?

If you turn to the back of the book, the endnotes will direct you to sources of evidence that you can use to support your careers programme and inform your evaluations. We've also made the point that the Gatsby Benchmarks do a pretty good job of pulling the existing evidence together and turning it into a practical framework that you can implement. But the Gatsby Benchmarks aren't the final word on what works in careers and it is valuable for you to review the evidence periodically.

Evidence is likely to be particularly useful when you are introducing something new into your programme. For example, if you are going to build employer mentoring into your careers programme you might find it useful to consult Tristram's publication *Effective Employer Mentoring*.[2] Once you have reviewed the evidence you can start to build, develop or change your programme to bring it into line with what the evidence suggests.

Resources: Evidence

There are lots of places to start if you are looking for evidence to inform your careers programme.

Google Scholar (https://scholar.google.co.uk) is a research-specific version of the Google search engine. It is a good place to start with any enquiry that you have about evidence.

The **Education Endowment Foundation** teaching and learning toolkit (https://educationendowmentfoundation.org.uk/education-evidence/teaching-learning-toolkit) provides an entry point to the wider literature on what works in education, and can be applied to many aspects of your careers programme.

Education & Employers is a charity which, unsurprisingly, focuses on bringing education and employers together. It offers an excellent research section at www.educationandemployers.org/research-main.

The Careers & Enterprise Company has published a lot of useful research including a series of 'what works?' papers focusing on different kinds of interventions. The organisation provides an archive of its research at www.careersandenterprise.co.uk/our-evidence/evidence-and-reports/archive.

The **International Centre for Guidance Studies** is an international research centre based at the University of Derby which publishes a lot of useful research in this area. The centre's website is at www.derby.ac.uk/research/centres-groups/icegs.

International reflections: Finding local experts

Career guidance is an international field of study and there is lots of research that we can draw on from around the world. However, nothing beats having access to local experts who understand your context. As a careers leader, it is important to find out who the key researchers, academics and thought leaders are in your country. Once you have identified them, keep up to date with their latest publications and reach out to them if you have questions. If you are undertaking a systematic evaluation of your programme they may be interested in what you find.

Developing a theory of change

The most important work that you do in evaluation is thinking about what you are doing, how you are doing it and what you hope will happen as a result. You probably thought about a lot of these things when you were first planning your programme (see Chapter 2.1), but we are going to ask you to revisit this from an evaluation perspective. To do this we are going to introduce you to a key tool that evaluators use called a 'theory of change'.

A theory of change describes the steps that you have to take to make something happen. So, if you are reading this book and it gets too dark you will probably get up, turn the light on and carry on reading. In this case the outcome that you are trying to achieve is being able to read the book in the dark. To achieve this you will need to go through a series of steps.

A theory of change for reading this book in the dark

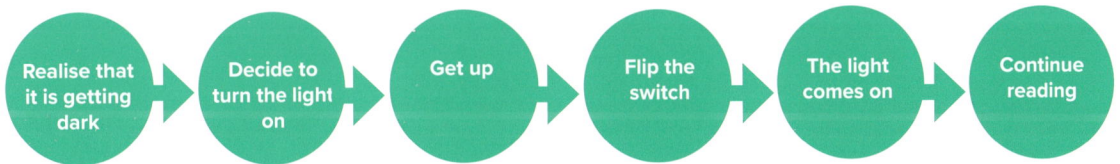

Realise that it is getting dark → Decide to turn the light on → Get up → Flip the switch → The light comes on → Continue reading

This diagram sets out a basic theory of change. It is only because you implicitly understand this theory of change that you know how to achieve your objective (to keep reading this book even when it gets dark). The theory of change also helps you to see when things go wrong. So, if for example you can't find the light switch, you know what the obstacle is and how to change it (look for the switch).

If we apply a theory of change to an aspect of your careers programme like helping students to transition to university we end up with a theory of change that looks like this.

A theory of change for supporting transition to university

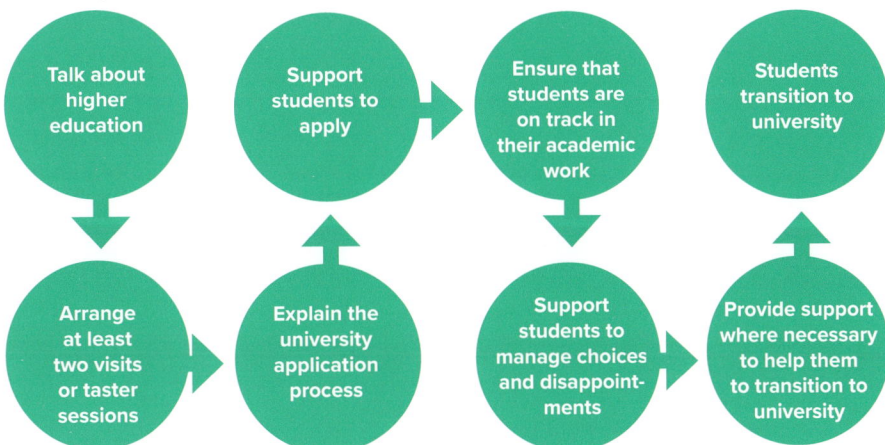

Talk about higher education → Arrange at least two visits or taster sessions → Explain the university application process → Support students to apply → Ensure that students are on track in their academic work → Support students to manage choices and disappointments → Provide support where necessary to help them to transition to university → Students transition to university

Inevitably, developing theories of change for careers interventions is a bit more complicated than the one that we created for turning the light on and reading a book. One of the complexities is defining the outcomes that you want to achieve. The example above is straightforward because it is about helping a student to access a choice that they are already interested in (going on to HE). But, when you are thinking about your whole programme it gets more difficult to define the outcome.

An example of a theory of change for your whole programme might therefore look something like this.

A sample theory of change for a whole careers programme

The school/college delivers an excellent careers programme → All students participate in the programme → Students build career knowledge and learn career management skills for their futures → Students achieve at school and make smooth transitions to the next phase of their life → Students achieve their career aspirations, build successful lives and make use of their education

Obviously, many of the links in this theory of change are easier to describe than they are to achieve or measure. None the less, it is important to start with a strong theory because it helps you to think about what you are trying to do and therefore about what you are evaluating against. So, in this case we have three ultimate aims.

1. Students achieve their career aspirations.

2. Students build successful lives.

3. Students make good use of their education.

As you start to think about these things you might want to refine them and consider how they might be measured.

If we take the outcome of students achieving their aspirations, we can see that if we are going to measure this, it is going to require a school or college to record students' aspirations while they are in education. It is also going to require some way of following up with these students to find out how far they have realised these aspirations a few years later. This might be difficult to do in practice, but just because it is challenging to measure doesn't mean that the aim isn't worthwhile. What is more, you might also want to reflect on whether it is OK for individuals to change their aspirations as they learn and develop. In this case you might want to adjust the aim to be something like 'students achieve their career aspirations or are happy with the way that their career develops'.

As this example shows, building a theory of change can be challenging. It is likely to be something that you continue to develop and iterate as you learn more and think about your programme and what you are trying to achieve. But, even if it changes, it is still critical to define your theory of change if you want to evaluate your programme. A theory of change creates a road map for what you are trying to do and allows you to see if you are on track.

Spend some time developing your theory of change and thinking about how you are going to communicate it to others.

Deciding on your evaluation approach

Once you have developed your theory of change you need to think about what kind of evaluation you are trying to do. There are two main types of evaluation.

1. **A process evaluation** (sometimes called a formative evaluation). This focuses on whether things are working in the way that you hoped and asks you to think about what is going wrong and how you might do things differently. A process evaluation is developmental and will help you to improve the quality of your programme.

2. **An outcome evaluation** (sometimes called a **summative evaluation**). This focuses on what has happened because of the intervention that you have put in place. This type of evaluation asks you to think about whether anything different has happened because of what you have done. It also enables you to think about whether the impact that you've had has been worth the effort.

At this stage you should also be thinking about what you are going to evaluate. It might be tempting to decide that you want to evaluate everything to do with your programme, but really understanding what is going on with every element is likely to be difficult and time consuming. While you might try to capture the overall effectiveness of your programme, you will probably want to focus in on one or two elements, usually new things that you have just introduced or older things that you are considering getting rid of or changing.

To give you the focus that you need you should define your **evaluation question** (or questions) before you start. An evaluation question should be specific rather than general and should be designed to be something that you can answer through your evaluation.

So don't ask: *Does our programme have an impact?*

Do ask: *Does providing students with labour market information result in them having broader ideas about possible careers?*

As the example above shows, setting an evaluation question is an important part of designing your evaluation. It will work alongside your theory of change and guide the analysis and reporting of your evaluation.

As you plan your evaluation you should be realistic about how much capacity and resource you have with which to evaluate your programme. You are the careers leader and have a lot on your plate! Evaluation is important, but you also need to organise the programme. In general, it is better to be less ambitious in your evaluation plans and complete your evaluation successfully than it is to plan to do everything and end up with a lot of half-finished projects.

Finally, you should think about the ethics and legality of your evaluation. The British Educational Research Association provides a code of ethics that you can use to guide your evaluation.[3] The key thing is to treat all participants with respect, ensure that they understand what they are involved in and consent to participate, and to think about any possible harm that may occur through your evaluation (e.g. by breaching anonymity), and manage these risks.

> **Link to Gatsby Benchmark 1**
>
> **Evaluation is a key part of meeting Gatsby Benchmark 1. Evaluation should be integrated into the planning and management of your careers programme. See Chapter 2.1 for further discussion of Gatsby Benchmark 1.**

Stage 2: Do

Collecting data

As you move into the 'doing' stage of your evaluation one of the key things is to collect data to help you to understand what is happening.

'Data' is a term that is bandied about a lot. Sometimes it can be difficult to know what people are talking about when they say that they are 'data-driven' or 'data-led'. In fact, data just means information that can be recorded or written down. It includes all sorts of information that might be useful to you in helping you to understand your programme.

Data includes notes that you have written on conversations, reflections, letters from parents, photos and recordings. It also includes numbers and statistics, but it is important to recognise that numbers are not the only valid form of data.

There are lots of tools that you can use to collect evaluation data. There are a few basic rules that should guide your thinking about data collection.

- **Make use of what you are already collecting.** Schools and colleges collect vast amounts of data from students, teachers, parents and other stakeholders. Your organisation will already be collecting information on student behaviour, absenteeism, academic attainment and immediate post-school or college destinations. Your students will also produce written work and presentations as part of the careers programme. You should get familiar with this data and think about how it might be useful in evaluating the careers programme. For example, you may believe that if your careers programme is working, students will be more engaged and less likely to have unexplained absences. Given the data that you are already collecting, you probably won't need to collect any new information to find out if this is true.

- **Don't collect anything that you won't analyse or use.** Inexperienced evaluators often try to collect every piece of data that they can. This leads to feedback forms after every session and surveys with hundreds of questions on them. The basic principle should always be don't collect anything that you aren't likely to use. So, if you aren't going to analyse your data by ethnicity, don't ask questions about it. Similarly, if you haven't got time to analyse thousands of feedback forms, don't collect them.

- **Don't reinvent the wheel.** If you want to collect data try to find someone else who has collected data already on a similar subject. If you can borrow the approach that they used (e.g. using the same survey questions) it is likely to improve the quality of what you do. It will also have the benefit of making your data comparable with theirs.

💡 Resources: Assessing students' career learning

It can be really useful to have a way of measuring what has been learnt by students through a careers programme. You can do this by assessing students against the learning outcomes that you have defined, using a framework such as the CDI's Career Development Framework for example (see section 2.4), and then using marks and feedback to help you to measure student learning and progress.

It can also be useful to have a quicker process to measure student learning. A common way to do this is using a standard set of questions which ask students to self-assess their own learning. The Careers & Enterprise Company have developed a tool called the Future Skills Questionnaire which is designed for this purpose.[4] This tool is integrated into Compass+ (**https://resources. careersandenterprise.co.uk/resources/compass**).

Tristram has been involved in developing an alternative questionnaire that is also freely available for use. This tool is called the Student Career Readiness Index (SCRI) and uses nine questions to measure how ready students feel to start their careers.[5] The SCRI is included as tool 4.1A at **https://indigo.careers/clh**.

- **Link your data together.** We all hate being asked the same thing repeatedly. If you already know a pupil's address, age or the subjects that they are studying, don't ask it again. This can be tricky, as it requires you to find a way to link all the data that you collect. All students have a unique pupil number or learner number that can be very useful for this purpose – but most students won't know this number, so you will have to find a way to connect the individual to their number. Often a combination of their name, date of birth and address will allow you to do this.

- **Collect once, analyse repeatedly.** If you store data well, you will find that it becomes more and more useful. If you collect information about a student's career aspirations one year it provides you with intelligence which you can use to shape your programme and improve the quality of the advice that you give to that student. If you collect this data over several years you can start to see how their aspirations develop and consider whether your programme is having an influence on these aspirations.

Link to Gatsby Benchmark 3

In Chapter 2.3 we talked about keeping good records on students' participation in your careers programme. If you have managed to do this, this will give you another valuable source of data for your evaluation.

If you follow these rules you should be able to avoid generating masses of unusable data. Of course, sometimes you do want to collect new data. We can't take you through every possible approach that you could use but the following should give you some starting points.

- **Your reflections.** If you get into the habit of keeping regular notes, you will generate a valuable source of data. For example, if every week in the year you summarised what you had done on the careers programme and identified two or three things that had gone well and two or three things that you would like to improve, you would have a lot of data about how to improve your programme.
- **Staff reflections.** We have talked about the importance of engaging other staff in your organisation in the careers programme (see Chapter 3.3). The colleagues who participate in the careers programme will have experiences, ideas and complaints that could help you to improve your programme. The challenge is to capture this kind of reflection in a way that you can analyse. This can be as simple as emailing people and asking them to send you their thoughts after an event, or even just taking notes at meetings. Alternatively, you could try running focus groups or even small surveys to gather this information.
- **Interviews.** These are usually one-to-one conversations where you ask someone a series of relevant questions about how they experienced your programme. Interviews can be very structured or more conversational in nature – there are pros and cons to different approaches and you should think about what works best for what you are trying to find out. You might want to interview students, employers, staff or any of your other stakeholders. Take detailed notes or record your interviews.
- **Focus groups.** These are similar to interviews but involve talking to groups rather than individuals. Focus groups allow you to gather more perspectives

and to hear where people agree or disagree and why. However, people can sometimes be reticent to share more personal experiences and reflections in a focus group context.

- **Surveys.** These are structured sets of questions that are usually (but not always) administered to larger groups of people either on paper or via the internet. You can structure surveys in a variety of ways. An important choice that you need to make is how much you are going to structure people's answers by giving them a number of pre-set choices and to what extent you are going to allow them to write what they want.

> ### Resources: Research and evaluations methods
>
> This book isn't the place to teach the basics of research methods, but thankfully there are a lot of other resources that you can use to help you with this.
>
> Louis Cohen, Lawrence Manion and Keith Morrison (2017) have produced the definitive *Research Methods in Education* book, which is published by Routledge.
>
> Robert Coe, Michael Waring, Larry Hedges and James Arthur's (2017) *Research Methods and Methodologies in Education*, published by Sage, offers an equally useful alternative.

Monitoring against your theory of change

The previous segment of this chapter talked about the different ways in which you could find and collect data. But, it didn't discuss what you are collecting data for or how to decide what is the best thing to collect. To decide that you need to go back to your theory of change.

In your theory of change you set out a series of things that you felt were important to take place if you were going to achieve your aims. When you get to this stage it is important to think about what information you need to monitor whether each of these stages has taken place in the way that you hoped.

If we review the example theory of change it suggests a number of things that we might monitor. The example on page 206 shows how you can use a theory of change to guide you on what to monitor. Collecting all of this data and relating it to your theory of change will give you a lot of the information that you need to evaluate your provision. However, you should also think about what else might be useful. Your evaluation questions will help to guide you on what else you might need – as will things that you notice in the monitoring data as you go along. For example, most of the information below is quantitative. It will tell you what is happening and how much of it is happening, but it won't tell you much about why. So, if you find out that 10% of your students are regularly ducking out of your careers programme you might want to run some focus groups with them to figure out why this is.

Monitoring against a theory of change

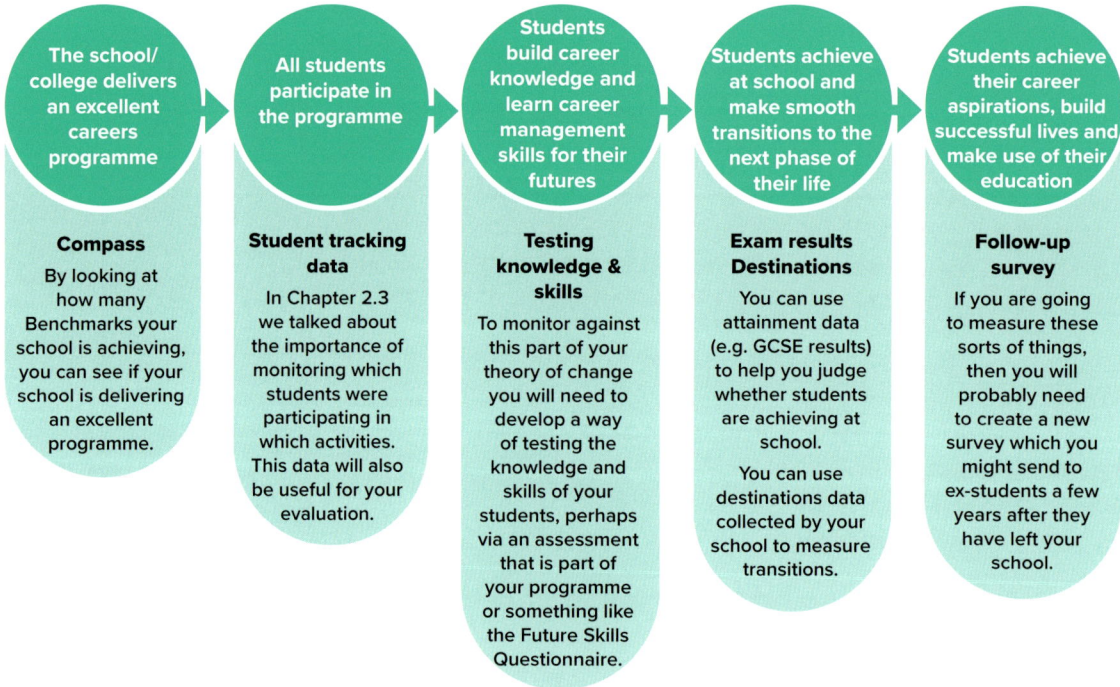

The school/college delivers an excellent careers programme	All students participate in the programme	Students build career knowledge and learn career management skills for their futures	Students achieve at school and make smooth transitions to the next phase of their life	Students achieve their career aspirations, build successful lives and make use of their education
Compass	**Student tracking data**	**Testing knowledge & skills**	**Exam results Destinations**	**Follow-up survey**
By looking at how many Benchmarks your school is achieving, you can see if your school is delivering an excellent programme.	In Chapter 2.3 we talked about the importance of monitoring which students were participating in which activities. This data will also be useful for your evaluation.	To monitor against this part of your theory of change you will need to develop a way of testing the knowledge and skills of your students, perhaps via an assessment that is part of your programme or something like the Future Skills Questionnaire.	You can use attainment data (e.g. GCSE results) to help you judge whether students are achieving at school. You can use destinations data collected by your school to measure transitions.	If you are going to measure these sorts of things, then you will probably need to create a new survey which you might send to ex-students a few years after they have left your school.

Stage 3: Check

Analysing data

As you develop your evaluation approach, you will need to focus the questions that you are hoping to address. You can't do everything – so ask yourself what this evaluation is really trying to find out. Both your evaluation questions and your theory of change provide you with a guide to this, but you might find that as your evaluation progresses you will want to refine these.

As you have been developing your evaluation you will have started to draw together lots of data. Every article that you have read, every data source you've discovered and every interview conducted will have produced new insights. The challenge in an evaluation is making sense of these insights, understanding the contradictions, and giving appropriate weighting to different perspectives. This process of disentangling the evaluation findings and making sense of them is what is meant by analysis.

Regardless of what you are researching, you should be systematic in the analysis of data. By systematic we mean that you should make sure that you attend to all the data that you collect and that you consider how to review all of it without giving undue weight to things which are very positive, very negative or just happen to be the last thing that you read. A range of software tools exist to support the analysis of both quantitative data (such as Excel, SPSS) and qualitative data (such as NVivo). Depending on how much data you have and how formal you want it to be, it can be useful to invest some time in learning how to use such tools because they can greatly increase the speed and accuracy of analysis. However, the tools will not, in and of themselves, analyse data.

A systematic approach to data analysis allows the evaluator to describe what the data are revealing, to quantify the different perspectives that emerge and to make connections and spot patterns. The process of analysing evaluation data is likely to be an ongoing process. It is not advisable to leave it until the end of a project, but rather to see analysis as a process that informs all stages of an evaluation.

The process of analysis needs to achieve the following tasks.

- **Quantification.** The process of assigning values and importance to elements of the data that you have collected. For example, some people might report that an intervention made them more positive about apprenticeships, while others might report the opposite. By identifying the size of these two groups it is possible to understand their relative importance.
- **Description and coding.** Understanding the patterns that exist within data. For example, in answer to a question about whom they see as a role model young people might give a long list of names. The process of describing and coding these answers would organise them into a limited number of codes, such as parent, friend, celebrity, teacher. Coding transforms data from just being many items of information into patterns that can be quantified and understood.
- **Making connections.** Identifying connections between different aspects of the data and between the data and other information that you have. For example, it might be the case that most people who answered 'yes' to a question are female and this might therefore be a relationship worthy of comment. It is also useful to note where the patterns that you spot are similar to those observed in previous research.

When analysing data it is important to consider all possible explanations for the findings. Evaluation should not be about confirming what the evaluator thinks already.

Useful questions to guide your analysis.
- What have we found?
- Why have we found it?
- What does it tell us about what we are evaluating?
- Could there be any other explanation?
- Is there anything that we don't understand or can't explain?
- How does this link to other research?
- How does this link to policy?

Develop recommendations

Once you have done your analysis you are in a position to think about what you want to change and develop in response to what you have found. The process of developing recommendations is a creative one – data will never tell you what to do, it will only give you information on what has already happened.

CASE STUDY

In her second year as careers leader Rita has put a lot of effort into evaluating the careers programme. One of the centrepieces of the programme is a day for Year 10 students when employers review student CVs, feedback on student presentations and give short talks to students. In her first year this was one of the activities that Rita enjoyed the most and she is confident that the evaluation will show that it was a huge success.

On the day Rita distributes short feedback forms to students, employers and teachers to capture their perspectives on the day. The initial feedback is really positive. Everyone enjoyed the day and would recommend it to others. However, when Rita digs further into the data the picture is less positive. Students tended not to agree with the statement 'I feel more prepared for my career', employers tended not to agree with the statement 'I would be likely to recruit a student from this school' and teachers tended not to agree with the statement 'I will be able to use some of the information from employers in my lessons'.

Rita isn't sure what to do. Should she cancel the day, rework it, spend more time briefing all the participants or do something else?

Reflective questions: What aspects of your careers programme would you identify for an in-depth evaluation? How would this feed into your career guidance development plan and the overall improvement plan for the school or college?

As the example above shows, evaluation can be really useful as a way to surface problems and give you ideas about what is working well or badly. It is important to state these problems clearly before you start trying to develop solutions to them. Once you have identified the problems you might want to suggest some possible solutions or recommendations, but you should also try to share these ideas with colleagues, students and other stakeholders and test them out before you solidify them.

Reporting

An evaluation should result in a report. This might be a brief summary of what you have found and the recommendations that you have generated in response to it. It could be a set of slides for a presentation. Or it could be a detailed written report. Regardless of the format, it is important to spend some time working through your evaluation data and thinking about what it all means. Producing a report provides a focus to your work and forces you to finish your analysis and put it together in a meaningful way.

When you are thinking about how to report on the work that you have done you should work through the following questions.

Who is this for? If you are going to write up what you have done you need to start by thinking about whom you are talking to. Putting yourself into the place of your reader will immediately make you a much better writer.

What do you have to say? A report should not just be about writing down everything that you've found out through your evaluation. You will always have a lot more information than you should put in a report. Focus on the big findings and the things that will be most meaningful to your audience.

What are you trying to achieve? You are writing a report for a reason. Maybe you want the governors to agree some radical changes that you have planned? Perhaps you want more resources to improve your programme? Or maybe you just want to convince everyone that you are doing a good job? Think about your rationales for reporting and use these to inform the way that you write it up.

How are you going to say it? There are lots of different ways to produce a report. It could be a one-page infographic or a 100-page report. You should think about these questions of genre and format before you start writing.

Finally, remember that most people don't read reports in full. The overwhelming majority of people will read only a couple of pages or even a few bullet points. Therefore, if you produce any report that is over four pages long, make sure that you include **a one- to two-page *executive summary*** and a **one- to two-paragraph *abstract***.

Stage 4: Act

Disseminating your findings

The final stage of the evaluation cycle is 'acting'. In this stage you need to take all the work that you've been doing and use it to make a difference.

Before your evaluation can make any difference at all people need to hear about it. It is your job to get people to engage with it and to think about the issues that it raises. There are lots of ways to do this, including the following.

- **Send it to people.** In most cases the audience for your evaluation will be small. You should be able to get it to most of the people that need to see it with an email. Your email should include a summary of what the report says and explain why they should take the time to open the attachment and read it.
- **Put it on the agenda of a meeting.** An evaluation is far more likely to get read and discussed if you create some time for it to be discussed. For example, getting it to a school/college SLT will guarantee that at least some key decision makers hear about it.
- **Set up a meeting.** Who is it critical to get to engage with the evaluation? Once you've figured this out, set up a meeting with them to make sure they put the time aside. If there is a group, e.g. all of the careers teachers in your school, then call a meeting and invite them along.
- **Publish it.** Making it available for the world to see will increase its impact enormously. This can be as simple as turning your MS Word document or PowerPoint slides into a PDF and putting it on your website. If you are feeling a bit braver (and have a bit more time) you might want to try to publish a version of it in a newsletter, blog, professional magazine or journal. Most magazines and journals are desperate for content and so they will be keen to feature what you've done, as long as you can adopt their style guide and connect it to their interests.
- **Produce bespoke summaries.** Careers programmes engage a wide range of stakeholders. Each of them is likely to find something different in your evaluation report. One way to handle this is to produce a bespoke summary for employers, another one for teachers and so on. Each of these can pull out the key relevant findings for the group that you are interested in talking to.

Implementing your recommendations

Finally, you need to implement your recommendations. Evaluation serves no purpose if you do it and then ignore what you have found. In practice this is incredibly difficult because time moves on quickly. A few things make it more likely that your evaluation will have an impact.

- **Act quickly.** Start implementing as soon as you have completed the evaluation.
- **Remember that evaluation is a process.** If findings and recommendations emerge as you are going through the year, start acting on them as soon as you can.
- **Allocate responsibilities.** Try to ensure that all recommendations are specific and allocated to an individual or group where possible. If something is everyone's responsibility, it is no one's responsibility.
- **Create an implementation structure.** Set up meetings and identify an implementation group to carry through the recommendations.
- **Tell people what you are planning to do.** Making your plans public will make you stick to them.

Development planning

All schools and colleges have an annual cycle of development planning. This should include all aspects of their work, and if the careers department is not asked for a development plan you should prepare one anyway. The contents will be informed by the results of your monitoring, review and evaluation. The plan should set out what developments you wish to make to your programme and any implications for staff development (CPD) and organisational changes. You should then list the actions needed in chronological order, clearly indicating who is to be responsible for each one and what the target dates are.

It is a good idea also to assess the climate for change, by identifying what factors may help, or hinder, the implementation of your plans. Finally, you should discuss the plan with your line manager, as you are likely to need their endorsement and support to put the proposals into practice.

Tools: Item 4.1B. Development plan.
A template for preparing a career development plan is provided in the online resources accompanying this book: **https://indigo.careers/clh**. You may find that your school or college has its own format, in which case you should use that, but if not, then this one should help you to present your proposals in a structured way.

In a nutshell

This chapter has looked at how you can evaluate your programme and use this evaluation to drive your programme. Key things to bear in mind include the following points.

- Evaluation is a process. It is something that you should be doing all the time rather than a one-off event.
- You should make sure that your evaluation plans are realistic and that you follow through on them.
- Developing a theory of change and some good evaluation questions is at the heart of effective evaluation.
- Effective evaluators make good use of existing data before they start trying to collect new data.
- There are lots of different ways to collect data. It can be useful to use a range of approaches to allow you to gather different kinds of data.
- Make sure that you analyse your data and write up and share your evaluation report.
- Evaluation is pointless if you don't act on what you find out.
- Use your evaluation findings to inform your development plan.

4.2 Looking after your own CPD

It is possible that you are using this handbook to support your participation in a training programme for careers leaders, or you may be reading it to enhance your knowledge and understanding of the role. In both contexts the book could be providing a source of either initial training or CPD. As we have indicated on several occasions in earlier chapters, the world of career guidance is evolving all the time and the landscape of education, training and employment that careers leaders are helping young people to navigate is forever changing. As a professional working in this sector you will need to continue to update your knowledge and skills throughout your career if you are to remain effective in leading programmes that provide young people with the careers support they need.

This chapter will cover:

- what CPD is and why it is important
- identifying your CPD needs and linking them to the development needs of the school or college
- the various forms of CPD
- taking responsibility for your CPD.

Introduction

People move into the role of careers leader from a variety of previous positions. Many are qualified teachers, others are qualified careers advisers, but an increasing number come from a range of other backgrounds. Some careers leaders are recruited from outside of education and bring a background in business, along with useful contacts and knowledge. It is also common for careers leaders to be recruited from elsewhere in the education system, for example from HE or those working in different roles within schools and colleges, including librarians, student support professionals, administrators and teaching assistants. Whatever the newly appointed careers leader has done before, he or she will need access to some initial training and support to get to grips with the new role.

Initial training

Initial training for careers leaders can take a variety of forms. It might consist of a short, often one-day, introductory course; it could be a longer training programme organised as a number of days spread over several weeks; or it could simply be a briefing from the previous post holder or a consultant. If you are lucky, someone will also have given you a copy of this book as soon as you started in your role.

In England, the Department for Education has recently introduced a centrally funded programme of careers leader training, managed by The Careers & Enterprise Company. As a new careers leader, you can complete a free, online induction module. It takes only a few hours to complete, at your own pace, and provides a foundation knowledge and understanding of careers leadership in schools and colleges.

You can then progress to one of the fully funded training courses, which are open to all secondary school, special school and college careers leaders (both recently appointed and those with more experience). These courses are designed to give you an understanding of the role and current best practice, and are provided by a range of universities and careers sector or education leadership training organisations who offer a choice of approaches but all cover the same outcomes. Typically, they are organised as a number of whole-day or half-day sessions over a period of a few months and delivered in-person, online or through a blend of both approaches. They offer the opportunity to gain a qualification, but there is also the option of completing the course on an 'attendance-only' basis without submitting assignments for accreditation.

> ### 🔅 Resources: Initial training for careers leaders
>
> The online learning introductory module for careers leaders can be found at **www.careersandenterprise.co.uk/careers-leaders/careers-leader-training/online-learning-modules**.
>
> Details of the careers leader training courses can be found at **www.careersandenterprise.co.uk/careers-leaders/careers-leader-training**

What is CPD and why is it important?

Initial training aims to give you enough to get started, but it can't prepare you for all eventualities. Once you get into the work you will want to further your knowledge, understanding and skills and to keep up to date with developments. This is what is meant by CPD. It plays a major role in equipping you to stay on top of the job and to lead an outstanding careers programme.

Your line manager and others may suggest CPD opportunities for you to pursue, and you are likely to be inundated with invitations to apply for various careers courses and conferences, but it is up to you to manage your own CPD, to identify what you need and to seek out opportunities for your professional development on a continuing basis.

💡 Resources: CPD for careers leaders

Neary and Johnson's 2016 book, *CPD for the Career Development Professional: A Handbook for Enhancing Practice* is published by Trotman. This is a practical handbook which provides information on ways in which CPD can be undertaken and which helps careers practitioners to direct their own CPD.

The professional association for everyone working in careers education and guidance in the UK, the Career Development Institute (CDI), provides a monthly CPD bulletin, an extensive programme of training courses and several online communities of interest. **www.thecdi.net/Developing-Yourself**.

In their handbook on *CPD for the Career Development Professional* Neary and Johnson quote Madden and Mitchell's definition of CPD.

> *Continuous Professional Development is the maintenance and enhancement of the knowledge, expertise and competence of professionals throughout their careers according to a plan formulated with regard to the needs of the professional, employer, the profession and society.*[6]

In the past, a distinction was made in the education system between 'initial training' or 'initial education' (i.e. the training or education received before, or on, entering the job) and 'in-service training or InSET' (training received once in the role). The definition of CPD above is wider than InSET, which can sometimes be seen as being limited to attending a course or participating in a training session organised within the school or college. One of the important elements that this definition brings out is that CPD is not just about meeting the development needs of the individual, but also about meeting the wider needs of the employer, the profession and society. This is important because in some schools and colleges CPD can be seen as something of a perk and rationed out in ways that do not take account of the needs of either the individual professional or the organisation. As a new careers leader, it is important that you be assertive about your need to access relevant initial training and CPD.

CPD can take a wide variety of forms, including, but extending beyond, attending courses. Not all CPD has a price tag attached to it, but all CPD will take up some time and energy. Consequently, it is important to plan your participation in CPD and to explain the value of it to your line management and colleagues.

Well-planned CPD should equip and enable you to do your job well, but should also assist the school or college to develop its careers provision and contribute to enhancing the careers profession as a whole and, in turn, its contribution to society. Society benefits if individuals are helped to make the right moves for them and they will be helped to do that if they have access to good-quality careers programmes led by careers leaders who have kept up to date with best practice in the field.

Identifying needs

The starting point in planning any CPD is to identify your own professional development needs. There are several ways of doing this. One would be simply to note things that you want to know or understand more about, or learn how to do. Another would be to review your current knowledge, understanding and skills against a suitable template. In England, The Careers & Enterprise Company and Gatsby Foundation's guide on *Understanding the Role of the Careers Leader* sets out the responsibilities of a careers leader and can be used to identify any gaps that you might want to fill by means of CPD.[7] The careers leadership section of the UK's National Occupational Standards for Career Development provides another resource to help you review and identify your CPD needs. This is particularly worth looking at if you are considering a qualification in careers leadership now or at any time in the future, as the Standards are used as a basis for designing professional awards.[8]

Once you have identified your CPD needs it is good practice to discuss these with your line manager. At a basic level, if the proposed CPD activity to meet those needs involves you being released from duties in school or college, or a cost to the school or college, you will need your line manager's permission and approval. But further to just allowing you to access the CPD, your line manager will be critical to providing the support to enable you to implement any developments in the school or college that follow from your CPD activity. During your meeting with your line manager, you should be prepared to discuss how your own professional development needs relate to the programme development and organisation development aspirations of the school or college. Your development or improvement plan may provide a further source for identifying your personal professional development needs.

Your CPD should not be determined entirely by what your school or college wants to achieve, but the closer the match between your own aspirations and those of the school or college, the greater the possibility that both will be supported and achieved.

Tools: Item 4.2A. Training needs analysis.
A template for identifying your CPD needs is provided in the online resources accompanying this book: **https://indigo.careers/clh.**

Finding CPD opportunities

Once you have identified your CPD needs you need to think about how you can find development opportunities that will help you to meet those needs. In some cases, it might be obvious, but at other times it might take some research. Google will sometimes answer your questions and find you a good opportunity, but in other cases there might be a need to ask around and see how other people have addressed this issue.

As you examine your CPD needs, consider the following questions.

- Is this a need that you could work on by yourself using self-study resources?
- Is there anyone in your school/college who could help you to meet this need?
- Is there anyone else in your immediate network who could help you to meet this need?
- Is there an obvious course or development opportunity that addresses this need?
- Are there any opportunities that are free?
- How much of a priority is meeting this need?
- How have other careers leaders developed in this area?

Forms of CPD

CPD is not only attending a training course or conference organised by an external organisation. That is just one of many forms that it can take. Neary and Johnson list an A–Z of over 60 different forms of CPD in their handbook. We won't cover that many, but what follows is a 'top 10' of the main types of CPD activity.

Reading
Reading relevant literature, articles and professional journals is a valid way of updating and enhancing your knowledge, understanding and skills relevant to the role of careers leader.

It is important that you keep up to date with developments in the education system, the employment market and in politics, as all of these factors will make a difference to the careers of the young people that you are working with. It can be difficult to make time for this, but try to put aside a little bit of time each week to read things like the *Times Education Supplement*, *The Guardian*, the *Financial Times* and relevant blogs.

> ### 🔆 Resources: Regular reading for careers professionals
>
> There are a few regular publications and websites that we think all careers leaders should be reading.
>
> *Career Matters.* The CDI's professional magazine, with four issues a year. **www.thecdi.net/career-matters/**.
>
> *NICEC Journal.* The *Journal of the National Institute for Career Education and Counselling*, published twice a year. It is an open access journal and has an archive of research going back over 20 years. You can access it at **https://nicecjournal.co.uk**.
>
> Other open access journals include *Nordic Journal of Transitions, Careers and Guidance* (**https://njtcg.org**), and the *Canadian Journal of Career Development* (**https://cjcd-rcdc.ceric.ca/index.php/cjcd**).
>
> There are also several blogs and online sources of information that are worth looking at. For example, Tristram writes *Adventures in Career Development* at **https://adventuresincareerdevelopment.wordpress.com**.
>
> The *Guardian* Careers section (**www.theguardian.com/careers**) is essential reading.

Shadowing and visits

You can learn a lot by visiting a workplace, a university or a college, or shadowing an apprentice or a careers leader working in another school. People will generally be open to meeting and showing you what they do. Just remember to thank them for their time and invite them to come and see what you do in return.

Mentoring

One of the most powerful forms of CPD is finding someone who is more experienced and willing to mentor you. Mentoring often emerges quite informally as just someone whom you talk to whose opinion you respect. Sometimes it can be useful to formalise it. Most people will be flattered if you ask them if they would be willing to be your mentor. This is likely to involve them meeting with you regularly (perhaps once a month), introducing you to some of their contacts and sharing some of their resources and experiences. Again, it is important to thank them for their time and to remember that in the future you should be willing to mentor someone else.

Conferences

Conferences tend to be large events (typically involving 50–200 people). They are often organised as one-day programmes of keynote speakers and workshops, but sometimes as two-day or more residentials. The conference themes will vary but will often emphasise developments in policy, research and theory and other topical issues.

Some conferences will offer you an opportunity to present your work. Once you've got something to present, you should take up this opportunity (if you dare!). You will generally find that conferences are supportive environments and that presenting your work to others can be a valuable CPD opportunity. One of the best things about presenting your work in this kind of forum is that it gives you a chance to reflect on it and to get some feedback from your peers.

Short courses

Local authorities, careers companies, private training organisations, professional bodies, The Career & Enterprise Company and others offer a range of one-day courses on particular aspects of career guidance and development. These range from introductory courses to help newly appointed careers leaders get started, through to workshops and masterclasses on specific elements of careers programmes.

Longer training programmes

These programmes are delivered over a number of days (typically 3 to 10) and organised over several months, allowing participants to reflect on the learning between sessions and to try things out. They tend to provide comprehensive coverage of the full set of careers leader responsibilities and all the main components of a careers programme. Some offer accreditation with a qualification, while others are not award bearing but instead give participants a certificate of participation. Such programmes are usually attended by newly, or recently, appointed careers leaders, or by more experienced careers leaders who want to refresh their programmes or gain a qualification. In England, the government-funded careers leader training courses come under this heading.

Online learning resources

In recent years, there has been a growth in online learning resources to support your CPD. Since the pandemic, the range and quality of online CPD opportunities available has exploded. All of the other forms of CPD that we have highlighted are now available in online and hybrid (a mix of face-to-face and online) versions.

Some online learning resources will be confined to providing information (essentially similar to reading a book online), but online resources are becoming increasingly interactive and embedded into our networks and communications. So, you might find interesting multimedia information via various YouTube channels, as well as gamified or interactive learning resources such as MOOCs (Massive Open Online Courses), which supplement self-study materials with the opportunity to interact with other students and, to a limited extent, with tutors. You might also access mentors, peers and experts through various forms of social media. Finally, there are some opportunities to study courses online provided by universities and other training providers. Generally, you will pay for such courses in the same way as you would face-to-face courses and they will typically involve both tutor support and some accreditation.

> ### 💡 Resources: Free CPD
>
> Career Guidance for the 21st Century (**https://careerguidancecourse.eu**) is a free online self-study CPD course for careers professionals funded by the European Union. It includes modules on careers education, the labour market, and professionalisation.

Accredited qualifications

You may consider whether to seek a qualification in careers leadership (depending on, among other things, what other qualifications you hold and how you might use the qualification). In England, the main qualifications for careers leaders are the awards used to accredit the careers leader training courses referred to earlier in this chapter, namely the Certificate in Careers Leadership awarded by the CDI and the various postgraduate awards from individual universities. Some universities offer modules designed to develop careers leaders beyond initial training. These are usually described as certificates (usually comprising two modules), diplomas (usually comprising four modules) and full master's courses, which often include a dissertation or extended project.

> ### 💡 Resources: Careers qualifications
>
> Details of the various qualifications and postgraduate awards can be found on the CDI's website at **www.thecdi.net/Getting-Qualified**.

If you are keen to pursue a postgraduate qualification, you have some choices to make which relate to your longer-term career aspirations (see Chapter 4.4). For example, you may pursue a course which focuses on educational leadership and management, or one which focuses on careers education and guidance. Both courses could be useful CPD for a careers leader but are likely to take your career in different directions.

> ### 💡 Resources: Leadership qualifications
>
> Examples of relevant school leadership qualifications include the National Professional Qualifications (NPQs) which are being reformed: **www.gov.uk/government/publications/national-professional-qualifications-npqs-reforms**.

Communities of practice

In Section 3 of this handbook we discussed the idea that the careers leader is one of the most highly networked roles in a school or college. To do your job you need to work with almost every member of staff inside the organisation and with a range of individuals and organisations in the wider community. Yet, in another sense, it is quite an isolated role. Subject teachers have department colleagues with whom they can share ideas and practice, but whom does the careers leader have to compare notes with? This is why, when careers leaders are asked about what kinds of support they prefer, they frequently refer to local and regional networks of careers leaders. The members of such communities of practice may share information and resources online but they may also come together from time to time to meet face-to-face or online, often with a structured agenda but also with space to exchange experiences and ideas.

In England, The Careers & Enterprise Company is establishing a national network of Careers Hubs, which bring schools and colleges together to work collaboratively and share practice. Some local authorities and multi-academy trusts employ strategic leads for careers who support individual schools and convene local meetings for careers leaders. The Career Development Institute (CDI) has an online Community of Practice for Careers Leaders (**www.careersleaders.thecdi.net**), and careers leaders themselves have set up the Facebook group 'Careers Leaders UK'. It is worth finding out what networks are available in your locality, and if there isn't one, consider starting one.

CASE STUDY

Dunchester Progress Academy is part of a multi-academy trust. When Rita took on the role of careers leader she struggled to find other careers leaders whose brains she could pick.

Once she got established in her job she contacted the careers leaders in the other schools within the trust and they have set up a WhatsApp group to keep in touch and ask each other about such matters as suitable speakers and resources. Recently she has spoken to the trust-wide leader for CPD and the group now meets once a term, usually on the premises of a different employer or learning provider. The group is now thinking about extending the invitation to heads of sixth, SENCOs and the careers advisers working in the different schools.

Reflective questions: What local networks are available to you? What other opportunities for sharing practice, including online, are you part of?

Professional associations

Many countries have a professional association for people involved in career development. The International Association for Educational and Vocational Guidance (**https://iaevg.com/**) is a global body that you can join in addition to any organisation that exists in your country.

In the UK, the Career Development Institute (**www.thecdi.net**) is the professional body for anyone working in careers. It supports careers leaders as well as careers advisers and careers coaches. The Institute provides a regular e-newsletter, publishes a practitioner journal, hosts a number of different online communities of interest and organises a programme of courses, conferences and webinars. By joining a professional association you gain access to this wide range of CPD opportunities.

Some members who meet the relevant requirements choose to join the CDI's Register of Career Development Professionals. This is open to anyone with a professional qualification in careers at Level 6 or above and members of the Register are required to complete a minimum of 25 hours CPD each year. **www.thecdi.net/Professional-Register-**.

Consultancy

You may, on occasions, bring an external consultant into the school or college to help you review and develop your programme. Perhaps the most common way in which you might engage with a consultant is if you decide to seek accreditation for your school's or college's careers programme through the Quality in Careers Standard. Although the principal focus will be on programme development and organisation development, you too will gain knowledge and understanding from the process, so this is another form of CPD.

After you have completed some CPD

Once you have completed any CPD activities it is important that you spend some time thinking about what you have learned. Often CPD will have alerted you to new areas that you will need to develop in the future, and it can be useful to update your training needs analysis in the light of this, crossing off the things that you are now confident in and adding anything new.

One of the key things with any CPD is trying to make the knowledge and skills that you have learned on a course stick. If you don't put what you have learned into practice quickly you will probably forget most of it. So the priority when you complete any CPD should always be to think about how you can put it into practice as quickly as possible.

Another important step in the process is that the outcomes of the CPD should be discussed with your line manager after the activity. The school or college will want to review if the investment was worth it, but they should also support you in implementing what you learned. It is good practice, therefore, before you participate in the CPD activity to arrange a debriefing and review meeting for soon after the activity.

Taking responsibility for your CPD

Committing to regular CPD is part of being a professional and it is up to you to take the initiative to seek out appropriate opportunities. The CDI recommends that you commit to a minimum of 25 hours of CPD a year and that you keep track of what you do. This gives you a rule of thumb for deciding whether you are getting enough CPD.

To keep track of your CPD you might want to create a portfolio of evidence. The evidence may comprise certificates of attendance, personal reports and reflective accounts of your experiences, records of items you have read and visits you have attended etc. Another good way to keep track of your CPD and to reflect on it is to keep a blog and to write a summary and reflection on all CPD that you participate in. You should also take the opportunity to review and discuss your CPD with your line manager during appraisal interviews and performance management reviews.

In a nutshell

This chapter has looked at your own initial training and CPD. Key things to bear in mind include the following points.

- Take advantage of any initial training, particularly where it is free of charge.
- Your CPD is your responsibility.
- Committing to regular CPD demonstrates the professionalism of the role of careers leader.
- Take opportunities to review your CPD with your manager.
- There are many different ways of accessing CPD. You should ensure that you access a varied diet of CPD opportunities.
- Try to link your CPD needs with the aspirations of your school or college for developing the careers programme.
- Make sure that you keep track of your CPD, reflect on it after you have completed it and act on it quickly.
- By participating in regular CPD you are helping to make sure that you are providing the best possible careers support for your students.

4.3 Looking after others' CPD

The previous chapter focused on looking after your own CPD. This one looks at your role in identifying the training needs of the colleagues with whom you deliver the careers programme, and supporting their CPD. A wide range of staff within the school or college will contribute to the careers programme. Your overall role is to lead and manage this team, and your responsibilities include helping them to access training and other CPD opportunities that will equip and enable them to play their part in delivering the programme.

This chapter will cover:

- whose CPD you need to support
- identifying other staff's training and CPD needs
- signposting and providing CPD opportunities
- mentoring and supporting staff
- delivering in-house training sessions
- bringing in external trainers.

Introduction

As we have demonstrated in earlier sections of this book, you cannot deliver a careers programme on your own. Tutors, subject teachers, PSHE teachers, course lecturers and other members of staff will all contribute to the programme. For most of these colleagues, their contribution to the careers programme will be in addition to their main role in the school or college, and you have a responsibility to support them. At a minimum this should involve careful briefings on what you are asking them to do, but it should also extend to making available relevant training and CPD.

In this chapter we will survey the full range of colleagues whom you should be supporting in this way. Some will be obvious, such as teachers delivering elements of careers education and tutors providing initial information and advice on study options; others will not necessarily come to mind straight away. We will discuss, firstly, how you could set about identifying their training needs and, secondly, ways in which those needs might be met. Finally, we will examine your role in planning and leading in-house training sessions.

> ### 💡 Resources: CPD for colleagues
>
> There are lots of CPD sources that you might want to engage your colleagues with – see Chapter 4.2, and don't forget the importance of the Career Development Institute (**www.thecdi.net**) as a hub for all careers-related CPD. If you want to think more about your role as a provider of CPD to your colleagues the following books might be useful.
>
> Shaun Allison's (2014) *Perfect Teacher-Led CPD*, published by the Independent Thinking Press, leads you through all of the key techniques for delivering CPD.
>
> Sara Bubb and Peter Earley's (2007) *Leading and Managing Continuing Professional Development*, published by Paul Chapman Publishing, provides a bit more theoretical depth on teacher CPD and school development.
>
> Siobhan Neary and Claire Johnson's (2016) *CPD for the Careers Professional*, published by Trotman, addresses these issues specifically with reference to the CPD of careers professionals.

Whose CPD is a careers leader responsible for?

In Chapter 3.2 we identified that careers leaders in most schools will probably have at most one or two colleagues whom they line-manage: the careers administrator and, where schools employ their own internal careers adviser, the careers adviser. The situation is different in schools that have developed a 'distributed leadership' approach, with a senior, strategic leader for careers line-managing two or three middle, operational leaders. In colleges careers leaders are even more likely to be managing staff and, in some cases, may be responsible for a whole department or even several departments if the role is undertaken by an assistant principal or person at a similar level. Regardless of how many people you directly manage, part of your role as their manager is to support their development and ensure that they have the right CPD to do their job.

Your relationship with colleagues who contribute to the careers programme will largely be one of 'project management', but it should also involve helping them to identify any training and CPD needs in relation to their work on the programme. In schools, the team may include form tutors giving information and advice and referring students for career guidance; PSHE and careers teachers delivering careers lessons; and subject teachers linking their teaching to careers. In colleges, the team might include: personal tutors giving information and advice, referring students for career guidance and teaching elements of career learning in the personal development programme; course lecturers linking their teaching to careers; and admissions staff providing pre-entry guidance.

But the list of colleagues whose CPD in relation to careers work you could support does not end there. Some of your fellow middle leaders with whom you work on the careers programme might want to further their own professional development in relation to their work on the programme. The list of such colleagues could include: in schools, the SENCO, the head of sixth form and the librarian/learning resource centre manager; in colleges, the head of learner support, the head of employer engagement and the head of admissions. You might also signpost the link governor for careers, and the senior leader with overall responsibility for careers, to relevant CPD opportunities.

> ### 💡 Resources: CPD for governors and senior leaders
>
> The free, online training modules provided by The Careers & Enterprise Company include one for governors and one for education leaders. Each takes about an hour to complete. **www.careersandenterprise.co.uk/careers-leaders/carers-leader-training/online-learning/modules**.

We know that, in addition to the formally planned careers activities and interventions, students are also influenced by informal conversations with their teachers and tutors. It is important, therefore, that all members of staff are kept up to date with the main developments in education, training and the labour market, and informed about the careers programme and support available in the school or college. Therefore, there will be occasions when the whole staff will need briefing and CPD on the careers programme and implications of developments in learning and the world of work.

Identifying CPD needs

Training needs can be identified in two main ways: (1) top down, where the careers leader identifies skills and knowledge gaps and seeks ways to fill them by providing CPD; and (2) bottom up, where individuals approach you for help in developing their skills and knowledge. In practice, the top-down and bottom-up approaches often work together as ideas emerge out of discussions and volunteers come forward to pick them up.

One of your responsibilities as the careers leader is to have a strategic overview of the skills and knowledge that are needed for your programme. As you plan your programme and then review and evaluate it you should think about where a lack of skills or knowledge is holding you back or limiting your programme. Perhaps you would like to run an enterprise competition, but the staff in your school or college are not confident in facilitating small groups as part of this kind of experiential activity. Or maybe you feel that you would like someone to run a session on the use of social media in your career, but no one does anything other than dabble on Facebook. In such situations you have a range of options. You might bring in a specialist to deliver the activity, see if you can get an employer to plug the gap or decide that someone in the school or college needs to become competent in this area. If you choose the final option, it is likely to involve a need for CPD.

Link to Gatsby Benchmark 1

Taking an overview of the skills and development needs of the staff in your school or college is strongly linked to the need to establish a 'stable careers programme'. Ultimately your programme is delivered by professionals, and so it is vital to attend to their capabilities as part of planning and developing your programme.

When the need for CPD is driven by a clear strategic need it should make it easier to unlock the time and resources needed. You should identify any CPD needs that arise from improvements that you propose to make in the school's or college's development plan and discuss it with other members of the SLT if it requires a substantial investment of time. For example, if you want to train all teachers and tutors in basic advice and guidance techniques you would probably need to agree this as a school or college priority.

Much of the CPD that you support is likely to emerge more organically. It might be based on concerns that you have about individuals' performance or on the developing interests of members of staff. For those colleagues that you line-manage, the question of training and CPD needs should be included on the agenda for your regular review meetings. For members of staff who contribute to your careers programme as a responsibility additional to their main role, training and CPD needs are likely to be identified during team meetings to review their contributions and to brief them on future activities. Their training needs are most likely to relate either to their current contributions or to things you will be asking them to do in the future.

It is also worth making some time each year to talk with the main contributors to your careers programmes and raise the issue of what further training and CPD they might need. Such conversations are likely to be informal and may be bound up with wider conversations about their own careers. As we discussed in Chapter 4.2, CPD is often a good route to boost your own career and it is in your interest to encourage others to consider whether a 'career in careers' might be something that they would be interested in. We'll discuss this further in Chapter 4.4 when we talk about the important issue of succession planning.

CASE STUDY

As part of her reflection on the careers programme Rita writes a list of all of the main members of staff involved in the programme. She creates one column where she notes all of the things that they are good at and another for their development point. So, Raj is a brilliant careers adviser, but he is a bit shy when you put him in front of the whole school. On the other hand Lucy, who heads up PSHE, is a hugely charismatic and compelling teacher, but she knows very little about careers.

Rita realises that there are both some individual development points that she would like to feedback to staff and some systemic gaps. For example, no one, including her, knows anything very much about apprenticeships. She uses this analysis to start building a careers CPD plan as part of her development plan for the programme.

Reflective question: What CPD proposals would you include in your development plan for career guidance in the school or college?

Making CPD available to your staff colleagues

Many of the training and CPD needs identified by your team can be met through you signposting them to relevant opportunities or making opportunities available to them. Examples include:

- passing on details of relevant training courses, conferences and meetings
- passing on copies of relevant articles/literature and links to online material
- arranging visits to or placements with learning providers and employers
- brokering access to external mentoring or coaching opportunities
- getting them involved in parts of the careers programme that they haven't previously contributed to
- inviting speakers into careers team meetings.

It can be useful to build up a list of key training and development opportunities and even to establish a mini-library of resources that you can lend out. If you write a blog, that can be used to update colleagues and draw attention to relevant courses and resources.

One opportunity that it is worth encouraging staff to engage with is undertaking a placement or other form of CPD delivered by an employer. Many teachers and other staff in education have mainly pursued their careers within education. Giving them the opportunity to connect with employers, even just for a day of job shadowing, can be an effective way to empower them to provide more career-relevant learning. The evidence suggests that increasing teacher interactions with employers can improve their knowledge and awareness, enhance their capacity to deliver learning and improve their practice.[9] College lecturers are far more likely to have worked in other sectors, usually related to what they currently teach. Encouraging them to reconnect with their former profession can be a valuable aspect of CPD and can enhance their curriculum teaching and their ability to deliver career learning.

In some cases, you might be asked to support people's requests for training and CPD. Depending on how your school or college is set up, you may have resources that you can allocate to your staff and other colleagues for training and development. More usually, substantial requests for funding for courses, or longer periods off timetable, will have to be submitted to the SLT or human resources department. In this case you may want to write a statement of support setting out why this CPD opportunity would be useful for the careers programme.

As the careers leader, you shouldn't feel that you have to say yes to every request for career-related training. Allowing people to access CPD can be motivational for them and serve to engage them in the careers programme, but these benefits need to be balanced with the needs of the programme and the relevance of the CPD opportunity to the individual. The need to say no sometimes comes with all leadership positions.

Mentoring and supporting staff

You can facilitate much of the CPD for your colleagues by directing them to existing opportunities, but there will be times when there are no suitable opportunities or when you think that you or someone else within the school or college could support them more effectively.

In many cases this can be handled as an informal relationship where you talk to people, share resources and provide some advice. In other cases, you might want to observe their practice and provide them with some feedback and pointers. Observations can be a particularly powerful form of mentoring and can serve both a developmental function for the individual (what could they do better?) and a quality assurance role for the programme (are they delivering effectively?). Some people would argue that it is better not to try to combine these two purposes into one observation, while others might approach observations more pragmatically. It is also worth noting that when you observe someone else's practice you almost invariably learn something about your own; as with all mentoring, observations are a two-way street.

It can sometimes be useful to formalise mentoring relationships to make sure that they are effective. In such cases you might want to plan an initial meeting where you discuss what you are hoping to achieve and build a plan together about how to achieve it. This would typically involve meeting regularly for a period and then having a review discussion to see how things are going and whether you have achieved your aims.

As the careers leader, you will be working with a wide range of people and often encouraging people to move into areas that they don't feel that confident in. This may mean that you get a lot of requests for mentoring and support. You should always think about whether you are really the best person to provide the support that they are looking for or whether there is someone else who might meet their needs more exactly. You should also be careful not to overstretch yourself, and try to engage other experienced staff in providing mentoring and support as well.

Leading in-house training sessions

Another way to provide CPD for your colleagues is to organise a school- or college-based training session. This could be for the whole staff or a subsection of it; it also could be delivered by you or a colleague. The opportunity to deliver a session in the school or college can be very impactful, as it signals the importance of the activity to your colleagues, allows you to address a large group all at once and means that you are all learning in the context in which you will be delivering the programme.

The process of planning and delivering such sessions is straightforward and is, in many respects, like planning a lesson for students, except on these occasions the students are adults and your colleagues. There are, however, some prior considerations. Firstly, you will need to secure the support of your senior leaders, particularly the member of the SLT who has overall responsibility for staff training and CPD in the school or college. Then, you will need to decide when and where to hold the training session. You should know what works best for your colleagues, and if you don't they will soon tell you. Should it be during the school or college day, or a twilight session? Should it be held in school/college, with the risk that staff might get called away, or off site, with the additional factor of getting to the venue?

Once you have settled on the time and place, and got the approval of the senior leadership, you can start to plan the session itself. And here it becomes very similar to planning a lesson for students. Key questions are the following.

- What do I want to get out of the session?
- What are the objectives?
- What content should I cover?
- What methods should I use – presentation, activities, discussion, etc.?
- Should I work with another colleague and/or visiting tutor?
- What refreshments should I provide?
- What equipment will I need?
- How and when will I notify them of the session?
- What should I ask them to do in advance, or bring to the session?

When it comes to delivering the session, again the usual good practice tips apply.
- Explain the purpose of the session and the anticipated outcomes.
- Allow time for your colleagues to seek clarification of what is expected.
- Keep to time.
- Make sure you explain what will happen next.

Most in-house training sessions will be for small teams of colleagues. You may, on occasions, consider running something for the entire staff, but many of the topics on which you want to brief the whole staff are probably best covered by means of an email, regular staff bulletin or a short input to a staff meeting.

The authors of this book are experienced providers of staff development. A useful practical tip passed on to us was, when planning an in-house training session think back to the similar occasions when you were a participant. What made them effective and enjoyable sessions and what made them less so? Build on the former and reduce the risk of the latter.

Procuring and organising external trainers

Sometimes you may feel that you don't have the expertise or time to deliver CPD to staff in your organisation, but that there is still a need to organise something for a group of staff within the school or college. In this case you will probably want to source an external trainer to come in and run a bespoke training course.

Bringing an external training provider into your school or college can be one of the most nerve-wracking aspects of careers leadership. Teachers, lecturers and other educational professionals can be a tough audience, because they will be quick to reach a judgement about whether a trainer is competent in the basics of teaching and educational practice. Most external trainers will also come with a price tag, which adds further pressure and will probably mean that you will need to justify the cost to your line management. Finally, no one likes to have their time wasted, and we've all spent time sitting in courses which just repeat the basics or provide nothing useful or of interest.

So, you need to make sure that when you bring in an external trainer you are confident that they will be a good fit for your needs. The following tips might be useful in helping you to do this.

Make sure that you are clear about what you want. It is important to be very clear about what the objectives for any CPD are. You should set out some learning outcomes and discuss them with your colleagues and with the trainer that you are bringing in.

Pick someone whom you have seen deliver training before. Nothing beats using a trainer whom you have seen deliver before. It is worth thinking whenever you participate in any training or conference about whether anyone would be worth bringing to your school or college. Most people on the conference circuit are open to offers of this kind.

Choose an individual or organisation with a good reputation. An established brand doesn't always guarantee a good product. But, if you use well-known trainers from reputable organisations you have a good chance of getting a good service. It is even better if you can get a recommendation from a careers leader in another school or college.

Don't always go with the cheapest person. There are several organisations that will provide you with free training. Sometimes this is because they are funded to work with schools, in other cases it might be a 'loss leader' where they provide you with some training and then hope that you will buy more training or their product. It is worth investigating these organisations – many of them will offer excellent training – but it is better to pay for something good than to get something of poor quality for free.

Investigate a few options. Ideally you will look for a few options. This will allow you to compare on price, experience and the nature of what they are able to offer you.

Participate in the training session yourself. This will enable you to respond to any questions from your colleagues that relate to practice in the school or college and to follow up points that may arise after the training.

Evaluate any training. We've already discussed the importance of evaluation in Chapter 4.1. This applies equally to any CPD that you are organising.

In a nutshell

This chapter has looked at CPD for your staff colleagues. Key things to bear in mind include the following points.

- One of your responsibilities as careers leader is to support the CPD and training of your colleagues contributing to the careers programme.
- You should consider the CPD and training needs of not only the staff that you line-manage and those who deliver aspects of the programme, but also the middle leaders, senior leaders and governors with whom you work.
- CPD and training needs will be identified by the individuals themselves and from the school or college development plan for careers.
- Many of the CPD and training needs can be met through directing colleagues to opportunities or creating opportunities.
- You may, on occasions, lead in-house training sessions for your colleagues.
- When you bring in external trainers, make sure that they are good and that you evaluate what they do.
- Remember: 'there is no development without staff development'.

4.4 Moving on

In this chapter we explore what will happen when you decide to move on from the role of being a careers leader. This raises concerns for both you and your organisation. For you it raises the question of what you have learned by being a careers leader and where you might go next in your career. For your organisation it raises the issue of how it is going to ensure that the programme continues and, ultimately, replace you.

Most people who are reading this book will probably be at the beginning of their journey in careers leadership. It might be tempting to ignore this chapter and return to it later. However, both your career development and the sustainability of your programme are not things that you can leave until the last minute. We'd therefore advise you to think forward and plan for the future from the start.

This chapter will cover:

- your own career aspirations
- thinking about what you have learned as a careers leader that will be useful in your career
- considering common routes from careers leadership
- planning for sustainability
- succession planning.

Introduction

When you start a new job it is easy for it to be all consuming. We have filled a whole book with ideas about what you should think about as you take up the role of careers leader. Figuring all of this out is likely to take up your time and energy. However, in this section of the book we've asked you to think more long term and to commit to a cycle of continuous improvement for your programme, yourself and those who you work with.

As you start to think more long term you will want to think about how the role of careers leader fits into your own plans. A lot of this will depend on where you are in your career and what you want to achieve. But, being a careers leader is an enormous learning opportunity which is likely to open you up to new ideas and experiences that will change the way that you think about your future.

It is not just you that will change. Your work and the careers programme that you develop will change your organisation. Many schools and colleges begin by viewing careers as a marginal part of their activities. But, if you have done your job well, careers will become more central to your organisation's mission, and this may open new opportunities for you and for the organisation.

Reflecting on how far you have come

If you've engaged with any forms of CPD you are likely to have come across the idea of *reflective practice*. Reflective practice is about thinking about what you have done and using it to guide your actions in the future. The approach to evaluation that we set out in Chapter 4.1 provides you with a formal structure for reflecting on how things are going for your programme. It asks you to think about what you are achieving and whether things are working in the way that you planned.

So now let's turn the mirror round so that you are looking at yourself. Are you happy with the way that you have been performing the role of careers leader? What have you liked and not liked? What do you think that you have learned from it? And where do you think that it is taking you?

Reflection is not about self-indulgent introspection. You need to try to ensure that you have some balance when you are reflecting, to ensure that you both celebrate your successes and learn from your failures. Importantly, you need to be very careful not to blame yourself for issues that are systemic and out of your control. For example, it may be that the governors have turned down your request for new funding to ensure that every young person gets access to high-quality work experience. This is probably not your fault. In fact, it may not even be the governors' fault, as pressures on education budgets inevitably mean that important things get deprioritised. Reflection is about thinking these things through and coming to a decision about what you might do about them in the future. In some cases, your reflection might tell you that this is not a battle you can win at the moment.

Evaluation is a helpful way to work through these issues in relation to your programme, but you need a parallel process of thinking about yourself. The irony of this is that as careers leader you will be thinking about the careers of young people all the time. But you may not be thinking about your own career. If you are attending to your CPD (see Chapter 4.2) this is a good start. But career development is about more than just becoming good at the job that you currently do. There is a useful symmetry in spending time on your own career development while you are working on the careers of others. After all, who wants to take careers advice from someone who hates their job?

We think that it is important that you can exemplify what you are teaching and demonstrate to students and colleagues alike that you take career development as seriously as you are telling them to. One way to do this is to use the Gatsby Benchmarks from Section 2 to help you to reflect and to guide your career development.

Benchmark 1. How far have you developed your own career plan? A career plan doesn't have to be based around a particular outcome, e.g. I want to become a head teacher. It could equally set out a plan of exploration and experimentation. But having a career plan will help you to guarantee that you are spending some time on your own career development and that you are doing it in a strategic and thoughtful way.

Benchmark 2. What sources of information are you using to inform your own thinking about your career? You might decide that you want to read the education press, subscribe to job adverts and build up a list of regular blogs and links to read. Finding the right information to support your career building is key, and you are likely to need to invest some time in putting this together.

Benchmark 3. How far are you critically examining your thoughts about your career? Are you just pursuing you current career direction because it is what someone like you would or should do? Take a step back and re-examine your options. Benchmark 3 is also about keeping good records about the career learning you have participated in. So, is your CV up to date? Have you got good records of all the CPD that you've done? Do you have somewhere to keep track of all the brilliant ideas that you've had in the night about your future, and what you can do about them? Blogging or journaling can be a useful tool for recording what you've done and encouraging reflection on it.

Benchmark 4. This Benchmark is about integrating career learning into the curriculum. For you this is likely to be about integrating career learning into your work and your wider life. Ask yourself whether you are opening yourself up to new experiences and taking on opportunities that push you to develop in new ways. Do your career aspirations fit with the rest of your life? Are you ensuring the right balance between work, family, leisure and other interests and responsibilities?

Benchmark 5. Chapters 3.3 and 3.4 discussed how being a careers leader is likely to bring you into contact with a wide range of new people. Are you using this network to inform your career thinking? Try to take the opportunity when you meet with new people to talk to them about their careers and consider what you can learn from their experience. Your network is also likely to be an important source of new career ideas and opportunities. Be open to these opportunities as they come along.

Benchmark 6. Becoming a careers leader is a major new piece of work experience. You should think about what you have done for the first time and what you have learned from doing this. You should also ask yourself which of your new tasks have been things you have enjoyed and which you have hated. For example, this may be the first time that you've taken on formal line management. Is this an activity that you find interesting and rewarding or is it something that you would rather avoid in future jobs? Reflecting on your experiences at work is likely to provide you with critical insights about your own career.

Benchmark 7. How far have you taken part in formal learning as part of your role as careers leader? Is this something that you would like to do more in the future? What have you learned about your academic abilities and your enthusiasm for formal learning? Do you think that you would be keen to gain more qualifications in the future, or would you prefer alternative routes to professional development?

Benchmark 8. Finally, whom have you talked to about your career? It is great if you can find an opportunity to talk to a careers adviser at some point. You may be able to convince the careers adviser you work with to see you or find a careers professional whom you can hire by searching the CDI register. In addition, it is important to have a lot of other career conversations with friends, colleagues and mentors. Talking about your career is a vital part of reflecting on what you want and where you should go next. If you really can't find anyone to talk to you can always buy a book like Corinne Mills's (2017) *Career Coach*, published by Trotman, which guides you through career reflection and planning in a similar way to a professional careers adviser.

Different ways to think about your career

You won't lag behind, because you'll have the speed.
You'll pass the whole gang and you'll soon take the lead.
Wherever you fly, you'll be best of the best.
Wherever you go, you will top all the rest.

Except when you don't.
Because, sometimes, you won't.

Dr Seuss[10]

As Dr Seuss reminds us, career is all about moving onward and upward and about being a success. Except when it isn't, and when it is about managing challenges and disappointments. Career is ultimately about the art of the possible. It is about making the best of what you have and dealing with the things that you face. If you manage it carefully, you'll have a good chance of doing interesting things and finding the things that you want. But there are no guarantees and no amount of planning will offer you everything that you want (even if you are sure that you can figure out what this is).

There is a range of different ways for you to think about your own career development. Careers are not just about climbing the ladder to try to get to the top. Not everyone wants to be a head teacher or college principal. What is more, 'top' jobs like those are very competitive, and so even if this is what you want you may find it difficult to achieve. Given this, it can be useful to have a plan B.

This kind of thinking about your career puts your long-term objective first and leads you to ask the question '*Where do I want to be in ten years' time?*' These kinds of questions can be useful in helping you to form ideas about your future, but they also have some dangers. Focusing on your long-term future can help you to analyse what kinds of career development to focus on, but they can also lead you to be dissatisfied with your current situation and become so fixated on one future that you ignore other possibilities.

It is a good exercise to think about where you want to be in 10 years' time, but you should probably view it as offering you a direction of travel rather than a destination. So, if you think that you might want to be a head teacher, try to take on some more leadership and management (as you have been doing by being a careers leader), and if you like this, then look for more opportunities to do more of it. But, remain open to the possibility that there are some things that you always wanted to do which you might hate when you actually start doing them. Equally, there are things that you might not even have thought of which will excite you and stimulate new career ideas. Career unfolds day by day as much as it follows a long-term plan.

An alternative way to think about career development is to review your current job and think about what things you like and what you would like to be doing more of. In some cases you will be able to gradually grow and transform your job to make it fit with the things that you like and enjoy, and gradually pass some of the other things on to other people (or get rid of them altogether). This process is sometimes called '*job sculpting*', as it is about sculpting your job until it is in the shape that you want it.

Even if you can't sculpt your job into the perfect shape you can still think about what you enjoy in your current role and use this as a guide for your career development. Rather than focusing on your 10-year plan you might want to focus on where to go next and how to make that move. Making a good, purposeful next move is probably more important than trying to develop the perfect 10-year plan.

💡 **Resources: Career development books**

There are a lot of resources to help you with your career development. Obviously, we think that the *You're Hired!* series and other careers books produced by Trotman (**https://trotman.co.uk/collections/all**) are an excellent starting point.

There are also some more educationally focused books like Jim Donnelly's (2002) *Career Development for Teachers*, published by Routledge, and David Hodgson's (2016) *What Else Can a Teacher Do?*, published by Crown House Publishing, which looks at how you can transfer the skills that you have developed in education to other fields.

Career possibilities for careers leaders

One of the good things about being a careers leader is that it opens so many possibilities. If you look back at Section 3 of this book you'll be able to see all of the jobs that you are doing. Many of them are not things that you would be doing in a more 'normal' teaching or lecturing job. You will be building a strategic vision and leading an area of organisational activity, managing staff, influencing colleagues, delivering professional development and training, networking with employers and post-secondary learning providers and very definitely becoming brilliant at time management and multi-tasking.

Once you've been working as a careers leader for a year or so, we'd suggest that you write a list of all of the things that you've done since you took on the role that you had never done before. You might surprise yourself!

CASE STUDY

Rita has now been the careers leader for two years. She has loved it and it has given her a huge range of new experiences. She's managed people, been able to be more creative in her curriculum design and has got out of school more than ever before. She is now starting to think about her future and it is causing her some anxiety. She has always thought of herself as a teacher, but she is starting to realise that there are other things she also enjoys. One thing that she has got a real kick out of is working with new careers leaders who are starting at other schools in her local area. She is wondering whether her next move might be into educational training, consultancy and advisory work. She puts out some feelers and arranges to talk to a few people who do this kind of work already.

Reflective questions: What parts of the job of careers leader do you particularly enjoy? What ideas does this generate about the direction of your future career? Who might you discuss these ideas with?

The new skills and experiences that you get as a careers leader open up new opportunities for you. We can't list them all, but the following seven possible career paths are designed to give you a few starting points.

Career path #1. Keep on keeping on! We think that being a careers leader is a great job. If you agree, you may be happy to keep doing it for a while or even for ever. When people think about career, they usually think about the idea of moving jobs and moving onwards and upwards. But, it is equally important to know when you are happy and stay put.

Career path #2. Going back to what you were doing before. If you think carefully, you can probably still remember your life before you became a careers leader. One option is for you to go back to what you were doing. Sometimes making a career move can be a good way to test out some of your career ideas. This doesn't mean that you must stick with it for life. Maybe you've learned that your previous job or profession was the one for you.

Career path #3. Moving up in your school or college (or another one). If you've done a good job as a careers leader you might have convinced everyone around you of your brilliance. In which case they may be interested in promoting you. Sometimes this might include you continuing as a careers leader but broadening your responsibilities and taking on new roles in addition. In other cases they might be keen for you to work some of the magic that you've worked on the careers area on another area. There are advantages and disadvantages to trying to move up in the organisation that you currently work in. In some cases, it might be easier to take your experience down the road to another school and use it to provide examples of the kind of work that you are capable of. One thing to remember is that it is possible to move from one kind of organisation to another – so everything that you've learned as a careers leader in a school might suit you to work in a similar role in a college, and vice versa.

The job of careers leader is a good stepping-stone towards senior leadership in a school or college, if that appeals to you. You will have formed working relationships with many different parts of the organisation and have had to take on a 'whole school/college' perspective. This provides just the experience that you need to make the move into an assistant head or assistant principal role.

Career path #4. Focus on leadership and management. As a careers leader you will certainly have developed your abilities as a leader and manager. You may want to take on more responsibility of this kind either in an educational setting or somewhere else. If this is the path that you want to pursue it is important to think about how what you have learned as a careers leader might need to be recontextualised as you move into other kinds of leadership and other organisations.

Career path #5. Focus on co-ordination and networking. The ability to build relationships with others and create good working relationships within and across organisations is very valuable. As a careers leader you will have had to do this quite a lot. You could take these skills to help other organisations to work more effectively. Jobs like 'business development', 'network management' and 'partnership management' are all likely to build on these skills.

Career path #6. Focus on careers. As a careers leader you will have started to become an expert in career development. You may feel that this is something that you want to pursue further. You might want to qualify as a careers adviser or specialise more in careers education. You could keep working with young people or move to deliver careers work in universities, workplaces or with adults. Equally you could offer what you've learned as a careers leader to other schools and colleges and become a consultant helping others to sort out their careers programmes, perhaps as a careers hub lead or the careers lead for an academy trust. Finally, you might want to do more research and writing on careers, perhaps even becoming a university lecturer or researcher. The careers field has a vast amount of jobs within it that should cater for most tastes.

Career path #7. Doing something else. Of course, you can do anything that you want. You can retrain and strike out in a completely different direction and apply for a job that has nothing to do with what you've done before. You may even find that through all of your networking you get offered something that you never would have thought of. Maybe one of the employers you work with asks you to come and head up her training and development department. Think carefully about these opportunities. Don't move just because you are flattered to be asked, but don't rule anything out either. Making a change can be exciting, and very few opportunities are one-way streets.

Finally, remember that the seven career paths set out above are not mutually exclusive. You may follow all of them at some point in your career.

Resources: Finding opportunities

When searching for career opportunities you might want to talk to headhunters and make extensive use of your network; however, it never hurts to keep an eye on the following jobs boards.

Careers in Careers (**https://jobs.thecdi.net**) – the CDI's jobs board.

Tes, formerly the Times Education Supplement (**www.tes.com/jobs**).

The Guardian (**https://jobs.theguardian.com**).

Jobs.ac.uk (**www.jobs.ac.uk**) – a site devoted to opportunities in HE.

We wish you luck with your career and hope that your time as a careers leader will take you to all of the places that you want to go. But, before you fly off, it is important for us to focus back on your programme and think about how to ensure that you leave a positive legacy when you go.

Ensuring that your programme is sustainable

The most common approach to organising the role of careers leader in schools is to identify a single individual to the position, usually a middle leader reporting to a senior leader who has overall responsibility for careers, but sometimes a senior leader. This model is also seen in many sixth form colleges and smaller FE colleges. It has the advantage of a single post, dedicated to careers, with fewer risks of responsibilities slipping through the net, but several careers leaders in this position have reported concerns about what could happen to the school's or college's careers programme if they were unavailable or moved on.

Even if the school or college has a 'distributed leadership' or 'careers leadership team' approach it is still useful to think about the issue of sustainability. But, this makes a useful first point: where careers leadership is shared among a number of people, issues with sustainability are less acute. Where all knowledge is vested in a single person there is a greater risk.

Schools and colleges need good careers leaders to lead, manage and develop their careers programmes, and that's why we have written this book, to support those important post-holders. However, those leaders should also set up systems such that the programme could be sustained, not forever but for a period, if they were to be temporarily unavailable for any reason. This means giving thought to developing policy statements, schemes of work and clearly documented procedures such as the referral process for career guidance, that would enable someone else to maintain the programme until the careers leader returned, or, if they had moved on in their career, was replaced.

Perhaps most critically it is important that you have shared some of your knowledge with the people around you. We have repeatedly emphasised the importance of the team of people that you will be working with as a careers leader. Collectively, these people should have most of the knowledge that you have. If you are off sick for a period, your line manager should understand enough of what you do to be able to work with the documentation that you have left and the team that you have built to run the programme. If you don't think that this is the case, then it is worth spending some time bringing them up to speed.

No one wants to be thought of as dispensable. We'd all like to believe that the world would stop turning if we weren't there to do our job. But, your students only get one opportunity to progress through the points of transition that we build into our education system, so the careers programme needs to continue even if the careers leader is not there.

Planning for succession

We've already talked about your career and the fact that at some point you are likely to move on. In five years' time you might be a senior leader, education adviser or consultant, HE lecturer, Ofsted inspector, researcher or something even more interesting. That means that you need to think about who is going to take over when you move on. It might feel that it is too early to start grooming your replacement, but if you postpone any succession planning until the point at which you leave, there is a danger that the programme may not be maintained at its current level and students risk suffering from a lack of continuity of support.

CASE STUDY

Rita has been talking to a lot of people locally about the possibility of moving into a role as a trainer and adviser specialising in helping schools and colleges to develop their careers programme. A local school improvement organisation is looking to take someone on part-time to focus on careers. Rita applies and is successful in getting the job. She goes back to her manager at Dunchester Progress Academy and talks it over.

They agree that she will stay on part-time for the next year and train up Albert, who is an English teacher who has been delivering a lot of careers education as part of the Dunchester programme. He will start as the assistant careers leader, with the idea that he'll progress to taking on the role next year as Rita moves on to become a full-time educational consultant.

Reflective question: What conversations have you had with your line manager about succession planning for when you might no longer be the careers leader?

There are a number of actions you can take to avoid things falling apart as soon as you move on. You should establish the systems and processes outlined in the previous segment of this chapter where we looked at sustainability.

It is also important to think about developing an assistant careers leader. As we are sure you appreciate, there is plenty of work to go round, and having a colleague with whom to share ideas would only enhance your programme. There is a variety of ways in which you could divide up the responsibilities, but investing in a second person would mean that there would be someone to take charge of the programme, if only on a temporary basis, until a replacement was appointed.

You should talk about this with your own line manager and get them to buy in to the idea that the careers programme should be more than just your responsibility. If they recognise the importance of broadening the skill and knowledge base within the school or college, and of planning for succession, they are ultimately recognising the importance of the programme. Your relationship with your line manager is also critical for managing the actual succession and handover. The better they understand what you do, the easier it will be for them to manage the transition and appoint the right person to replace you.

Finally, it is important that your work be well documented. We've encouraged you to create and publish a plan, to keep good records and to regularly reflect on what you do. If you have been doing all of this it should be relatively straightforward for you to produce a handover pack and a new job description for your replacement.

The ultimate test of your work is that others will advocate for it and carry it on after you have moved on.

In a nutshell

Even if you are new into the role you should be thinking about how long you want to do this for and considering what will happen to your programme after you leave. Key things to keep in mind include the following points.

- You are encouraging other people to think about their careers, and so you should make sure that you spend some time thinking about yours.
- You should reflect on what you have learned from being a careers leader and consider how this might inform your career development going forward.
- There are a lot of ways to think about your career. Planning to climb to high-powered positions is just one small aspect of career development and is certainly not for everyone.
- Being a careers leader opens a lot of opportunities.
- Remember that as you are planning your career you also need to plan for your succession and for the future of the organisation after you leave.

Section 5:
Final thoughts

Final thoughts

This book sets out the role of the careers leader in a comprehensive and systematic way. In it we have tried to offer advice and ideas on what constitutes a good careers programme and what your role is as a careers leader. We've tried to be definitive, offering you everything that you need to know, without being prescriptive. Ultimately only you will know what it is like to be a careers leader in your school or college, and ultimately only you can decide how the programme is best organised.

As we draw to a close, we would like to emphasise our belief that a focus on the careers of young people is one of the most valuable ways in which you can spend your professional life. It is challenging and, at times, frustrating, but in putting your energy into young people's futures you are empowering them to build a meaningful life, and are investing in the future of your country and of the world.

If there is one message that we'd like you to take away from this book above all, it is that you are not alone. We've tried to draw on all the experience of careers work that we have and the experience that we've borrowed from others. But this is only the start of your journey. You should try to connect to other careers leaders in your area, join your professional association and link up with careers leaders from across the world online. There are a huge number of people experiencing very similar triumphs and pitfalls to you every day, and if you link up with them we can all help each other.

We'd also urge you to remember that careers work in schools and colleges is intensely political. Every time the government changes, the context of your work shifts. There is a very good case for being informed about what is happening at the policy level, and an equally good one for trying to be involved in it. Read parties' manifestos at election time, write to your political representatives about your concerns, and take any opportunity to ensure that the profile of careers education and guidance is kept high.

We're sure that you will have your political views, just as we have ours. But careers education and guidance has had both high points and low points under governments of all types and all colours. The only thing that keeps politicians engaged and committed to this agenda is the willingness of professionals (and students) to speak up for what is right. We hope that you will join us in doing this as we move forward.

Careers leadership as part of whole school development

Throughout the book, we have argued that career education and guidance matters for young people, for schools and for societies. The model of careers leadership that we have proposed is not based around a single individual doing everything, but rather around the careers leader as a catalyst of school transformation. Before we finish, we want to say a little bit more about this and to encourage you to have difficult conversations with head teachers, college principals and governing bodies.

Careers is about focusing on the life, learning and work of individuals. The process of developing an individual and supporting them to make a difference through their work, in their community and for their country and the world should be at the heart of education. Of course, getting good grades matters, but it is a means rather than an end in itself. Ultimately, education must be about preparing people for life and inspiring them to become lifelong learners. Many of the school and college mission statements we have seen talk about these aims, and the careers programme plays a central role in achieving them.

Schools and colleges are under enormous pressures to meet targets, perform for inspectors and deliver results, results, results! As a careers leader, you have a lot to contribute to this agenda of school improvement and school development. Careers programmes can engage young people in learning, provide them with motivation and help to clarify why they are learning what they are learning. A young person who has a clear vision of the kind of future that they want will understand what grades they need to achieve and work harder to achieve them. There is evidence that careers programmes enhance educational outcomes as well as supporting social and economic outcomes.[1]

But, results are not everything, and, as a careers leader, you have an important role in reminding others in the school or college's leadership of that. The careers programme focuses our mind on achieving our students' potential and on considering the contribution that they are going to make to the world. These ideas should also influence the vision and mission of the school or college and shape the way things are run.

All of this reminds us why it is important to push the careers programme forward, and ensure that it is included as a key part of the school or college development plan. Careers should not be pushed to the side or viewed as an added extra; it should be at the heart of the purpose of the school and always on the mind of the school leadership team.

Creating this kind of culture change isn't easy. But when you took on the role of the careers leader, you also became a campaigner for educational reform. Good luck!

Reflecting on what you have learned

We are going to finish by summarising the main messages that we have tried to convey through this book. You might want to think about whether you agree with our summary and whether there is anything else that you would raise or highlight.

Careers matter. Individuals' careers are the path that they use to make their way through life, learning and work. They are valuable and complex and need to be nurtured and supported if people are going to achieve what they want from life.

Schools and colleges can make a difference. Schools and colleges have the power to make a big difference to the way in which young people's careers begin. We know a lot about what works, and by providing young people with a steady and varied diet of career learning opportunities (the Gatsby Benchmarks) we can put them on the right road.

The role of the careers leader is critical. Careers programmes in schools and colleges don't just happen by accident. They need to be carefully designed and implemented. In many cases someone will have to fight to get careers onto the agenda and to ensure that the careers programme is properly resourced. This person is the careers leader. Good careers leaders need to be able to create vision and lead their colleagues, to manage people and projects, to co-ordinate the activities of diverse staff and build networks with external supporters. This is a difficult job, but it is one which is immensely satisfying when you do it well.

Careers programmes are built over years. Setting up your school's or college's careers programme is just the start. Once you've got it in place you need to carefully evaluate your programme and commit to a process of continuous improvement. A key part of this is developing your own skills and knowledge as the careers leader and committing to the development of the rest of the staff you work with. To achieve this, you will have to become an experienced mentor, trainer and leader. Finally, while you can play a key role in delivering the careers programme you have to make sure that it is not entirely built around you. Careers leadership is good training for a wide range of jobs and when you move on you should try to make sure that your programme is sustainable and that you have planned for succession.

Very final thoughts

Throughout this book we have sought to define excellent practice in running careers programmes and being a careers leader. We have tried to always remain practical, highlighting ideas that we think work and setting out models and frameworks that you can pick up and run with. But inevitably, a book like this is just theories, ideas and advice. It is now time for you to put the book down and start to turn theory into practice.

We wish you good luck with it and believe that you will make a big difference to the young people you are working with. We also hope that you feel that you are interested in continuing to develop your own career in this field. There is no more worthwhile way to spend your life than in supporting the futures of the next generation.

Endnotes

Section 1

1. See Hooley, T. (2014). *The evidence base on lifelong guidance*. Jyväskylä, Finland: European Lifelong Guidance Policy Network (ELGPN). www.elgpn.eu/publications/browse-by-language/english/elgpn-tools-no-3.-the-evidence-base-on-lifelong-guidance

2. Zytowski, D. G. (2001). Frank Parsons and the progressive movement. *The Career Development Quarterly*, 50(1), 57–65. https://doi.org/10.1002/j.2161-0045.2001.tb00890.x

3. Holland, J. L. (1959). A theory of vocational choice. *Journal of Counseling Psychology*, 6, 35–45. https://doi.org/10.1037/h0040767

4. Super, D. E. (1980). A life-span, life-space approach to career development. *Journal of Vocational Behavior*, 16(3), 282–298. https://doi.org/10.1016/0001-8791(80)90056-1

5. Savickas, M. L., Nota, L., Rossier, J., Dauwalder, J. P., Duarte, M. E., Guichard, J., ... & Van Vianen, A. E. (2009). Life designing: A paradigm for career construction in the 21st century. *Journal of Vocational Behavior*, 75(3), 239–250. https://doi.org/10.1016/j.jvb.2009.04.004

6. Roberts, K. (2009). Opportunity structures then and now. *Journal of Education and Work*, 22(5), 355–368. https://doi.org/10.1080/13639080903453987

7. If you are interested in the contemporary debates in career guidance, we suggest the following books: Hooley, T., Sultana, R. & Thomsen, R. (Eds.) (2018). *Career guidance for social justice: Contesting neoliberalism*. Routledge; Mann, A., Huddleston, P. & Kashefpakdel, E. (Eds.) (2018). *Essays on employer engagement in education*. Routledge; Robertson, P., Hooley, T. & McCash, P. (2021). *The Oxford Handbook of Career Development*. OUP.

Section 2

1. Mann, A. & Huddleston, P. (2017). Schools and the twenty-first century labour market: Perspectives on structural change. *British Journal of Guidance and Counselling*, 45(2), 208–218. https://doi.org/10.1080/03069885.2016.1266440

2. Mann, A., Rehill, J. & Kashefpakdel, E. (2018). *Employer engagement in education: Insights from international evidence for effective practice and future research*. Education Endowment Foundation. https://educationendowmentfoundation.org.uk/public/files/Employer_Engagement_in_Education.pdf

3. Gatsby Charitable Foundation. (2014). *Good Career Guidance*. London: Gatsby Charitable Foundation. www.gatsby.org.uk/uploads/education/reports/pdf/gatsby-sir-john-holman-good-career-guidance-2014.pdf

4. There is lots of research on the value of employer engagement in education, and a good place to start is Mann, A., Stanley, J. & Archer, L. (Eds.) (2014). *Understanding employer engagement in education*. Routledge.

5. Department for Education. (2021). *Careers guidance and access for education and training providers*. Department for Education. www.gov.uk/government/publications/careers-guidance-provision-for-young-people-in-schools

6. Hanson, J., Moore, N., Clark, L. & Neary, S. (2021). *An evaluation of the North East of England pilot of the Gatsby Benchmarks of good career guidance.* iCeGS, University of Derby. www.gatsby.org.uk/uploads/education/ne-pilot-evaluation-full-report.pdf

7. The Education Act 2011. www.legislation.gov.uk/ukpga/2011/21/part/4/crossheading/careers-education-and-guidance

8. The Technical and Further Education Act 2017. www.legislation.gov.uk/ukpga/2017/19/contents

9. Skills and Post-16 Education Act 2022. www.legislation.gov.uk/ukpga/2022/21/contents/enacted

10. Education (Careers Guidance in Schools) Act 2022. www.legislation.gov.uk/ukpga/2022/13/contents/enacted

11. For evidence on the impact of career guidance on attainment see Hanson, J., Moore, N., Neary, S. & Clark, L. (2021). *An evaluation of the North East of England pilot of the Gatsby Benchmarks of good career guidance.* University of Derby. https://derby.openrepository.com/bitstream/handle/10545/625634/Gatsby%20pilot%20evaluation_final.pdf; Hooley, T., Matheson, J. & Watts, A. G. (2014). *Advancing ambitions: The role of career guidance in supporting social mobility.* The Sutton Trust. https://derby.openrepository.com/handle/10545/333866; Mann, A. & Dawkins, J. (2014). *Employer engagement in education: Literature review.* CfBT Education Trust. https://files.eric.ed.gov/fulltext/ED546811.pdf

12. The Careers & Enterprise Company. (2016). *Moments of choice.* London: The Careers & Enterprise Company. www.careersandenterprise.co.uk/media/m31lm1qo/moments_of_choice_report.pdf

13. For more on career guidance and social justice, read IAEVG (2013). IAEVG *Communiqué on social justice in educational and career guidance and counselling.* http://iaevg.net/iaevg/IAEVG/nav16ee.html?lang=2&menu=1&submenu=9

14. Equality Act 2010: Guidance. https://www.gov.uk/guidance/equality-act-2010-guidance

15. For resources on the gender pay gap visit the Equal Pay Portal at www.equalpayportal.co.uk

16. Hooley, T., Sultana, R. & Thomsen, R. (2021). Five signposts to a socially just approach to career guidance. *Journal of the National Institute for Career Education and Counselling*, 47, 59–66.

17. Berrington, A., Roberts, S. & Tammes, P. (2016). Educational aspirations among UK young teenagers: Exploring the role of gender, class and ethnicity. *British Educational Research Journal*, 42(5), 729–755. https://doi.org/10.1002/berj.3235, provides a good entry point to the literature on young people's aspirations.

18. Unique Pupil Number. www.gov.uk/government/publications/unique-pupil-numbers

19. Statistics: destinations of key stage 4 and 16 to 18 (KS5) students. https://www.gov.uk/government/collections/statistics-destinations

20. Collins, J. & Barnes, A. (2017). *Careers in the curriculum. What works?* The Careers & Enterprise Company. www.careersandenterprise.co.uk/media/oq0bqhmp/careers_in_the_curriculum_report_what_works.pdf

21. Law, W. & Watts, A. G. (1977). *Schools, Careers and Community.* Church Information Office.

22. This updated version of the DOTS framework has its origins in the three sets of curriculum guidelines that were published in England between 1995 and 2003. School Curriculum and Assessment Authority (1995), *Looking forward. Careers education and guidance in the curriculum*. SCAA; Qualifications and Curriculum Authority (1999), *Learning outcomes from careers education and guidance*. QCA; and Department for Education and Skills (2003), *Careers education and guidance in England. A national framework 11–19*. DfES.

23. Australian Government. (2020). *Australian Blueprint for Career Development*. www.dese. gov.au/school-work-transitions/australian-blueprint-career-development

24. Kompetanse Norge. (n.d.). *Karrierkompetanse*. www.kompetansenorge.no/kvalitet-i-karriere/karrierekompetanse

25. Department for Education. (2011). *Personal, social, health and economic (PSHE) education: A mapping study of the prevalent models of delivery and their effectiveness*. Research Report DFE-RR080. DfE.

26. Hooley, T. (2021). *Career education: every teacher has a role*. myfuture Insights series. Melbourne, Education Services Australia. https://myfuture.edu.au/docs/default-source/insights/2020/career-education-every-teacher-has-a-role.pdf

27. Office for National Statistics. (2020). Self-employment in the UK and its characteristics. www.ons.gov.uk/employmentandlabourmarket/peopleinwork/employmentandemployeetypes/datasets/selfemploymentintheukanditscharacteristics

28. Mann, A., Huddleston, P. & Kashefpakdel, P. (Eds.). *Essays on employer engagement in education*. Routledge.

29. If you want to get to know Bourdieu better, the Wikipedia page is an excellent starting point, https://en.wikipedia.org/wiki/Pierre_Bourdieu

30. Bourdieu, P. (1986). *The Forms of Capital*. www.marxists.org/reference/subject/philosophy/works/fr/bourdieu-forms-capital.htm

31. Education & Employers. (2019). *The case for employer engagement in state schools*. www.educationandemployers.org/wp-content/uploads/2019/04/Research-summary-website-version.pdf

32. Kashefpakdel, E. T. & Percy, C. (2017). Career education that works: An economic analysis using the British Cohort Study. *Journal of Education and Work*, 30(3), 217–234. https://doi.org/10.1080/13639080.2016.1177636

33. Jerome, J. K. (1889). *Three men in a boat*. J. W. Arrowsmith.

34. Buzzeo, J. and Cifci, M. (2017). *Work experience, job shadowing and workplace visits: What works?* The Careers & Enterprise Company. www.careersandenterprise.co.uk/media/wknmpwvm/what-works-report-work-experience.pdf

35. UK Commission for Employment and Skills. (2015). *The death of the Saturday job*. UK Commission for Employment and Skills.

36. Holford, A. (2016). *Youth employment and academic performance: Production functions and policy effects*. IZA Discussion Paper No. 10009. https://ssrn.com/abstract=2803841

37. Miller, A., Watts, A. G. and Jamieson, I. (1991). *Rethinking work experience*. Falmer Press.

38. Kolb, D. A. (1984). *Experiential learning: Experience as the source of learning and development*. Prentice-Hall.

39. Data from the Office for National Statistics *Participation rates in higher education 2006–2020* shows that the proportion of 17- to 30-year-olds entering HE has risen steadily from 42% to 51% between the academic years 2006/07 and 2019/20.

40. Data from the Higher Education Statistics Agency (HESA) shows that in 2019/20 5.3% of students did not continue beyond the first year of entry.

41. Article in *The Guardian* (6 September 2016), 'Why one in 10 students drop out of uni in their first year'. www.theguardian.com/education/shortcuts/2016/sep/06/why-one-in-10-students-drop-out-university-in-first-year

42. Egan, G. (2002). *The skilled helper*. Brooks Cole.

43. Alexander, G. (2010). Behavioural coaching – the GROW model. In Passmore, J. (Ed.), *Excellence in coaching: The industry guide* (pp. 83–93). London: Philadelphia: Kogan Page.

44. Neary, S., Marriott, J. and Hooley, T. (2014). *Understanding a 'career in careers': Learning from an analysis of current job and person specifications*. Derby: International Centre for Guidance Studies, University of Derby. https://repository.derby.ac.uk/item/937vv/understanding-a-career-in-careers-learning-from-an-analysis-of-current-job-and-person-specifications

45. Careers Profession Task Force. (2010). *Towards a strong careers profession*. Department for Education. www.gov.uk/government/publications/towards-a-strong-careers-profession

46. Everitt, J., Neary, S., Delgardo, M.A. & Clark, L. (2018). *Personal guidance. What works?* The Careers & Enterprise Company. www.careersandenterprise.co.uk/media/xuzdfl2s/what-works-personal-guidance.pdf

Section 3

1. The Careers & Enterprise Company & Gatsby Charitable Foundation. (2018). *Understanding the role of the careers leader: A guide for secondary schools*. The Careers & Enterprise Company. www.careersandenterprise.co.uk/media/uhtkww5h/understanding-careers-leader-role-careers-enterprise.pdf

2. The Careers & Enterprise Company & Gatsby Charitable Foundation (2018). *Understanding the role of the careers leader: A guide for colleges*. The Careers & Enterprise Company. https://resources.careersandenterprise.co.uk/resources/understanding-role-careers-leader-guide-colleges

3. Andrews, D. & Hooley, T. (2017). '… and now it's over to you': recognising and supporting the role of careers leaders in schools in England, *British Journal of Guidance & Counselling*, 45(2), 153–164. https://doi.org/10.1080/03069885.2016.1254726

4. Andrews, D. & Hooley, T. (2019). Careers leadership in practice: a study of 27 careers leaders in English secondary schools. *British Journal of Guidance & Counselling*, 47(5), 556–68. https://doi.org/10.1080/03069885.2019.1600190

5. Andrews, D. (2019). *Careers education in schools* (Second edition). David Andrews.

6. Andrews, D. (2019). *Careers education in schools* (Second edition). David Andrews.

7. Sutcliffe, J. (2013). *8 qualities of successful school leaders*. Bloomsbury.

8. Kellerman, B. (2008). *Followership: How followers are creating change and changing leaders*. Boston: Harvard Business School Publishing.

9. Acas. (2018). Top tips for better management. www.acas.org.uk/index.aspx?articleid=2966

10. Oomen, A.M. (2018). *Parental involvement in career education and guidance in senior general secondary schools in the Netherlands*. University of Derby.

11. Andrews, D. & Barnes, A. (2003). Career development of careers co-ordinators. *Career Research & Development: the NICEC Journal*, 9, 3–9. https://doi.org/10.20856/jnicec.0902

12. The six principles of networking were first introduced in Hooley, T., Bright, J. & Winter, D. (2016). *You're hired! Job hunting online: The complete guide*. Trotman.

Section 4

1. For more on the history and meaning of this phrase visit https://en.wikipedia.org/wiki/Standing_on_the_shoulders_of_giants

2. Hooley, T. (2016). *Effective employer mentoring*. The Careers & Enterprise Company. https://resources.careersandenterprise.co.uk/resources/effective-employer-mentoring

3. British Educational Research Association. (2011). *Ethical Guidelines for Research*. London: BERA.

4. Tanner, E. & Finlay, I. (2021). *Future Skills Questionnaire: The development of a tool to measure young people's career-related learning and skills*. London: The Careers & Enterprise Company. www.careersandenterprise.co.uk/media/cmrkm4xc/1448_fsqdevelopmentreport_v7.pdf

5. Dodd, V., Hanson, J. & Hooley, T. (2021). Increasing students' career readiness through career guidance: measuring the impact with a validated measure. *British Journal of Guidance & Counselling*. https://doi.org/10.1080/03069885.2021.1937515

6. Madden, C. & Mitchell, V. A. (1993). *Professions, standards and competence: A survey of continuing education for the professions*. Bristol: University of Bristol. Cited in Neary, S. & Johnson, C. (2016). *CPD for the career development professional: A handbook for enhancing practice*. Trotman.

7. The Careers & Enterprise Company and Gatsby Charitable Foundation (2018). *Understanding the role of the careers leader. A guide for secondary schools*. London: The Careers & Enterprise Company. www.careersandenterprise.co.uk/media/uhtkww5h/understanding-careers-leader-role-careers-enterprise.pdf

8. The National Occupational Standards for Career Development are maintained by the Career Development Institute and can be accessed at www.thecdi.net/National-Occupational-Standards.

9. Dodd, V. (2017). *Teacher CPD delivered by employers. What works?* The Careers & Enterprise Company. https://resources.careersandenterprise.co.uk/sites/default/files/2021-09/what_works_cpd_for_teachers_report.pdf

10. Dr Seuss (1990). *Oh, The Places You'll Go*. Random House.

Section 5

1. Hughes, D., Mann, A., Barnes, S.-A., Baldauf, B. & Mckowen, R. (2016). *Careers education: International literature review*. Institute for Employment Research/Education and Employers Research. https://warwick.ac.uk/fac/soc/ier/publications/2016/hughes_et_al_2016_eef_lit_review.pdf

Index